POLICE JUVENILE
ENFORCEMENT

POLICE JUVENILE ENFORCEMENT

By

C. J. FLAMMANG

Associate Professor
Police Training Institute
University of Illinois
Formerly Police Consultant
The University of Tennessee
Coordinator, Police Science
Fresno City College, California
Seargeant, Juvenile Bureau
Fresno County Sheriff's Department
California

With a Foreword by

The Honorable William Sylvester White

Presiding Judge
Circuit Court of Cook County, Illinois
Juvenile Division

CHARLES C THOMAS • PUBLISHER
Springfield • Illinois • U.S.A.

Published and Distributed Throughout the World by
CHARLES C THOMAS • PUBLISHER
BANNERSTONE HOUSE
301-327 East Lawrence Avenue, Springfield, Illinois, U.S.A.

© 1972, by CHARLES C THOMAS • PUBLISHER

ISBN 0-398-02280-1

Library of Congress Catalog Card Number: 70-187653

With THOMAS BOOKS *careful attention is given to all details of
manufacturing and design. It is the Publisher's desire to present books
that are satisfactory as to their physical qualities and artistic possibilities
and appropriate for their particular use.* THOMAS BOOKS *will be true
to those laws of quality that assure a good name and good will.*

Printed in the United States of America
PP-22

To

MONA and LUCRETIA

Sisters and Nurses, who dedicated
their lives to the service of children.

FOREWORD

ARTICLE I of the Juvenile Court Act of the State of Illinois states:

The purpose of this Act is to secure for each minor subject hereto such care and guidance, preferably in his own home, as will serve the moral, emotional, mental, and physical welfare of the minor and the best interests of the community; to preserve and strengthen the minor's family ties whenever possible, removing him from the custody of his parents only when his welfare or safety or the protection of the public cannot be adequately safeguarded without removal; and, when the minor is removed from his own family, to secure for him custody, care and discipline as nearly as possible equivalent to that which should be given by his parents . . .

The juvenile court was a notable step forward—at least conceptually—and I believe practically, but has fallen short of its promise. The whole juvenile justice system is under attack both from the press and in the courts, in part because the available institutions and programs simply do not come close to living up to the underlying philosophy of juvenile courts. We must return to the *parens patriae* philosophy which holds that our treatment of juveniles should be rehabilitative rather than punitive. Most of the people in juvenile corrections believe this, but their tools are limited. We need more group homes and halfway houses where children may be supervised but remain in the community. We need more diagnostic centers for psychological testing, for industrial and vocational appraisal, guidance, and assignment. We need more competent social scientists, psychiatrists, psychologists, and social workers. And we need more informed citizens involved in programs such as the Juvenile Court of Cook County's newly instituted corps of volunteers where concerned and compassionate men and women serve as friends of probationers on a one-to-one basis. Law enforcement officials and court officials and private citizens must work together to save our youngsters. Books like this, which provide an understanding of problems of our youngsters and which analyze our procedures for meeting these problems, are more than welcome. They are urgently needed.

WILLIAM SYLVESTER WHITE

PREFACE

ONE begins the writing of a technical book with enthusiasm and the optimism that it will serve to enhance the reader's insight into the specific field or endeavor. Upon completion, a true sense of humility replaces the earlier emotions, and a recognition of the finality of the effort begins to transcend the original excitement.

To be satisfied defies progress. This writing effort has resulted in the realization that the comprehensiveness of the approach utilized still does not encompass all of the areas of police work with juveniles. Juvenile work is a demanding and complex police operation involving a multiplicity of skills and knowledge.

This book represents an attempt to provide the police student with an exposure to the basic armament with which to adequately perform the varied tasks comprising the police juvenile operation. In order to successfully present the necessary information, the writing was given a two-pronged focus.

Juvenile work requires an understanding of the growth and development of the human entity. It necessitates a familiarity with the many psychosocial factors which tend to influence behavior. The effects of the family, the educational system, the peer group, and the culture upon the individual must be viewed from the perspective of behavioral determinents. The police juvenile officer has to be in the position of understanding the nuances of the conditioning and development of youthful behavior.

The reader will discover an extensive treatment of the normalcy of childhood maturation, with an inclusion of subject matter indicating environmental influences affecting behavior. The potential of the family unit as a vehicle of socialization is given emphasis, and this reflects the author's conviction of the importance of the family as the focal point for childhood development. At the same time, the culture and the society in which the child finds himself has not been neglected. The effects of a complex urban and industrialized social system upon the many institutions of socialization and upon the individual will be found to provide insight into the breadth of factors that may affect the very personality of the individual in his attempt to establish his identity within this structure.

For the most part, this information has been presented in a manner conducive to an ease of understanding. Where it appears to be somewhat technical, the reader may be assured that the difficulty of the material defied simplification without a loss of accuracy and completeness.

The second portion of the book addresses the juvenile justice system. The basic philosophy of the juvenile court law is examined, including a survey of those institutions that represent its adjudicative processes. Both the juvenile court and the correctional services of the probation and parole system have been subjected to a realistic appraisal. Just as the strengths of the system have been articulated, the apparent weaknesses have also been discussed. This has been intentional, for it is necessary for the police officer to understand the capabilities and limitations of the total system in order to be able to work within its present structure. Furthermore, if the police are to become an effective instrument for change, their leadership must be based upon their expertise. The voice of law enforcement will not be heard until it has developed the baritone of knowledge.

The need to conceptualize the objectives of the police juvenile enforcement enterprise has led to the presentation of material that covers the administrative aspects attendant to specialized juvenile units. Included within this subject matter are the responsibilities of the unit commander. Thus, the reader will be presented with an overview of the tasks of management as related to juvenile work. No longer can the police act in an independent and isolated manner. Rather, the role of the police in juvenile work must be carried on within the larger framework of the community's effort to control delinquency. This broader perspective has been woven as the central theme throughout the managerial presentation.

If law enforcement is to act as an institution for societal intervention in the lives of youth, then those individuals who will carry out that mission are extremely important in any consideration of the police juvenile mission. The requirements for and the responsibilities of the position of police juvenile officer have been set forth in a way that will alleviate misunderstanding and will facilitate an effective comprehension of the magnitude of that position. It is now necessary for the police to make a significant contribution to the area of the control and prevention of delinquency. The capability of the police to make such an impact will begin with, and in large measure be carried on by, the individual police officer acting in the role of the juvenile specialist.

Attention has been given to many of the more important duties of the juvenile officer. Areas of concern and areas of controversy are not only examined, but recommendations are made that may serve as guides to policy formation. No portion of the juvenile enforcement operation has been intentionally omitted.

Nor has the future direction of law enforcement in its involvement with youth been slighted. The alterations in strategy that will become more evident within the next few years have been postulated in an attempt to stimulate those persons engaged in police juvenile work, to refine their thinking and venture into the challenging world of innovation and improvement.

This book is an honest effort to transmit to the student of police juvenile enforcement the work of others and the additional thoughts of the author, all of which have been evaluated in light of the author's active police experience and further years of tenure in police education and consultation. It is hoped that the reading of this book will not only be an educational experience, but that it will also be a pleasurable one for those interested in the juvenile aspects of police work.

In the course of the advancement of human knowledge, few persons have been destined or privileged to act independently of others. This fact is emphasized herein. The author's ability to be so presumptuous as to attempt to write a meaningful book in the area of police juvenile enforcement is really the representation of the efforts of many others. Some of these individuals are persons who are known to the author and who have contributed to the many opportunities for professional growth that the author has experienced. Included within this group are several persons who must be acknowledged and to whom the author is indebted: Sheriff Melvin A. Willmirth, Fresno County, California, who provided the opportunity to become actively engaged in juvenile law enforcement; and Harry More, now the chairman of the law enforcement program at San Jose State College, who afforded the chance to instruct in-service personnel in a Delinquency Control Institute in Pennsylvania. To these persons and others, the author is grateful.

One person stands out as the most single significant influence in providing the author with the basics of police juvenile specialization. He is representative of the desired professional police officer, and he is undoubtedly the outstanding juvenile specialist ever encountered by this writer. He did more to form the expertise in juvenile enforcement that is now enjoyed by the author than any other individual. Lieutenant Edward Margosian, Fresno County Sheriff's Department, not only personifies excellence in police work, but he is also a good friend.

In closing, the author would like to publicly thank his wife, Donna, for her inspiration and support during the long months of manuscript preparation and to point out her active role in typing the final material, proofreading, and indexing. Without her effort, this book would never have been written.

C. J. FLAMMANG

CONTENTS

POLICE JUVENILE
ENFORCEMENT

PART I

Chapter One

THE PROBLEM

THE increase in criminality stands as one of the nation's most crucial problems. It is obvious that one method of reducing criminal acts is to attack the roots of crime. No such attack can be contemplated without consideration of the long term effects of juvenile delinquency.

Crime is a youthful occupation, and the antisocial behavior of the juvenile not only adds to the burdens crime places upon society, but deviant behavior is subject to learning principles. Thus, delinquent behavior may be reinforced. This reinforcement of socially unacceptable behavior is subject to a time horizon effect. The criminality learned as a juvenile may hold over to adulthood.

With the advent of World War II, many persons in the fields relating to the behavioral sciences, education, and psychology predicted an increase in the deviant behavior of the youth of the nation. Time, affluence, and social change have proved them to have been correct. Following the end of hostilities, the nation entered a period of unparalleled prosperity. The addition of the crop of "war babies" to the society gave a new perspective to the importance of youth, and that perspective has felt no diminishing effects. Thus, youth has emerged from a period of depression and war as one of the most important single groups in the country. The prosperity of the nation has enabled these youngsters to have experienced material values of grand proportions. This has been true even for those who have endured the privations of lower economic life. The *poor* child of today enjoys more of the frills of life than the majority of the children of the depression years.

Yet, in the face of such a period of prosperity, there still exists deprivation. It is more subtle than was experienced a generation ago, and more harmful. Prosperity has been accompanied by technological advancements increasing the material living standard. It has also placed a new emphasis on the need for training and education. Competition is a keen awareness to which every youth is exposed. One cannot live in a candy store without wishing for some sweets. The same is true of the youth of an affluent nation. In a society such as ours, it is very possible to be adequately housed and fed but to undergo deprivation from other areas of life experiences; such as education, parental affection and interest, and the establishment of a feeling of self-worth.

The results of a materially oriented social system can be found within the various manifestations exhibited by the youth. Included in these examples is the increase of youthful criminality and delinquent acts.

The dimensions of the problem are not entirely clear. The nature of delinquency is still subject to controversy. Control and prevention are presently society's weakest tools. What is needed are answers to many of the perplexing questions that arise when the dilemma is subjected to analysis. How widespread is delinquency? How many youth are actually involved? What type of acts are most likely to be committed by any age group or sex? What type of person becomes delinquent? What type of person, committing what type of act, ceases antisocial behavior by adulthood? What is early detection, and is the social system capable of performing that task? These are but a few of the questions which must be answered. Anyone may easily consider more, just as the solving of any one of these will uncover more.

One thing is known. Juvenile delinquency occurs in every area of the country, every community, every social class and ethnic group, among the rich and poor, the educated and the uneducated. It knows no bounds, nor is any child immune. If one is to assume correctly that youth represents the nation's most valuable asset then delinquency must be controlled, if not prevented or reduced. To assist in this end is the reason for this book.

DEFINITION OF DELINQUENCY

Beginning with the definition of delinquency, one immediately encounters problems.[1] There are a multitude of variations in the conceptualizations necessary for the development of a definition. From the legal standpoint, one may be considered to be delinquent at any of several points along the path of the judicial process. From a much broader base, delinquency may be defined in terms of any childhood behavior that goes beyond the bounds of social acceptance. Depending upon which definition is utilized determines the acts that are deemed delinquent, as well as the number of youth who are delinquent.

Thus, under one definition, a child of four years entering the open garage of the neighbor and removing an inexpensive toy to his own yard may be considered delinquent. The same could be true of the child of eight who talks back to his parent. Or of the youth of twelve who absents himself from school on one occasion without permission or excuse.

Another definition may require social recognition of delinquency only after official contact with the police. The youth whose name is taken by an officer when found lounging on a corner would be delinquent. Or the girl contacted by police after failing to return home at the time set by the parents for a dating situation would become a delinquent statistic. The young child talked to by the police or fire department personnel because of playing with matches could be a defined delinquent.

A more narrow definition has been advanced by the Children's Bureau:

> Juvenile delinquency cases are those referred to courts for acts defined in the statutes of the State as the violation of law or municipal ordinance by children or youth of juvenile court age, or for conduct so seriously antisocial as to interfere with the rights of others or to menace the welfare of the delinquent himself or of the community.[2]

Under such a definition, the youth would have to be of juvenile court age and have been referred to the court for some type of action. It should be noted, however, that such a definition is still much broader than some persons would advocate. From this view, the youth who was referred to the court but for whom the court acted in such a manner as to adjudicate in his favor would still be a delinquent.

Of course, the act—the delinquency itself—would have been

properly defined as a necessity to bring about the court referral.

Savitz sees delinquency as all acts legally set forth, binding all youth of juvenile court age who have attained the age of reason or responsibility.[3] This latter age is usually statutory.

Under both definitions, delinquency not only includes criminal statute violations, but also actions which if performed by adults would not be an offense. As opposed to the Children's Bureau definition, Savitz purports the delinquency to be inherently a part of the act; and occurring within the act if such an act is performed by a person who is a culpable juvenile. The federal agency incorporates the juvenile court referral as a criteria for a delinquent act.

Youths are legally held accountable for many acts for which adults are not under the juvenile court laws. This requires the need to differentiate between the delinquent act of the youth (those actions such as truancy, runaway, incorrigibility) and the violations of criminal statutes which apply to all persons.

In this book, the term *juvenile criminality* will refer to those crimes universally deemed to be prohibited actions, such as murder, rape, robbery, burglary, arson, theft, and assaults. *Juvenile delinquency* will be used to describe the acts of youth of a noncriminal nature; or criminal statutes of a lesser degree than enumerated, and which vary in penalty from jurisdiction to jurisdiction.

It must be pointed out, however, that a much broader definition of delinquency exists that goes beyond that of the legal nature. It is of importance to the behavioral scientist who considers delinquency as acts that deviate from the social norm so as to place the youth in the position of being a danger to himself, his interests, or the community. This is not the concept of delinquency to be utilized herein, but it has been included in order for the reader to recognize the need for determining the *use* of a definition before accepting any given one.

For the purposes of this writing, a delinquent act would be any legally prohibited act of a youth whose minimum age would be the age of reason and whose maximum age would be the upper jurisdictional limit of the juvenile court; and, that act would not include crimes of a serious nature or crimes of violence. These latter offenses would be deemed *criminality*. In keeping with such a legal definition, a delinquent would be any youth ajudged a ward of the juvenile court for any act not including dependency situations.

From this latter definition, a delinquent would be a juvenile over which the juvenile court has placed wardship. This would arbitrarily exclude all youth handled by the police, but released prior to any juvenile court action; as well as those youth who appeared in juvenile court, but against whom the court took no action.

This definition precludes anyone other than a legally constituted juvenile court from declaring a youth a delinquent.

THE EXTENT OF DELINQUENCY

Any attempt at describing the extent of delinquency is at best a hazardous situation. Obviously, from the problems inherent in defining delinquency the measurement of extent is found to be varied and complex.

To discuss extent, one must be interested in what is known, not what is thought. Opinions, no matter how perfected, are of little value in making the determination at hand. It is necessary to evaluate those sources of statistical information that are available. Regardless of the limitations of such statistics, they do represent what is *known* about the extent of delinquency, and such data are absolutely essential in the determination of the extent of the problem.

Somewhere in the area of 400,000 youths appear in juvenile court annually, and their numbers equal almost 2 percent of the total number of youths in the age group between ten and eighteen years.[1] These years represent the years during which a child is most likely to appear in court.

This percentage is an annual consideration. The percentage increases if the total juvenile court years of jurisdiction are taken into account. Thus, in the eight year span of high juvenile court appearance rate, around 20 percent of the boys, and 8 percent of the girls will appear before the judge. Some authorities estimate as high as one in every six male youths will make a juvenile court appearance for a delinquent act before reaching his eighteenth birthdate, a rate that is higher than that for completion of high school.[4]

Added to the burden are the additional children who are the result of the increase in the population. By 1980, it is estimated that youth within the age bracket indicated will number about 47 million.[5] If the present percentage of youth appearing in court annually does not increase, the additional numbers of youth, a part of the normal population increase, will severely strain the existing services.

The problem becomes more acute in the face of the fact that the percentage of children appearing before the juvenile court is increasing.[1] This increase has been an annual occurrence for every year but one since 1950.

The practical implications of such a drain on the judicial process in the face of increased youthful population, as well as increased delinquency trends, are such as to stagger the imagination. Added to this burden are the additional youths handled by the police and other agencies who are released without a court appearance. This group is estimated to be three times the number who appear in court. Most conversations with police juvenile officers would tend to confirm the suspicion that such an estimate does not attain the proportions the actual caseload incurs.

If the self-reported delinquency is considered, the amount of socially unacceptable actions of youth ascends rapidly. Self-reported delinquency studies indicate that upwards of 90 percent of the youth will admit to one or more acts which would bring them under official control.[4]

Arrest statistics can give only a partial picture of the extent of the problem; however, the FBI's *Uniform Crime Reports* for 1967 is worthy of review.[6] Youths are found to be responsible for a substantial share of the nation's crime, although it is also probably true that they are more easily apprehended than the adult offender. The arrest statistics of the *Uniform Crime Reports* are the result of the cooperative reporting of the arrests made in various crime classifications by more than 97 percent of the nation's police agencies.

In 1967, the total arrests by age in the seven major felony classes (Homicide, Forcible Rape, Robbery, Aggravated Assault,

Burglary, Larceny, and Auto Theft) were illustrated by the following facts:

1.	Ages Under 15 Years	23.1 percent of the arrests nationwide.
2.	Ages Under 18 Years	49.0 percent of the arrests nationwide.
3.	Ages Over 18 Years	51.0 percent of the arrests nationwide.

It is apparent that the juvenile accounts for a disproportionate percentage of the total arrests made during a given year. In fact, just less than 50 percent of all arrests made in the United States for a major felony crime in 1967 were youth under eighteen years of age.

Additionally, during that year the arrest rates were highest for the 13 to 14 year age group, reaching a startling 13.6 percent. The rates decreased and stabilized at about 9 percent for the 15 to 16 year age group and continued to drop with the increase in age until the 25 to 29 year age group when the rates again increased to over 9 percent.

From this data, it may be inferred that the police will encounter most juveniles during the junior high school period, with a gradual tapering off during the high school years. There will be an increase in criminality within the 25 to 29 year age group. This will appear for several reasons, among which will be the fact that many of these persons have been institutionalized and released and are now recidivists.

During the same year, the offenses cleared (or cases closed) by the arrest of persons under eighteen years of age accounted for 22 percent of the robberies, 40 percent of the burglaries, and 51 percent of the auto thefts.

In the category of criminal homicide, the year 1967 saw 9 percent of those arrested for murder to be under eighteen years of age, and 37 percent were under 25 years. Of the long term arrest trends for murder, youth accounted for a 56 percent increase in arrests for homicide from 1960 to 1967. The increase for adult offenders during the same period was only 39 percent. During the same seven year period, the arrest trends for youth involved in aggravated assaults increased 121 percent.

From 1960 to 1967, police arrests for all offenses and all age groups increased 11 percent, while for the under eighteen year age group for the same period arrest trends for all offenses rose 69 percent. During the same period, the number of youth in that age group increased only 22 percent.

While there are many inherent problems that affect the reliability of the FBI statistics, the figures do point out a continuing involvement of youth in criminal acts as well as a continuing increase in the trend toward their involvement. The figures cannot be ignored.

The costs are high, with the most notable being the human cost. For those children who become involved in the judicial process due to a minor offense, the effects of the involvement might be the deciding factor between delinquency and nondelinquency; while those who are caught up in the serious offenses are in need of long and skillful treatment quite often absent in our society. Added to the costs in human misery are the financial burdens of crime that attain fantastic proportions yearly. No nation can endure such staggering losses indefinitely.[3]

THE NEED FOR POLICE KNOWLEDGE OF DELINQUENCY

The police, because of their unique first line contact for society with a delinquent youth, are in a strong position to perform many functions aimed at the control and prevention of delinquency. This is an enviable position and it is one that can become more meaningful and important if performed with the degree of professionalism modern society needs. It is incumbent upon the police to provide such services and in such a manner as to perform the most successful service for each juvenile contact.

It is no longer possible for the police to continue to perform the juvenile function of law enforcement without a degree of sophistication that can only be attained through knowledge and understanding. The facts are the opposite. Too many police agencies are perpetuating the former fallicies and erroneous conceptions regarding delinquency and the delinquent. These errors are even spawned in the training academies through the repetitious use of outdated and poorly organized material that emphasizes procedures instead of understanding.

It is not enough to teach the officer when to issue a citation, when to reprimand and release, or when to refer to juvenile court. The time has come for the police to be able to have an intelligent understanding of the facets of growth and maturation; attitude development; the effects of various family deficiencies; cultural, educational, and social deprivation; and the myriad of delinquency conditioning factors that are experienced by a child in a complex, industrial society.

The day of the statement "I don't like to work with juveniles" is long since over, but the police officer does not know it. That remark is heard over and over in squad rooms and radio cars throughout the country. Yet, it is a fact that at least 50 percent of the arrests an officer makes will involve a juvenile. No officer can work an eight hour shift without encountering a juvenile situation, whether the juvenile be a suspect or a victim.

The police emphasis on arrest and case clearing in juvenile matters is mute testimony of the failure of law enforcement to adequately prepare for professionalized service in juvenile enforcement. The inability of the police to focus proper attention on the protection of the juvenile is a constant reminder of law enforcement's self-imposed limitations.

The belief that the patrol division can perform the responsibilities of the police in juvenile enforcement can lead to only superficial handling of a juvenile case. The need for specialized juvenile officers to augment the routine police patrol has not been altered.

Full recognition of the responsibilities of law enforcement in dealing with the juvenile and delinquency has never been as crucial a need as now. The many areas of community effort in which the police can show decisive leadership has not been tapped. Police involvement in developing new and useful programs of delinquency control is just beginning to surface and only in the most progressive agencies.

Many controversies still exist within enforcement itself concerning numerous aspects of the police role in juvenile enforcement. Included are questions concerning police involvement in recreation, the fingerprinting of juveniles, and police-juvenile counselling. These and other areas of juvenile enforcement must be reconciled with the need for solid law enforcement and the best interests of the child and the community.

The police image, especially among the youth, is another area of concern. The activities of youth directed toward social dissent is causing more confrontations with the police. Many of these situations have given rise to poor police procedures, and such tactics have served to widen the breech between the youth and the law enforcement services.

Poorly trained officers result in poorly handled situations, even on the individual basis. Each such police action results in a further alienation of the police and the youth. Each such action results in a reinforced learning situation on the part of the officer involved.

Many police juvenile contacts are inadequate due to the officer's lack of confidence in what action should be taken. This lack of confidence is the result of poor training, not only in procedures; but more so, in the understanding of the youth and the direction societal intervention should move. Juvenile work is so varied, the problems encountered so complex, that it is impossible for an officer to be given preinstruction on how and what action to perform in a given circumstance.

This indicates that police juvenile enforcement is an unstructured situation. Police officers, working in a semimilitary unit, are familiar with very strictly structured situations. When they are faced with broad and unstructured situations their perception is easily distorted. When this occurs they are found not only to over react, but also to under react. Consequently, it is known to police everywhere that many juvenile situations are handled poorly by the failure to take the necessary action as often as taking too harsh a course.

In order to facilitate the proper use of the discretionary police decision involved in juvenile enforcement, it is necessary that each officer know and understand the many ramifications of youthful development, as well as the effects of the ecology of the juvenile in question. This means knowledge, and understanding of that knowledge. The information contained in the next few chapters is geared to provide a basic awareness of the juvenile problem.

NOTES AND REFERENCES

1. Ruth Cavan: *Juvenile Delinquency.* New York, J. B. Lippincott Company. 1962, pp. 5, 6, 15-22.
2. Juvenile Court Statistics, 1957, Children's Bureau, Statistical Series No. 52, Children's Bureau, Washington, D. C., 1959, p. 4.
3. Leonard Savitz: *Dilemmas in Criminology.* New York, McGraw-Hill, 1967, p. 15. (See Chapter 3 for an extensive presentation of Statistics and Research regarding juvenile delinquency in the United States.)
4. Robert W. Winslow: *Juvenile Delinquency in a Free Society.* Belmont, California, Dickenson, 1968, p. 2.
5. *Statistical Abstract of the United States, 1959.* U. S. Government Printing Office, Washington, D. C., 1959, p. 6.
6. *Uniform Crime Reports, 1967.* Federal Bureau of Investigation, Department of Justice, Washington, D. C., 1968, pp. 121-122.

Chapter Two

GROWTH AND MATURATION

D EVELOPMENT is continuous and cumulative. The manner by which a child interacts with others at age five or ten may be of great significance in understanding his behavior at age fifteen or twenty. Changes in the nature of the child coupled with changes in his environment combine to cause the child to be quite different at various stages in his life.

With juveniles, one is confronted with children and youth who are in any one of four stages of development; or more complicated, in the process of leaving one and entering the other. Each stage is characterized by differing physiological changes, emotional development, and maturation rate. Not all children develop at the same speed, and either advanced development or developmental lag may create severe problems leading the youth into difficulty with society. There are marked differences between individuals as each advances through the periods of the life cycle; however, there are enough traits that are universal to enable a generalized outline of the various periods of growth and development and their effects on the child. Each stage adds to the development of the eventual personality of the youth; the personality that will appear in his adult life.

It should be understood at the outset that as the child proceeds toward adult maturity, his personality and actions will be subject to change in the various stages through which he passes. Consequently, he may be cooperative and polite at one time, and exasperating and belligerent during another period. This inconsistent behavior often disturbs adults, but it is a normal experience in the life of every child.

The process of development occurs from infancy to adulthood, and both the delinquent and the nondelinquent child progresses

16

through the various stages, which are the preschool period, middle childhood, puberty or early adolescence, and adolescence. For most humans, physical and mental maturation are achieved along somewhat uniform lines, allowing for generalized predictions of the effects of each period encountered. Deviations do occur, but they are usually found to be within a narrow range. Only a minority of individuals deviate so much as to need excessive societal intervention.[1]

The periods of development do not end abruptly, but rather are subject to a blending, and delineation is difficult. Yet, if one but pauses to view each stage, there are marked changes in the lives of children during the various periods.

THE PRESCHOOL YEARS

The preschool years may appear to be of little concern to police officers, but this period is one in which major personality trends often are clearly evident. Habits are beginning to form, and some of these pertain to socialization of the individual and may determine his social relationships for the larger portion of his life.[2]

The period is characterized by rapid physical growth from the helpless infant to the active and noisy child of five or six. The physical growth emphasis is on the large muscles causing them to mature prior to complete voluntary control. At the end of the period, the child is able to run, jump, and skip quite well, but may still knock things over and appear to be clumsy.

The social progression of the individual, from the protection of the womb to backyard play, is rapid and conflicting. The infant at first is little more than an animal, but social stimulation brings about early signs of response. Thus the infant of several months will respond to the human voice, and by eight or nine months the child will reach out toward adults. Interestingly, during this same period the infant, when placed with another, will often treat the other as a toy. By eighteen months, the child will recognize the other as the same *kind*, and social relationships will emerge. By four years, the period of associative play will have transgressed to a cooperative play.

During the infancy stage, physical needs are predominant. It is here that the first satisfactions of human drives are either attained or denied. It is also during this period that frustration and anxiety are first experienced. Because there are so many routine needs to be met, and due to the infant's inability to meet any of them himself, his first learnings of trust and confidence in others takes shape during the early months of his life. If these needs are met to the satisfaction of the child, the development of these early socialization experiences will be positive and meaningful. On the other hand, if the child is neglected or rejected, the early seeds of maladjustment will be sown. The maladjustments may be seen in the later preschool period by the child's withdrawal from social contact or his literal attacks on his environment, including people.

The learning assimilated during this period is fantastic. The child learns to walk, verbalize, to feed himself, dress himself, and perform most of the basic functions necessary for life. He is capable of making simple requests, formulating demands, and utilizing his investigative drives by asking questions and through exploration. His desire to learn is punctuated by frequent clashes with the adult world; and he is introduced to discipline, wherein he learns to obey simple commands.

The preschool child attains a certain amount of freedom, but this coupled with his inquisitive nature and active needs brings him into conflict with his authority figures. Thus, the child learns to react to his new found freedom in conformity to the cultural standards as demonstrated by the parents. He learns to utilize his freedom in the safety of the limitations they have placed upon him. This is one of the most important lessons in the life task of socialization.

Since most of these activities are experienced in conjunction with the association of child and mother, the role of the mother becomes one of extreme significance. More of the importance of that role will be discussed in Chapter Three.

The move from the helplessness of infancy to the active and boisterous child of five years is accompanied by much thwarting, resulting in emotional outbursts.[3]

Some children do not respond to discipline or authority, and these failures to adjust may be manifested through efforts at resistance, such as kicking, yelling, and other forms of emotional tantrums; or the child may respond by almost complete passivity or refusal to conform. These reactions may be merely spontaneous, or they may be artfully directed at the irritation of the adult authority figure, usually the mother.[1]

Generally speaking, one may expect the child to proceed through this period with the eventual attainment of a limited social humaness, capable of leaving the home and entering the school situation.[4]

THE MIDDLE CHILDHOOD PERIOD

The child is now ready to enter school, his first introduction to a formal, social institution. Here he is expected to conform to rules and regulations. There is little time to be paid to his individual demands, as was the case when he was in the confines of his home. Having reached the age of five or six, social tolerance of his transgressing behavior is now limited. These limitations on tolerance will continue to parallel his age development. The actions of the youth, which before were tolerated or even thought to be cute, are now condemned. The child is expected to behave according to the standards for his age. Failure to do so brings about censorship and results in a responsiveness to social expectations.

The peer group receives attention for the first time, beginning with limited friendships in the first grade and extending through the development of large group activity by the eighth to the tenth year. These peer group associations are not all smooth, as many of the groups tend to form and dissolve quite rapidly. The effects of such dissolutions are minimal for children of the middle childhood period, and much less frantic than such situations during adolescence.

The peer group becomes a place wherein conformity can be experienced with less difficulty than in the larger environment. There are common experiences to be shared, and equal rights tend to exist. The rules are loose and flexible, and condemnation not as severe as in the formal institutionalized setting. It is a place for the development of companionship and loyalty. It serves as a market place for the exchange of ideas. The peer group gradually becomes the primary reference group for the child, and will remain so until adulthood is reached and marriage replaces its need. Until that time, the importance of the peer group on the life and development of the child will increase in intensity with each additional year.[1]

Physical development is fairly even during the middle childhood years. It is characterized by the growth of the long bones of the arms and legs, giving a slender look to a formerly pudgy child. The increase in the size of bones and the development of large muscles causes this period to be one of almost constant activity. This activity is not just emotional release, but is an organic need of the stage of development. The child has increased strength and mobility. Fatigue is almost unknown. Most activity will be with other children, and is usually accompanied by noise, emitted verbally if not otherwise. Such activity brings the child into adult conflict, again causing the individual to adjust to discipline and conform.

Although they learn large muscle skills easily, their ability to perform intricate motor control tasks is still limited. Yet, at about age ten, the nervous system has attained its maximum development. The child has an active imagination, and will often exasperate parents and others by beginning a project that he is incapable of concluding.[5]

During the latter portion of the middle childhood period, the drive for emancipation from the family takes on new meaning. No longer is the adult word received without question, and in some cases belligerence and outright rebellion occur.[6] Thus, the child becomes increasingly independent of the parents. He now begins to make certain decisions on his own. Moral judgments and the refinement of conscience take place. The child may begin to compare the standards of his home with those of his friends.[7]

Many of these attempts at emancipation are thwarted, and others cause anguish and guilt. It is a period of emotional struggling. The child is straining to free himself from those whom he loves and who are the closest to him. His reactions may be emotional or even physical, with the child developing annoying habits or suffering from sleeplessness.[8] The more aggressive youngsters cease to be the complacent children of before, and actually may appear to be daring and reckless in their adventures.[3]

Most middle childhood delinquency is still handled by the parents, in the neighborhood, or by the school. Only in the more severe cases of serious malicious mischief, theft, burglary, or incorrigibility is the child brought to the attention of the police.

It is well that officers understand that delinquency during this period takes on several forms, with much of it either school or family oriented. The child who has a quick temper or who fails to achieve in school may become a problem within the school. The dislike of the academic setting may lead to truancy, as well as truancy being the result of peer group association.

It is quite possible that theft is the result of the failure of the child to have a full comprehension of the meaning of personal property; or, it may be the result of cultural or family deprivation. A family or neighborhood in which much theft occurs has a difficult time producing youngsters who value private ownership and condemn larceny. Many thefts are the result of acts of impulse, as well as sign posts that indicate a failure to develop clear concepts of right and wrong. If allowed to continue or go unchecked, such thefts will be reinforced, and the pattern will take on new meaning through the introduction of preplanning.

An aggressive child may become openly hostile to authority figures. The same can occur with a milder child who cannot accept discipline. In some instances, children in the latter years of this period of development may reach toward physical combat with parents, adult neighbors, school officials, or police. This is not from the desire for the combat, as much as it is from the desire to show a lack of respect for an unaccepted authority figure.

Many children become involved in delinquent acts almost by accident, usually while pursuing an otherwise legitimate purpose. Cavan classifies such activity as *recreational delinquency*.[1] It is characterized by youth acting either on impulse or with no thought given to the consequences. Such is the case in many instances of damages involving the use of BB or pellet guns. It is also seen in the background of many malicious mischiefs, especially to vacant or deserted buildings. Often youths report that the activity, although destructive, was "something to do."

If police encounters continue throughout the latter part of this period of development, more serious antisocial behavior may be expected in later years. It is the duty of the police to attempt to determine those children with serious maladjustments, and seek the best remedies the community has to offer at the earliest possible time. This is one of the more acute problems of police juvenile enforcement. Most agencies are overloaded with serious cases of criminal violations, causing the officers to expend their energies in those areas rather than to take the time necessary to perform the task of early detection in situations involving youthful and minor infractions. This may appear to be an argument for more police officers; on the contrary, it is a plea for better training and more effective utilization of police man hours.

THE PUBERTY YEARS AND EARLY ADOLESCENCE

Central and undoubtedly most important in the process of change is the onset of puberty, which ushers in the growth and maturation of the sex organs. It is a time when old personality patterns break down to make room for new. In general, the taller and heavier child, as well as those who are healthy, appear to reach puberty earlier.[2]

Because individuals do not mature at the same rate, there can be wide differences between children regarding the time when puberty begins. Individual differences will never be as great as they are during this period. For the child entering puberty at an early age, many distressing problems may occur. The same is true for the child who lags in advancement into puberty. The early pubescent may find new importance because of the increased development, but lack the mental and emotional maturity to use it to advantage. The early blooming girl may find difficulty adjusting to her physical changes. She may be overcome by the attention she derives from boys much older, and the ramifications and consequences of such situations are usually tragic.

Puberty begins in girls with the onset of menarche and ends several months later with the ability to reproduce. The menstrual cycle may begin anywhere from age eleven to age fifteen. For boys, the period of puberty begins prior to the development of secondary sex characteristics, usually somewhere between twelve and sixteen years.

The male voice deepens during puberty, and for some youngsters the sqeaking vocal noises caused by an involuntary change in pitch may be the cause of much embarrassment. At the same time, the fact that a late developer still maintains a high pitched voice in a group of deep voiced peers can be an extreme source of ridicule and anxiety.

Girls lose their childish ways and turn to more adult pursuits and actions. These changes often separate old friendships if the former chum has a lag in development. Deep emotional problems may infect either party, unless they are assisted by others in understanding the normalcy of the breech.

There is an increase in growth at the onset of puberty evidenced by rapid increases in height or weight. The growth rate for the different parts of the body are not even, however, and consequently, some part of the body may appear not to belong because of an immediate, extreme size differential. The feet and hands, as examples, will increase disproportionately to the body, attaining almost full growth in a very short period. The nose will take on its adult shape, yet be fitted to a childish face. These changes in extreme sizes, tend to magnify the part, causing awkwardness and embarrassment.

It is odd how a boy of thirteen whose feet have grown almost overnight is fitted with a brogue type of shoe with excessive leather extending outward beyond the sole, and emphasizing the increased size. Such a youngster has been placed in the position of appearing as if he were wearing snowshoes.

There are some physiological changes of the visceral organs which may affect the child's physical capabilities. The heart has developed in size, but the arteries remain much smaller. This causes the heart to work harder to force the proper amount of oxygen to the body. Exercise may result in dizziness, or even heart enlargement if not moderately controlled.[5] At the same time, the youth may appear to be large and strong. The energy required for growth tends to reduce the stamina of the youngster, and these physiological factors cause the child of this period to appear lazy. This brings about criticism and conflict with the adults around him who are judging him by his size alone. Very often, such children are not active and need considerable rest. The contrast between the activity of a few months or a year before amplifies the picture of laziness.

The fact that the puberty period is full of so many quick physical and emotional changes causes the child to have rapid mood alterations. There may develop certain hostilities toward adult authority, and the concern of the family, teachers, or others regarding the lassitude of the individual tends to accentuate the problem.

States of depression are not uncommon, and negative attitudes are constantly displayed. This is the period of "moping around." It is a time when no activity or recreation seems to bring about the response the adult world deems should occur. Critical attitudes directed toward adults encompasses most of the respected authority figures, from parents to the police. Both boys and girls appear to be suspicious and unfriendly, as well as sensitive and belligerent.[3]

The drive toward independence becomes stronger as this period progresses, and will attain its greatest magnitude during the adolescent years.

All of these factors bring the youth into conflict with the adult world and the social environment. Because of a certain amount of freedom, increased size, and the advent of the junior high school experience, the youth with maladjustments is often seen by the police on an official basis during this period. In some areas, the junior high school has become a substation of the department with juvenile officers and detectives coming and going at random.

Many persons tend to believe that delinquency, as a police problem, is most frequently encountered on the high school level. This is just not true. The early manifestations of delinquency begin to emerge during the junior high school years when the youths are approaching puberty or are in the early adolescent stage. All of the problems attached to these stages of development are locked together in one school situation. The peer group importance has increased to the extent that there is a constant struggle for status. This means that word-of-mouth exchanges between students are of more importance at this time than at any other.

The school is no good. The teachers are all slobs. Parents don't care, or are too strict. Girlfriend and boyfriend encounters flourish and die. Sex is a common conversation topic, as well as a subject for experimentation. Smoking is introduced as a sign of adulthood. Drinking is attempted by the bolder, more aggressive child. Glue sniffing and some drug abuse is commonplace. The automobile is a desired item, but for the majority, legally far from attainable.

The child has been removed from the stability of one classroom and one teacher in the neighborhood elementary school where he was well known with a circle of close companions with whom he had shared life for some time. In its place, the youth finds the multiple class and instructor situation that is a standard part of the junior high school plan. The school is no longer a neighborhood environment, but is the result of the amalgamation of several areas. Some of his old friends have been lost to other schools. Others have been separated through the growth process. New friends are made, but are no longer persons necessarily from his neighborhood, or known to his parents.

The youth of this age is a great one for learning first names only. This lessens the opportunity of the parents knowing the nature of the child's companionship.

The popular thing is to find the school, an adult institution, and the adult world a drag. This is reflected in academic achievement and extracurricular participation. The "nothing to do" cult is evident, adding to the apparent lethargic attitude displayed.

The gym, with its locker room, becomes a place of invitation for theft. The lunch money, furnished by obliging parents, becomes a new found barter. It is not unusual for groups to develop who demand payment for protection, collections coming from lunch money.

Rivalries between groups occur. Sometimes these are fad oriented, while on other occasions they are neighborhood or ethnic group factions. From these stem fights and disturbances. Interschool rivalries occur when older brothers get involved, or when a junior high school sweetheart is lost to a high school student.

For those students who have difficulty in achieving in the regular school program, the notoriety of a negative act will gain status among the "out group." Thus, the stigma of police contacts or court action is reduced, and in many instances raises the degree of influence within a group.

For the adult world, very little of the truth of these encounters is ever received. If directly involved, the youth will preface all statements to parents and others with "They said I . . .," while if not involved "They said he . . ." will begin the recounting of the facts as told to this third party by the suspect or one of his friends.

It is during this period that most attitudes are refined and imbedded in the individual. Not only should the police recognize the need for effective control efforts directed toward the youth with delinquent manifestations; but, law enforcement should further be aware of the need for instituting and maintaining effective relations with the early adolescent in general. By so doing, the police may make use of the natural state of attitudinal development existing during the junior high school years. Much can be done to offset the police community relations problem by appropriate activity with children in this stage of development.[9]

ADOLESCENCE

It has been pointed out by a noted sociologist that while physically at a prime, and equal to any adult, the adolescent finds himself socially inferior.[10] Striving for emancipation, he is obliged to his parents for certain care and support. School attendance laws, as well as the holding power of education, compel him to remain a schoolboy. This is a much different situation for the adolescent that he would have encountered a few generations ago.

The adolescent's physical growth has been completed, or most certainly has slowed down. But, for the majority, many unsolved personality problems have held over from the period of puberty and early adolescence. Sexual interests and appetites have fully developed, but the ability to partake on a manner wholly acceptable is still denied. The sex orientation of our culture continually presents itself to these youth who are physically if not emotionally equipped. Society is not willing to tolerate overt sexual experience for the adolescent until the later teen years. For some youth, this waiting period is a considerable length of time. The time lag between physical and emotional maturity brings about widespread sexual experimentation, not all of which is without negative consequences.

Much time is spent in searching for an individual identity. This involves the finalizing of the personality. Additionally, worry over a variety of problems, including school achievement consumes much energy.[11] Anxiety over sex, further education, immediate employment, and vocational goals are common causes of concern. Social status seems a constant worry. The adolescent is often plagued with feelings of inadequacy. For boys, the draft or military service is a problem. Always there looms the attempts at freedom.

For most, freedom is an abstraction that will come with adult status and legal drinking. For the minority who cannot wait, the answer is found in running away. These situations are a concern to parents and dedicated police officers. While the majority of runaway juveniles are returned home with minor repercussions, some are subjected to various delinquent activities during their absence.

The adolescent is full of deep and sensitive thoughts. This is a period of questioning the "whys" of existence, and the "wheres" of direction. Confusion and uncertainty over religion and moral issues are a part of the problems to be faced.

The identification of the masculine and feminine roles take place during adolescence and are a part of the life task of the reestablishment of the self-image. This is the point of departure into the adult world; a world in which society expects the male to be a man and the female to be a woman. Adolescence is the time to finalize the sex typing of the individual.

The peer group has now become the most important reference group in the individual's life, fully taking over the position once held by the family. As a consequence, the parents must compete with that group. If this competition is at complete odds with the prevailing group thinking, the parents may find that they have been isolated from their offspring as the group defends itself by closing out the unwanted, and becoming a society within a society.[1]

For some adolescents, the desire to emancipate is one of inner conflict caused by their fears of being separated from their parents and the security offered in the family unit. In such cases, the hostility displayed by the teenager is more of a cover for inward fears than the venting of true feelings against the parents. Adolescents are seeking a new posture within the family. They are trying to bring about a reevaluation of their position and relationship with their parents. They no longer wish to be treated as children, but rather as semi-equals within the household. They crave love and wish to give affection, but they want this to be on a mature level of mutual respect.

The adolescent is going through an experience of insecurity, with himself and the world around him. He must bring into mature focus all of the life tasks required for adulthood, and this is a tremendous job. In some instances, he must do this with little or no understanding and support from those who are the closest to him. He experiences loneliness and frustration, fears and anxieties. Normal drives and urges are ever present, but are yet forbidden. He shirks from the adults who could offer him the guidance and assistance he needs. He is often depressed, feels valueless, doubts his own abilities, and has little certainty regarding direction.[12]

Some adolescent delinquency is an outgrowth of earlier delinquent activity; a hold over from the middle childhood or early adolescent period. Other delinquency in adolescence is brought on by the stresses of that stage of development. In either case, adolescent delinquency seems to be a means of negative conformity. It is persistant utilization of planned delinquency. It is no longer impulsive behavior and it tends to exist over a long time period. The youthful adolescent who has several known delinquent acts in all probability has been involved in many more. As these acts become progressively more serious, he may continue to do minor infractions and have these latter episodes overlooked. A boy who has turned to committing burglaries seldom draws serious censorship for a few acts of truancy, or an occasional disturbing the peace. This new found tolerance is prevalent among parents, school authorities, and the judicial process.

Many of the opportunities for adolescent delinquency are choice situations. The adolescent delinquent seldom makes that choice on the basis of a moral judgment, but usually based on a *pleasure index*. The more confirmed the delinquency, the more often the pleasure index will be weighed against apprehension and punishment. On the basis of the pleasure to be derived, the adolescent delinquent will act. It is this phenomenon that causes one youth to be involved in a certain offense with a second youth on one night, only to drop out and have the second youth team with another for a different type of act the following evening. This constant shifting or adding crime partners causes juvenile investigations to be complex and lengthy.

Successful acts of an antisocial nature bring status with the peer group. As the delinquency progresses, the pattern of the acts become subject to more selectivity. This patterning of life organization after delinquent behavior can become so set as to be followed by a criminal career.

On the otherhand, if the desires and goals of the adult world appear to be more satisfying and pleasureful than the pleasure derived from delinquency, the youth may cease the negative pattern and being striving for those things that will bring about the normal adult satisfactions. At that point, the youth has returned to the mainstream. Regardless of the claims and accounts of those favoring rehabilitation, the majority of those youths who turn away from what appears to be confirmed delinquency have done so on their own merit, utilizing the pleasure index to determine the course of their future.

One other important characteristic of most adolescents is their inability to project toward the future. Youth tend to live in and for the present with little consideration given to future outcomes. This is not only in reference to a lack of long range planning, but it also implies little regard for the literal tomorrow. What is important is *now*. Coupled with the recklessness of youth, the juvenile has a natural capability to perform any deviant act with but a limited amount of external encouragement.

ADJUSTMENT

Since little of what the human desires or strives for is ever attained to the degree of the original motivation, life is a period of need for successive adjustments. Maladjustment appears as a conceptual term, indicating the wrong or erroneous adjustment to a particular set of circumstances. As most severe delinquency is the result of a maladjustment, it is important that the police officer understands the meaning of adjustment, what it implies, and how it occurs.

In this discussion, little attention will be paid to the numerous manifestations of maladjustment; instead, adjustment toward normalcy will be outlined. Through the recognition of normal adjustment patterns, abnormal adjustments should become clearer perceptions.

For many persons, adjustment is some abstract state of contentment; a feeling of being right with the world. In reality, adjustment is a process. It is the process of alteration of one's inner forces to bring about stability and to maintain equilibrium in the face of external environmental forces. To avoid confusion at the outset, it must be noted that adjustment also has a social factor. It cannot be just the release of inner tensions, but must be a rational act that will conform to the needs and demands of society. In some instances, this may be an easy task, while in other cases it may be a compromise that does not fully attain the desired results of the individual.

It becomes apparent that adjustment does not equal happiness or necessarily bring about any state of good feeling. It is a behavioral process necessary to the life tasks. It is not a rock behind which a person may hide. It is not a security blanket. Some adjustments are very difficult to make, but every adjustment accomplished is an addition to the inner strength needed for modern living. The selective development and utilization of an individual's strengths and potential, attuned to the cultural orientation of the society, is an essential part of human adjustment.[7]

Assistance in conceptualizing adjustment may be discovered

by consideration of the basic components of a positive adjusted person. These are elements necessary as basic to the well adjusted individual.[3]

The first requirement is the existence of basic values that serve to guide the individual. These are the motivating forces that perform the service of directing behavior while furnishing basic purpose for existence. Each individual needs rational reasons for determining the worth of the life adventure to overcome temporary setbacks, to endure hardships, and to continue to compete for goals and attainments which are desirable and reasonable.

Having a goal in life, or wanting something very desperately, will assist in guiding the individual along certain lines, but is not enough to bring about fulfillment. The second consideration basic to adjustment is the ability on the part of the individual to see himself in a real sense. This means the person must be able to determine his strengths and weaknesses. He must realistically determine his capabilities and potential. If there are handicaps that may be overcome, the person must make the effort to do so, recognizing that if the weakness is permanent, he must alter his goals and learn to live with reality. Most importantly, he must be realistic in evaluations of his abilities and the establishment of aspirations.

The setting of too extreme a goal is probably the root of more failure than any other single factor. Most agency personnel, counselors, and educators have experienced that tragedy of being contacted by a person with enthusiasm seeking a goal that for him is an impossible dream. It is difficult to advise such persons of the realities involved without defeating them. Police officers, in the course of their juvenile contacts, will often come upon such situations. To deal with these requires patience, tact, and understanding. Having the insight to be able to suggest areas with greater success potential, toward which to guide the individual is a much needed asset. This requires the officer to be more than casually acquainted with local resources, vocational requirements, and other reasonable opportunities.

In some instances, a youngster's unrealistic goals are the result of parental pressure. In desiring the best of the good life for their child, parents may set standards of achievement or future goals that are too high or too remote to be meaningful to the child. These situations should be discovered and remedied, as the child faced with such unrealistic ends, may react through delinquent patterns in seeking an escape.

Realistic appraisal of oneself is usually associated with attempting too much, or with trying to perform tasks for which the individual does not have the necessary capacities. There is another side to the coin. Too low of a self-image may bring about just as severe circumstances as the opposite. This may be the problem in a situation in which a child with normal or higher intelligence is an underachiever academically. It may be related as a conditioning factor to other failures. In such cases the appraisal is still unrealistic, but due to different reasons.

The third test of adjustment is the control of emotions so the individual is not overcome nor without emotional response. This means the individual should be capable of emotional expression in keeping with the situation, but should not be so emotional as to deny vitality to himself. The same is true of a lack of emotion, which also strips the personality of vigor.

The well-adjusted individual is able to provide affection, but just as importantly, to gracefully receive such feelings from others. He is able to respond to people and to his environment. Being upset will not give rise to an overwhelmed and defeated reaction. This does not mean that such a person would never appear upset. On the contrary, being able to exhibit negative emotion is necessary as long as such a response would not be evident in his ability to perform during a crisis, and passes away afterward.

Having empathy toward others is a measure of the well-adjusted individual. Sensitivity is the fourth requirement of adjustment. The person would not be an extreme extrovert, nor an introvert. He would be gregarious, enjoying people not only in a social setting, but also on the job and in other contacts. It entails being comfortable around people, caring for them with a concern that is a part of the individual's personality. He could see himself as others view him, and know when his actions were becoming ill mannered. Most importantly, such a person would care about others. He would have compassion for those with life difficulties, or who had suffered from the hardships of living.

By caring, his own behavior would be aligned with social requirements. His inner self would be gratified and deepened through his concern for the feelings of others and his sensitivity to their responses. The adjusted man never uses people to achieve his own ends.

The final test of adjustment to be considered is the ability to maintain an effective equilibrium between the individual's behavioral drives and controls, and the external forces encountered within the environment. This requires the ability to equalize the effects of the environment upon the personality of the individual. As the forces of the environment are constantly changing, the individual is required to withstand these pressures, thrusts, and pulls, without giving way. By doing so, the person is able to adjust himself to the world about him, harmonizing his life to cope with the situations he continually must face.

PROBLEMS ENCOUNTERED IN ADOLESCENT SOCIAL DEVELOPMENT

Social development will alter drastically during adolescence. Socialization will be very different; and, accompanied by the youth's lack of maturity, his desire to free himself from his family, and the normal circumstances encountered during these years, the social life of the individual will take on new dimensions.

In contrast to the peer group of the middle childhood years, the new emphasis will involve heterosexual activity. This is probably the most important problem of adolescence, the development of heterosexual social response.[2] During the adolescent period, the development of adequate relationships with the opposite sex must occur. The importance of this life task cannot be underestimated. It ranks with the problems of vocational needs. Many persons never achieve a satisfactory relationship with the opposite sex, and numerous marital problems can be traced to this failure to adjust. Not only are marriage problems the result of poor heterosexual relationships, but also other problems are encountered, many during the period of adolescence. In addition to emotional stress, the chances of participating in a normal and mature social life are drastically reduced if this adjustment is not adequately made. In extreme instances, severe personality maladjustments may be encountered.

Girls are usually more active in this process, and at an earlier age. This earlier social and sexual maturation of the female must be recognized, and should be considered a factor in many of the incorrigibility problems in which girls are involved. One serious outcome of this factor is the contact by the youthful adolescent girl with older boys.

Most teenagers eventually locate activities that will bring about girl-boy relationships. But, even those adolescents who arrive at an adequate adjustment heterosexually do so through the experience of many complicated situations and factors. It is not a smooth transition. The peer group develops into a heterosexual group with membership composed of both sexes who experience new and congenial activities. The influence of the group cannot be overstated. It is the primary reference source for teenage activity. Fads of dress, grooming, speech, and activities all gravitate from its existence.

The group tends to be small, composed of both sexes with amicable interests. Its closeness is evidenced by the fact that one is either admitted or completely kept out. There is no in between. The social life of the members of the group rotate about the group. Even the act of dancing is mostly limited to group membership. Certainly, parties and other social functions are experiences of the spontaneous restrictions. Such a clique exerts very strong pressures upon the member. It creates many problems for the participants. There is a paradoxical attempt to lose identity while attempting to identify and gain status. Group status demands acceptance of group standards. This often mystifies adults, especially the parents with whom the group standards comes into conflict on many issues. In such conflicts, it takes a strong parent to withstand the pressure of the group. For the most part the group will be victorious.

No longer is the close friend of the same sex, but inevitably become the girlfriend or boyfriend of the opposite sex. The trend is to "go steady" and much of the individual's time and social activity is monopolized by the presence of the other. The temptation to be with each other excessively is great, and this is just what does occur in the majority of the relationships.

These relationships do not run smooth. The search for heterosexual identity, coupled with the normal problems of maturation and extreme sensitivity, lead to many outbursts and other emotionalism. The falling in and out of love is a constant reminder of the difficulties being experienced by youth. These feelings are new and the youth is found to be on unfamiliar ground. The blundering encountered is inevitable.

Conversation is aimed at discussions of the opposite sex, especially among group members where evaluation of each other is almost constant. This discussion is usually quite frank when it is conducted by members of the same sex. This is often upsetting to adults, but is a much healthier approach than was vogue many years ago. The same is true of the frequent contact and activities with the opposite sex. Though immature, these searchings for experience of a heterosexual nature are quite natural and necessary for the development of a healthy personality. Without these contacts and acquaintanceships, the youth tends to rely on an imagination activated by media such as television. This places the experiences derived in poor prospective and is conducive to fantasy experiential activity. Fictionizing life's realities is a dangerous game for anyone, but it becomes more of a problem during the adolescent period of development.

Television, movies, pulp magazines, and other media present love and sex in an unrealistic and extravagant setting. It is easy for false standards of heterosexuality to develop. Habitual adolescent daydreaming may result in social isolates. When this occurs, it should be viewed as a symptom of a sociopathic personality development. It is a sign of the individual's withdrawing from the struggle to formulate heterosexual adjustment.

The middle childhood youth experiences most of his associations with persons of the same sex. There will be a certain carry over of these types of associations in the adolescent period. Close observation of these associations will uncover important differences in these relationships in the later period.

Because of the dominance of heterosexual activity during the adolescent period, this need will dominate the homosexual relationships. This is very prevalent among girls where the shy or unpopular girl will have difficulty in remaining close friends with a girl who has become involved with boys. With boys, activities are very strong determinants of friendship with other males. This is quite true where athletics are the central focus. Other interests in school activities, or even hobbies, may bring youth of the same sex together. The varieties of the contacts involved tend to wear away at the older acquaintanceships, and assist in forming new ones. This may cause some problems with the individual's relationship with his parents. In the event the original childhood friendship was the result of exposure brought about by the parents relationship with the parents of the other youth, concern for the feelings of the other child's parents may precipitate parental displeasure.

As a refuge from the failure to make a healthy heterosexual development, some youth find comfort in a same-sex companionship. This must not be interpreted to mean these youth are on the verge of homosexual development, but rather there has been an adaption from the need to become involved in heterosexual relationships, and security has been found in the same-sex acquaintanceship.

Not all persons can be popular. The critical dimensions involved in adolescent evaluation precludes many from popularity. The deep feelings of youth are a part of their criticism, not only of adults, but of other youth who are not members of the group. Many youth are cut off from full social participation, and for a variety of reasons. These reasons range widely from real to imagined inadequacies.

One of the most significant criterias for the development of adolescent friendships is economic. Contrary to the self-proclaimed noneconomic value system presented by youth, their actions do not equal their statements. Social and economic simularities are the most striking likenesses of secondary school friendships. Friends also seem to be alike in interests, ability to perform certain tasks, and social behavior.

The satisfaction of drives or desires has much to do with the development of the personality. The need for companionship, recognition, and a feeling of self-worth is great for the adolescent, and occupies prominence in much of what he attempts. The frustration of loneliness and isolation can be severe. This is why group activity and participation is so important during this period.

Success experiences, not only in the social development of the individual but in other areas of the teen existence, is an important phase of normal maturation. Continual rejection, failure, or defeat may cause chronic emotional maladjustments, manifested in a variety of ways from nervous habits to delinquent behavior. Adolescence is a time of extreme and rapid change. It is accompanied by many real and imagined problems. Adjustment is the key to successful completion of this period of maturation, but it is not a process that is easily accomplished alone. The youth of this developmental stage are in need of understanding and support, of guidance and counselling, and of patience and affection.

NOTES AND REFERENCES

1. Ruth Cavan: *Juvenile Delinquency.* New York, J. B. Lippincott, 1962, pp. 41,43,45,47, and 49.
2. Sidney L. Pressey and Francis P. Robinson: *Psychology and the New Education.* New York, Harper and Brothers, 1944, pp. 25, 200, and 237.
3. Louis Kaplan: *Foundations of Human Behavior.* New York, Harper and Row, 1965, pp. 9-11, 45, 47, and 49.
4. A Gesell and F. L. Ilg: *Infant and Child in the Culture of Today.* New York, Harper and Row, 1943, p. 247.
5. E. B. Hurlock: *Child Development.* New York, McGraw-Hill, 1956.
6. Benjamin M. Spock: The school-age child. Some behavioral, anthropological and physical implications of the latency period. *Abstracts and Reviews of Selected Literature in Psychiatry, Neurology, and Their Allied Fields.* Hartford, Conn, The Institute of Living, February, 1955, p. 51.
7. A. W. Blair and W. H. Burton: *Growth and Development of the Preadolescent.* New York, Appleton-Century-Crofts, Inc., 1951.
8. F. Redl: *Preadolescents, What Makes Them Tick?* New York, The Child Study Association of America, 1959.
9. See Appendix.
10. Kingsley Davis: Adolescence and the social structure. *Annals of The American Academy of Political and Social Science.* 236:8-16, 1944.
11. F. Patterson *et al.*: *The Adolescent Citizen.* New York, The Free Press, 1960.
12. E. Douvan: Independence and identity in adolescence. *Children, 4:* 186-190, 1957.

Chapter Three

THE FAMILY AND BEHAVIOR

N O other group holds the potential for affecting behavior as does the family.[1] The family, as the basic and primary societal unit is the filter system through which one passes onward into the broader culture[2]. The family is the basic group wherein socialization of the individual occurs. Within the family, the early lessons of trust, respect, and discipline are learned; all with profound effects upon the child.[2] It is here that the foundation for future interrelationships with others occur. The success of the early familial experiences will have lasting effects upon the individual.

To view the family as a purely social unit is too narrow a dissection. It must be seen in its entirety. The family is a biological and psychological as well as a social unit.[1] It is well that these areas be explored.

BIOLOGICAL FACTORS

Not enough is known about the effects of heredity upon the individual. For a long time, heredity was seen as the main cause of antisocial behavior. With the advent of psychological theories, the importance of heredity lessened; however, the development of science and medicine in the area of chromosome research has again opened new avenues into the significance of heredity. If heredity is a factor in deviant behavior, the family's importance as a biological unit cannot be overlooked. Biochemical research is on the threshold of providing answers to some of the questions that relate to the importance of heredity.

It is known that genes carry certain elements of protein that affect behavior.[3] Some metabolic insufficiencies have been found to have genetic origins. *Mongolism* is thought to be the result

38

of an abnormal number of chromosomes in the fertilized egg.[4] Advanced research into the molecular arrangement of the individual chromosome is leading science into an area of predictability and possible control of generic formation.[5,6]

Much effort has been expended in research into the behavior of individuals classified by body type. Conceptions in this area date back to the time of Hippocrates, but body type theories have received modern impetus from such persons as Kretschmer and Sheldon. The latter has done intensive research along the lines of body build and behavior. His endeavors resulted in an extensive classification of *somatotypes.* Sheldon's basic breakdown of builds were under the following classifications: *ectomorphs, mesomorphs,* and *endomorphs.*[7]

While some studies have attempted to utilize body build as a criteria for behavior, there is no empirical evidence at this time to indicate that an individual's actions relate more than indirectly to his hereditary physical characteristics. As an example, the Glueck's found that a large percentage of the delinquents studied were *ectomorphic* or thin and reserved. One criticism of the Gluecks study has been its emphasis on correlation, which does not determine cause. Thus, *mesomorphic* types may correlate to delinquency, but this does not establish that being of that body build *causes* delinquency. It may be that delinquency causes the body build, or that there is no relationship between the two at all.

The Minnesota Multiphasic Personality Inventory was administered to persons classified under Sheldon's method, and no significant traits were found to exist.[9] An adaptation of Sheldon's classifications was utilized in a study of the relationship between body build and emotional disorders.[10] In this study, it was found that there was a tendency for such disturbances to occur in cases where the individual had more tissue composed of fat than muscle.

In Hooten's study of crime among people with Nordic and Alpine ethnic backgrounds in the United States, the researcher discovered the former group to have a high incidence of forgery, fraud, and embezzelment; while the latter tended to show a high rate of robbery.[11] Hooten felt that the crimes were related to the biological origin of the individuals, but the findings may have been related to experiential exposure instead. Persons of Nordic backgrounds came to this country a century before the influx of the Alpine groups. The Nordics tended to be artisans and middle class merchants. Their exposure was to business and this ecology could easily explain the high rate of business-type crimes. The opposite is true of the Alpine group who came to the United States as a result of the Industrial Revolution and were factory workers.

As a fact, the theory that criminality is inherited has been discounted. That science may uncover new and startling issues in its quest into the genetic origins of man remains as a reminder for all to be aware of the need for open-mindedness. At this time, heredity may be said to have definite influences upon the individual, but more in the area of capabilities. The interaction of the human to his environment tends to determine the direction of his actions. That this interaction is influenced in part by hereditary factors cannot be denied. That these factors determine behavior has never been established.

PSYCHOLOGICAL FACTORS

Delinquency is rooted to emotional maladjustment; and, emotional growth is psychologically oriented. Social conflict often results in emotional stress, and such outcomes are the result of subtle psychological conditioning.[12] The home is where psychological conditioning occurs during early childhood. The experiences of the child at age five or ten years may be the underlying influence upon behavior at age 15 or 20.

The home and family exerts influential pressures upon children during their most flexible period of development. A child identifies with other persons, in large measure, on the basis of how the child is treated.[2] This is true of parental relationships. The child will feel and act toward his parents as he has identified with the parents. If the parental model is one that presents security, respect, and affection, the child will identify with those qualities through satisfaction. This satisfying of the needs of the child causes him to seek out persons who act in such a manner. Through the development of such relationships, the child will come to know fulfillment. The need fulfillment overcomes emotional instability and conflict. It produces stability, and an awareness of the needs of others. Thus, a child so exposed will tend to develop meaningful personal relationships; not only with his parents and family, but in other life experiences.

The foundations of adjustment set during early childhood tend to demonstrate control over the individual in later life. Later years experiences are but a continuation of the foundations built during early childhood. Development is a continuous process. It is identified by its quality of superimposing upon what has gone before. Yet, there is a danger in assuming that the family exerts an absolute cause of delinquency when family relationships are psychologically unsound. It is quite well known that in any group of identified delinquents or nondelinquents, one may find children in either group who come from well-structured families and those who come from psychologically disorganized groups. There are several explanations for this contradiction.

First, the same family that presents undesirable psychological traits in one area may also foster very satisfying and acceptable relationships in another. The good traits of the family may overcome the poorer ones allowing the child to develop along patterns of acceptable behavior.

Secondly, the environment external to the family may provide the necessary psychological development, wherein the child is sheltered from the poor effects of his family situation. While family influence is extremely important, the influence of the culture and society may have profound effects.

What must be kept in mind is the complexity of family relationships. Although quite subtle, very intricate patterns of interpersonal relationships are fostered in any family group. The danger of assumption lies in oversimplification. It would be quite easy to point to early family relationships as the *cause* of delinquency; however, present knowledge forbids this conclusion. The correlative effect of familial experiences cannot be argued, but to assign causation to these factors is improper and without valid foundation.

SOCIOLOGICAL FACTORS

The family is a social unit: a social institution. As such, it exerts an influence upon behavior in numerous ways. The family into which a child is born gives to that individual a heritage which is not only biological and psychological, but that is also strongly social in nature. It is within this group that the young child must interrelate for the first time. It is here the child is already, before his birth, predestined to certain social advantages or disadvantages. After entering the unit, the individual is subject to the experiences of family conflict and cleavage, and these are often events over which the child has little or no control.

Many social variables are determined by the family. These include race or ethnic background, which may or may not have behavioral consequences depending upon the individual family unit's own adjustment. The size of the family is a factor that the individual child will merely influence, but will not control. Where the family lives, the neighborhood, the child's associates, and the schools that will be attended are important social determinants. Whether or not there is a record of criminality in the family. Health and mental illness backgrounds. The economic status of the family. These are all important factors in the structure of a family unit and they are the basis for the formation of many values that orient the family and its member's behavior.[1]

While the factors represented in the social structure of the family correlate to delinquency, assumptions regarding causation should not be made. As with psychological theories, the control of the social variables is impossible. Without a control of variables, one cannot state that any given pattern or situation will lead directly to delinquent behavior. It is known that a child of a minority group ethnic background, from a slum home with one or both parents absent in which there is a background of criminality, has a high predictability for delinquency. At the same time, it is known that such a child may not become delinquent. On the contrary, he may become a productive and successful member of society. To recognize these factors is one thing; to see them as a *cause* is quite another.

The most important function of the family as an institution is the socialization of the incoming generation. This entails the interpretation of the values of the society and the perpetuation of the society through the media of the societal values. This value transmission is basic to the continuation of an orderly society, but it is subject to the affect of the individual family's interpretation.

Social values are contained in society in a pure form. Values can be verbalized, they may be promulgated, and they may be guides for living; but they cannot be self-perpetuating. They must be carried into the society through the human vehicle, and that vehicle is imperfect.

The development of attitudes and ideals begins early in life. Babies are seen to have a preference for games and toys before the first year. Attitudes between sisters are definite and distinguishable by the third year.[13]

Originally, values are accepted on the basis of who presents them. The child accepts the values of those persons who are closest to him. The primary group in this value guidance system is the family. It is important then how the family views a value, what values have meaning, and the values to which the family does not subscribe. The child's early exposure will be within the family, and this entails the family interpreting the values that will be transmitted from the society to the child.

Not only does this system give rise to the discarding of some values, but it also permits the warping of those accepted. Therefore, the socialization of the individual will differ greatly, depending upon which values have been presented to him and in what manner.

In a society subject to a rapidity of change, values are also subject to change. This is certainly true of modern America. The overall value system of the society is in a constant state of alteration. This not only leads to conflict, but it also erodes the controlling nature of the value system. The social limitations so readily accepted by one generation begin to fade in the design of a new generation. Thus, the boundaries of the value system are not as clearly defined, and the values are subject to broader interpretation.

With increasing age and environmental exposure, the child begins to see the flaws in his existing value structure. At the same time, growth and maturity increase his ability to perceive weaknesses in the persons formally held as examples. Father is no longer as strong and full of wisdom, and mother's tenderness and love is tarnished with the bitterness of adult error. This is the time when the child begins to find his heroes among personality figures beyond the home. It is the awakening of the peer influence.

With increased insight, the individual's value system may alter. The alteration may be either toward or away from what is adjudged by the family to be accepted values. This is a point of child-parent conflict, and in severe cases of interfamily conflict. The family can only present the values it holds, and the presentation can only be in the manner in which the value is held. The family cannot transcend its own influence. It cannot shut out the environment into which the child will enter.

How well society's values are transmitted to the child from the family depends upon how well the family understands and perceives the values. Subcultural values complicate the process. The fact that modern American society is a diverse society breeds diverse values. This increases the confusion and the complexity of the family role of socialization. There are some who claim the family is abdicating its role of value transmission to other institutions. When one ponders the complexities of the social value system of an urban society, it would be little wonder if abdication became a reality.

THE MOTHER ROLE

The importance of the mother role cannot be discounted. For most people, the mother figure remains as one of the most influential of life's experiences. It is expressed as a culture through the various recognitions of motherhood, climaxed by the national observance, Mother's Day. The only American art included in the massive collection at the Louvre in Paris, is the famous painting of the artist's mother done by Whistler.

The early role of the mother is to develop the trust and willingness to love in the person of the young infant.[14] This is accomplished by the mother's efforts to meet the needs of the child in the early developmental stage. Through the meeting of the child's needs, the child begins to trust both the persons around him and his environment. This in turn develops security in the child, and the early beginnings of a sense of worth are awakened. In turn, the child is then able to open himself to the desire to be loved and eventually to love.

If these needs are not met by the mother figure, the child will undergo feelings of rejection and insecurity. From these may spring the seeds of serious maladjustments, which may culminate in actions such as isolation from social contacts or even open hostility toward the environment.[2]

As the child develops, he must learn to submit to restraints placed upon him. Thus, while the child gains a certain amount of autonomy with growth and age, conformity to the cultural limitations of an obedient child must occur. This conformity is learned early in life through the imposition of the standards of the culture upon the child. The person carrying out this developmental instruction is the mother. The mother's role is to bring about a willingness to conform by forming the desire to behave in a manner that carries an expression of love.

The mother's reward and punishment method must equal, but not exceed the mother's demonstration of pleasure or displeasure with the actions of the child. If the earlier lessons of love, trust, and tolerance have been properly instilled, then the child will have a desire to please those whom he loves. This desire will be manifested greatly in the child-mother relationships. The mother's role during this period is to guide the child, with love and understanding, into his role as a child and a developmental citizen.

The mother role is so important and complex during the early childhood of the offspring that further consideration will be limited to mother deprivation in an attempt to demonstrate the mother's importance by indicating the outcomes when no person adequately plays that role. When an infant is deprived of the love and affection received from the mother or mother substitute, the reaction is one that indicates a loss of something quite vital to the child. Depending upon the extent of the deprivation, the reactions range from emotional to physical symptoms; such as rashes and skin disorders, respiratory problems, refusal to eat, excessive crying, and in extreme cases, infant autism.[15]

Research into the effects of mother deprivation have established definite patterns of reaction to the absence of an effective mother role. For the most part, these studies were performed with children placed into institutionalized situations during which time no mother substitute was provided.[16]

The first pattern identified is a *tantrum* stage in which the child cries, throws himself, kicks, shakes the crib, and attempts to bring about a reduction of tensions and conflict through physical demands. As the normal demand techniques fail to bring the mother figure, the physical demands become more extreme.

With continued deprivation, a dispair reaction begins to take the place of the physical display. This *passive* stage is characterized by a reduction in physical activity. Crying is only occasional, and not as severe as during the original stage. No apparent demands are made upon the adults the child has contact with, and the total child appears to be waiting for a return of normalcy into his life. During this stage, the child is aware of what is taking place within his surroundings. He knows what is being done for him or what is not being done for him. The difference is that the child apparently does not care whether something occurs or not.

The third pattern is a *withdrawal* stage. This withdrawing is from most social participation. The child becomes absorbed in his immediate surroundings, such as a toy or some other object. There is an almost total lack of response to outside stimuli, and often the child develops one or more mannerisms characteristic of withdrawing. These include body rigidity, unusual hand movements, a rocking motion that tends to continue, and various facial expressions that tend to be fixed. Direct contact with an adult may bring about terror reactions. Obviously, the child is close to psychotic reactions during this stage.

The final pattern occurs if no relief of the deprivation is evident. This is the *autism* stage, a form of childhood psychosis. The child that would suffer such prolonged deprivation as to develop this defect would be difficult to treat with any measure of success.

Several things must be pointed out about maternal deprivation. First, the mother figure does not have to be the natural mother, nor does it even have to be a woman. What is important is the ability to perform the mother role. Secondly, the deprivation does occur, to varying degrees of severity, when the mother is in the home. Thus, it is important for the student to recognize that maternal rejection or failure does happen, although the mother is physically present with the child. The results tend to be serious, and many infants have been found to have suffered from developmental retardation in situations where the mother was unable to give the love and affection necessary to adequately perform the mother role.[17,18]

THE FATHER ROLE

Because of the culture within which an urban society is bound, the father, of necessity, has a limited role during the infancy of the child. This limitation is due to the economic role of the father as the family bread winner. With the increase in the number of working mothers, this role is probably in a period of transition, and modern young couples may be in the process of sharing the parental-infant relationship more than in the past. The effects of this alteration, if it is occurring, have not been measured. Whether such arrangements are good or bad cannot be set forth at this time. At the same time, the general pattern existing in this nation is that the responsibility for the early child care is that of the mother, while the need to find economic security by working out of the home is the lot of the father.

Due to this cultural arrangement, the father's role is somewhat diminished during the infancy of the child. For many persons observing child rearing patterns in the society, the full recognition of the importance of the father never extends beyond that of the disciplinarian. While discipline and authority should emanate from the father figure, this by no means is the limits of the importance of the father role.

Of the many effects of fatherhood, the one that seems to be of significant importance is in the sex typing of the child.[19]

During the late infancy and early middle childhood stage, the sex of the child begins to be introduced to the child by the parents and other adults around him. Thus, he learns that certain toys are for boys and others are for girls. The same lessons are taught the child regarding clothing, use of bathrooms, dressing and bathing, and numerous physical motions and actions. What it is to be a boy or girl becomes meaningful at this early life stage. The child has the task of identifying with the sex he has biologically acquired. From this introduction, the child's play is steered toward a homosexual peer group relationship. As the child gets older, society's tolerance of a child's deviation from the normalcy of the role attributed to that particular sex is reduced. Dolls, tolerated for the boy of five, are taboo for the same child when he is ten or twelve. Tree climbing by an eight-year-old girl is deemed healthy exercise. The same actions at twelve or fourteen bring concerned reactions by the parents and influential adults.

At an early age the father becomes a meaningful person to the boy child. The father is the example of manhood. He is the one who brings the outside world into the children's life. The father is the image of strength, aggressiveness, leadership, and other emotional responses that are masculine in nature. During the middle childhood years, boys more than girls need identification with the masculine role. This identification is found in the person of the father figure. The boy receives the pattern of his own manhood from the father, and this begins during the middle childhood years.

Most certainly the father role is decisive during puberty and the adolescent years. This is true not only for male children, but for girls also. Just as the boy finds his masculinity through the father, the girl discovers those male qualities that are desirable in the same manner. The image of the father, that of the supportive protector of womanhood, becomes the standard by which the teenage girl is able to judge her male acquaintances. Just as the teenage courtship and dating period is one of experimentation with the opposite sex, the male criteria held in the mind of the adolescent girl as she has pereceived it in her father becomes the basis for her ability to enter the dating situation with more than just prudish armament.

The father who has performed his task well has set standards of male behavior toward the females in his life so as to prepare the adolescent girl with the knowledge and understanding of how she *should* be treated by her male companions. It is a fault of many mothers, desiring popularity for their daughters, to push girls into advanced situations for which the girl is not prepared to handle. The father, in many cases, actively overcomes this feminine trait. This is an unconscious, but natural counteraction and it has a counterpart in the mother's influence in the life of the adolescent male.

The daughter will learn what to expect of male behavior from her father and she will be able to determine how she should act in response to masculinity from this association. The successful transition from homosexual to hetersexual relationships will be made easier due to this sex typing of the female by the father. The fulfillment of this role reduces the girl's building of fantasies and unrealistic standards for choosing a mate.[20]

Inadequate father-child relationships are manifested early in a child's life and often found to be the root of the passive or isolated child's problem during early school years.[21] Poor father relationships may be the cause of academic failure among intellectually sufficient adolescent boys.[22] It has long been known that much of the delinquency, especially sexual, engaged in by adolescent girls is related to less than satisfactory father-daughter relationships.[23]

From the information presently available, the role of the father in the child rearing patterns of the American culture cannot be discounted. The importance of the role far exceeds the authoritarian aspects so readily seen. The father image importance has come to be recognized as one of the more serious problems existing in the minority group family, primarily the Negro. Thus, leaders in the efforts of that ethnic group to upgrade family life in the ghetto are attempting to deal with the lack of a meaningful male image. Many problems encountered by young male and female Negroes, and which have been manifested in antisocial behavior, may be traced to the poor esteem with which the Negro male has traditionally been held.

The father figure, in primitive as well as many other cultures, has long been established as the person to take complete control of the adult preparation of a male child. This aspect of historical family life may be identified in the ritualistic rites of attaining manhood. The male child, at or around the age of puberty, was in effect given to the father to be taught the things of manhood, with the mother a bystander who had little say in what transpired.

In the present day American culture, there is more and more concern on the part of many disciplines in the behavioral sciences that the mother image exerts too much influence upon the male child, and for too long. With fathers just reaching the apex of their careers during the adolescent years of the male child, the male influence is further removed from the home for vocational and business reasons. In lower class America, the father often is not even in the home leaving a void in masculine influence. More and more, the society, at all levels, is becoming matriarchal in nature. Part of youths' difficulty in accepting the reality of the world, its sorrows and pain, may be attributable to an overextended maternal influence.

INTERFAMILY RELATIONS

The thought that one may act in a certain manner, as long as it does not harm others, is an oversimplification of the complexities of interpersonal relations. As most often determined after the fact, the problems, behavior, or actions of any one person have effects on others. This is true within the family unit, just as it is within the larger ecology. One fact is pronounced pertaining to family relationships. Due to the close proximity and the intricate ties between members of the primary social unit, the psychological climate of a family is a fragile and complex unity. Any breakdown or diffusion of interfamily relations can have a drastic effect upon the equilibrium of the unit with far reaching impact upon the individual members.

Children of emotionally maladjusted parents are affected by the concepts, attitudes, and values of those parents throughout the lives of the offspring.[24] Very often, children so exposed in turn infect their own children with the residue of the ills of their childhood. Familial relations are capable of extending into unborn generations.

While some experts, such as Bossard,[4] have identified numerous patterns of interfamily relationships, only those that occur with frequent regularity shall be discussed. Consideration will be given to *rejection, dominance, overprotection,* and *overindulgence.*

Rejection

The ability to reject a child is latent in most persons, and may be manifested for any number of reasons ranging from multiple pregnancy to the mere fact the child resembles someone whom the parent has a deep hostility toward. The truth is the biological fact of parenthood does not cause one to be a parent. Rejection can occur openly and consciously, as in severe cases of child abuse.[25] Quite often it is subtle and unrecognized, even by the rejector. In between is the parent who is rejecting the child, recognizes that fact, and who may be making a conscious effort to reduce the tension. In such cases, the effort is usually futile as the rejected child may have begun to perform in attention-getting ways producing mannerisms that aggravate the rejection. In such cases there is a cycle developed that runs a pattern of rejection, counter rejection, annoyance, and new rejection.

It is important to realize that rejection of a child occurs more often than is thought, and it is a phenomenon that seldom is the result of a psychosis. Rejection may occur even when not intended. Every time a young child, excited and thrilled over a new discovery or experience, comes into a home bursting with the energy of the moment and wanting to share the joy of living with the parent only to be subdued for upsetting the sanctuary of adulthood, that child has been rejected. The scene just described is portrayed over and over in homes throughout the land daily. Children coming in from school with a crumpled paper drawing of the home, or the summer vacation, or any one of number of items utilized by primary grade teachers to bring about creativity and expression, are turned off by parents too busy with the chores of living, or worse, not even at home when the child gets there from school. The father, who relaxing after a tedious day reading his paper or listening to the news doesn't have time to listen to the child's description of an incident in the child's life, has added to a sense of rejection.

The saving factor in such circumstances is the parents' ability to both explain the reason for the ignoring, and to redeem the equilibrium of the parent-child relationship at another time by providing the time and attention the child craves.

Children are not deceived when rejected. They are quick to notice rejection, and they know when they suffer it. The emotional responses of the parents are deftly sensed by the child, and as the child has the basic human need to be wanted and loved, rejection is the sign of the antithesis of desire and affection. This can do no less than hurt. Rejected children are deeply scarred emotionally. It is not unusual for such children to desire to cause hurt in return. Because the parent is usually beyond the reach of a direct, hostile attack by the child, other avenues of striking back must be found. This is the reason so many delinquent youth tend to be rejected youth. It is also the reason why so many rejecting parents were themselves rejected children.

An example of extreme rejection occurred in a case of child abandonment in Bakersfield, California. The mother and common-law stepfather of a four-year-old girl, while driving through that community, placed the child by a fence along the freeway several miles outside of town. The stepfather told the child to hold onto the fence and not to let go until a policeman came. This occurred during early morning hours of darkness.

The girl remained along the busy highway for a number of hours of darkness, while the temperature remained quite low. Just after dawn she was found by the California Highway Patrol. After a number of days of nationwide publicity, the parent and stepfather of the child were identified and arrested in another jurisdiction. The two were transported to Bakersfield to stand trial.

In the meantime, the real father of the little girl, living in another state, heard of the youngster's plight. He also learned that the other children, except one, had been placed in protective custody. The child who had not been accounted for was an eight-year-old boy. The real father had not heard of that child for about eight months. As it turned out, that child's whereabouts were presently not known. The real father and the authorities questioned the possibility of foul play and an investigation into the whereabouts of the eight-year-old began.

The ultimate in rejection then took place. The mother and stepfather, contacted by investigators in jail, on advice of their counsel not only refused to discuss the location or fate of the child, *but they refused to acknowledge the existence of the child.* Almost a month and a half later, the mother admitted the child was hers and that the stepfather had beaten the child to death. She indicated that the body had been disposed of in a desert grave, and a recovery of the decomposed remains was later made by authorities.

Dominance

Domineering parents manifest this pattern of parent-child relations in several ways, and for different reasons. More often than not, the parents are rigid persons with narrow values and unbending standards. They demand conformity to these values and standards and many times the child is incapable or unwilling to meet these demands. Such parents tend to hold behavior expectations that far exceed the age and normal activity of the child. They want the child to accept too much responsibility at too early an age. The actions of the parents are rationalized on the basis that the parent, seeing the continued rise of juvenile delinquency, is not going to have that occur to his children. The children are going to respect people and property. They are going to get along in school. They are going to behave. The individual differences that exist within children are not taken into account. The child's ability is ignored. Performance as it relates to living up to parental expectations is the measurement, not of success, but of good or bad.

Such a demanding situation, constantly faced, can have extreme effects upon the personality of the strongest adult. It is no wonder that children are damaged by such actions. Some children will bend to the parental will, attempting to remain within the limits of behavior and performance that have been set down. Others will find themselves in an untenable situation where they can neither please or succeed. In either instance, the child will suffer personality disorders that may lead to delinquent acts or maladjusted adulthood.[3]

Another method of dominance takes shape in the lives of talented children who are pushed, sometimes ruthlessly, toward goals of achievement that will bring to the child success and fame. Instances of this nature have been seen in the arts, sports, and other vocational areas. The child succeeds because of a talent, but only after years of a regulated life controlled by the parents as they constantly direct the child toward the final goal. Very often these children are quite successful vocationally. It is in their social ability they tend to falter, explaining to some extent the reasons for the eccentric actions of many such persons.

Overprotection

Often confused with giving the child too much, overprotection is a situation in which the parents attempt to shelter the child from the realities of living. It is an overwhelming desire on the part of the parents to keep the offspring from being hurt physically, mentally, or emotionally. Overprotection is manifested by the desire to do too much for the child. It is the performing of simple and routine daily tasks that every child should do for himself at various ages.

Overprotection may be seen in the making of the child's bed and the straightening of his room or the refusal to allow the child to become involved in the process of growing up by denying the child access to normal activities. It may be seen in the boy who is denied a paper route because it requires him to arise too early for the deliveries. Overprotection may be manifested in the athletic youngster who is held out of sports because of possible injury, or in the youngster who is allowed partial participation only, such as being a member of the school band but not being allowed to go on overnight band trips.

In its ugliest form, overprotection is the waiting on a healthy teenager. It may be the father who hires the grass mowed with a fifteen-year-old son sitting idly by while another youngster mows it for money, or a mother who continues to do the dishes with several adolescent daughters in the home. These forms of overprotection are the worst, as they are daily acts that erode the very being of the child resulting in a plastic personality. The child becomes so accustomed to having things done for him that he expects the same from his peers. The inability to make friends follows, as other youngsters will not wait on him as he expects. Such children often grow into lonely and isolated persons.

For police officers, as well as others encountering cases of overprotection, they find the parents difficult to work with, due to the convinced sincerity of the parents. In situations of over-protection, the parent feels that he is taking the best course of action. Who can argue with wanting to protect a child? Who can condemn parents who wish to insure that the child does not get hurt? The fact that these parents have gone to extremes is not easily recognized by the participants. The fact is that they are hindering their child's ability to grow up, and in some cases are openly attempting to keep the individual a child in the face of the inevitable.

It seems the more one attempts to point out the folly of the parents actions, the more they will rationalize and become defensive. Professionals must recognize that such parents have been wheedled and cajoled by friends and relatives for years without success. One of the better approaches to be utilized by officers recognizing this type of situation is to explain to the youngster what is happening rather than to try to change the parents. Through the youngster's understanding of the error and motives of the parents, a possible adjustment may be made by the youth.

Overindulgence

This pattern of family relationships is one that may occur at any level of society, although it is often seen in its more stark examples among the well-to-do or upper-class. The overindulged child gets everything he desires, at least to the parents' ability to provide material items for him. Not only does the child receive material demands, but he also seems to get his own way in other respects within the home.

The three-year-old who accompanies the parents on a visit to another couple's home, and during the adult card game or conversation enters the room announcing that it is time to go home, only to have the parents get up and leave, is an example of extreme indulgence at an early age. Another sign is the older child sitting in the room while the parents visit with adult company watching television and telling the adults to be quiet, as they are interrupting his program. Naturally, the child who is bought off with expensive items, to perform in school or otherwise accomplish a task that would be a normal expectation for a youngster is a prime example of overindulgence.

Many of these children have a difficult time adjusting in school. They have unstable academic and deportment histories. They do not make friends easily, as persons around them do not tolerate their demanding ways. On their part, such youngsters do not like many people, as they measure affection by the amount of giving to their whims and demands. Overindulged children grow into egocentric adults who are as demanding on spouses and fellow workers as they were on their own parents. They represent the typical spoiled child.

THE ORDINAL POSITION OF THE CHILD IN THE FAMILY

Among the factors that must be attributed to interfamily childhood development is the position the child holds in the family unit. There appears to be some significance to the position or the order in which the child enters the family. Whether a child is first, middle, or the lastborn, or whether he is the only child seems to have significant bearing upon the development of the individual's personality.

When a child is born into a family, there is not only the familial influence which is brought to bear upon the newborn child, but there is also the influence the newborn child brings into the family unit. This interaction of individual upon unit and unit upon individual is very important in the development of the child's personality, and will have effects upon the development of personalities of other siblings.

There is no precise scientific information available at the present time that would indicate that ordinal position alone affects the development of the child or extends a significantly important influence into the atmosphere of the home. Some behavioral scientists are beginning to attempt a variety of studies to link the importance of birth order and the ultimate outcome of the individual. Certain factors have been discovered during various recent surveys and studies on large groups of people.

Relating to achievement, it has been found that firstborn children tend to appear in predominate numbers as *succeeders*. They are apparently highly represented in *Who's Who*, as an example of this success. Even among U. S. Presidents, five who have been assigned attributes generally considered to be necessary for successful administrations were firstborn children. Twenty-one of the original 23 astronauts included in the space program were either firstborn or only children.[26]

The Oldest Child

For most parents the birth of the first child culminates a period of expectation and excitement. The new child enters a family unit that has prepared a place which is definitely child centered. This child-centered environment tends to be in existence until sometime during the period extending from the second to the fifth year of the child's life. It has been found that a sharp decline in this child-centered situation occurs during that period. Parental attention declines and finally attains a more moderate level even though no other child arrives during that time.[27]

This child-centered atmosphere allows a period of development for the firstborn child during which he has no rivals. When a rival sibling enters the scene, the firstborn child is in a position of reflecting the threat being made upon his security. Thus, every firstborn child faces dethronement. How parents handle this dethronement will have much to do with the eventual effect it will have upon the firstborn. With the arrival of a second child, a real crisis is developed in the life of the first. Reactions to this crisis may occur in several ways. Most notably in a younger child will be alterations or changes in eating or toilet habits, or by crying or various other attention getting devices. An older child who may have already begun school may produce anxiety symptoms such as problems with sleep, stuttering, negativism, or even fantasy. As long as these devices gain attention, the firstborn will continue to employ them.

Entering the parents' life at a time when being a parent is probably the most exciting, the firstborn child is really a wanted child. Usually this child receives attention that other children coming later will not receive. However, the firstborn has higher expectations being placed upon him by the parents. He is also the child who teaches the adults their parenthood. Their tenseness, their inability to cope with situations, their need for *his* approval is often apparent. Many times the parents themselves have a need for the child to show them that they are performing correctly. These encounters usually occur between the older child and the new parent.

With the coming of the second child, the firstborn has lost his *onliness*. Gradually the first born adjusts to having other siblings within his environment with whom he must share and care for to assist in meeting the new child's physical needs. This latter is stressed to the older child. The oldest child becomes a big brother or sister, and must assume responsibility toward the younger child or children in the home.

Among the eventual outcomes of the effect of the ordinal position of the firstborn child, there tend to be two recognized extremes. One is the acceptance of responsibility and leadership thrust upon the oldest child by his parents and carried over into his adult life. The other extreme is the resentment of the oldest child leading to hostility toward any competitors, thus leading him into conflict with society.[28]

The Middle Child

Quite noticeable in the early development of the middle child is the parents' calmer approach to the environment prevailing about the child. The high child-centered feeling of the parents has disappeared. They are most prepared, physically and emotionally to cope with the problems of infancy. Actions of the young child, which before were causes for concern, are now accepted as normal infant behavior.

This means that the middle child's environment and relationship with the parents should be conducive to optimum behavioral and personality development. Such an atmosphere of calm is not totally recognized by all members of the family unit. The displacement of the firstborn child, which has brought upon him certain anxieties, is often brought to bear upon the middle child, and in some cases negates an otherwise adequate environmental situation. Consequently, although the middle child undergoes less strict parental action and response, this same loss of child-centered feeling on the part of the parents means a loss of attention toward the child also. This loss of parental attention affects not only the middle child, but also the firstborn. This places the children in the position where their interaction is increased.

In the event of existing hostilities and resentments upon the part of the older child, subtle, devious, and sometimes open methods of displaying the hostility can be manifested overtly within the children's relationship.

The middle child undergoes a calmer atmosphere with his parents. At the same time, parental attention is lessened. The combination of these factors throws the middle child and the firstborn together in a new relationship. At no time is the middle child able to compete with the older child physically, mentally, or emotionally. Therefore, being placed in a position of developing a relationship with the older child, the younger one is also in a position of not being able to enter into meaningful competition with the older offspring. This difficulty is increased if the older sibling is one who demonstrates responsibility or other meaningful attributes.

With the advent of younger siblings, the middle child becomes wedged between the others. He is always faced with the presence of the older siblings, and living within the reality of the existence of a "baby of the family." The baby's position and demand for attention cannot be disputed, nor is the middle child able to compete with the younger siblings for this lends itself to unfairness. It has already been established that the middle child cannot compete with the older sibling, and therefore, from ordinal position alone, the middle child appears in a situation resembling a "no mans land." How the middle child reacts to this position depends in great part upon the personalities, attributes, and characteristics of the other siblings. The more competent and successful the other children may be, the more difficult it will be for the middle child to attempt to compete. If the accomplishments of the firstborn child are not impressive, the middle child may show an aggressiveness and an attempt to enter into meaningful competition with the older child. In most instances it is apparent that the middle child would like to see a change within the power structure of the family unit. In this way he may be seen to be a revolutionary, as he desires the power within the family to change hands. This is true whether or not the middle child takes any overt action to see such a struggle occur.

There is one problem that tends to continue to exist in the life of the middle child. That problem is the one he faces from the very fact that he can never "catch up." Even after leaving the family, an older child, who is also successful, presents great influence back into the family unit. He is held as an example, he is called upon for assistance, and his counsel is sought. In these situations the departure of the firstborn child does not clearly remove his influence from the relationship that existed between he and the middle child. The middle child may live within the wedge most of his life.

The Lastborn Child

The youngest child enters into a unique family relationship. He enjoys the position of the baby of the family, and will never truely relinquish that title. With such a title are certain advantages. These include the experiences the parents have had in the raising of other children. Also is the fact the parents are more prepared than at any other time to handle a new child, and this preparation often includes economic security. The lastborn child is in the position to receive additional material advantages. Another facet of his life is the attention given to him by the older children within the family. Everyone, it seems, gives of themselves for the benefit of the baby. They pick him up if he cries or falls, they get his toys, they fight his battles and they see to his general comfort. Because of the experience of the older children, the lastborn child is guided through events that the firstborn faced alone. The youngest child does not face school alone, find his way by himself, or even make friends on his own. Always surrounding him are his older brothers and sisters who lead him to school, advise him of the nuances of this new situation, and through their friends aid him in the development of his own group peers.

With all of these advantages, life can become casual for the lastborn child. As with all situations, with every benefit there is a cost. The same is true in the life of the lastborn child. The ease with which he may live, the extra advantages he may have, also contain factors that are likely to cause undesireable characteristics. Among these is found the unwillingness of the parents to allow the child to grow up. The temptation is great for the parents to resist the growth and development, and to deny the individuality of their last child. At the same time, the ease with which he lives and the additional material benefits he has gained tend to induce the young child's desire for independence. Herein is found conflict. How does the parent explain to the other children if they allow the youngest child to perform a certain function at an earlier age than the other children were allowed to perform the same function. Resentment on the part of the other siblings can occur as they look backward and watch the younger child receive things and be given privileges which they were denied. The experience of having the totality of the family unit reacting for the benefit of the younger child can cause expectations of dominance or of having his own way to become established within his personality.

Because he is given his own way, the baby of the family develops likeable traits, and may be quite pleasant to be around. At the same time, this child may develop into a very dependent person. While he has a personality that is attractive, he is also prone to lean on others throughout his life. He may be a very demanding person as an adult, always willing to have others give to him, but not willing to give of himself in return.

The calmness of the family unit atmosphere which the youngest child experiences may tend to keep that child from becoming achievement oriented.

The Only Child

The only child finds himself in the position of being the firstborn, entering the family at the time when the parental child-centerd atmosphere is at its highest. The child-centered situation will decrease, as in other family situations, but the only child will never be dethroned. Many of the problems encountered by the only child will be the result of the parents' approach to the raising of this one sibling.

Probably one of the more dangerous encounters of the only child is the ever-presence of adults. This child is often developed into a "small adult." He accompanies his parents to adult functions, goes with them to homes where he sits and listens attentively to adult conversation, and otherwise engages in adult-oriented activity at an early age. In so doing, the only child is subjected to an adult orientation which is not conducive to ready acceptance by his peer group.

The fact that the only child has no one with whom to compete within the family brings him to the place where he does not readily compete in a peer group situation. He will expect other children to give in to his demands and to treat him as he is treated at home. Very few children are willing to be that condescending. The failure to compete is recognized when the only child enters school, but becomes more intense in the later school years.

The personal feelings of the only child were found by one investigator to be highly associated with a sense of not belonging.[29] Not having to compete at home, the only child is burdened with a problem of peer adjustment and often encounters an inability to adjust to the give and take of peer group relationships. The easiest way to overcome the problem is through detachment. He encounters resistance to his demands on his peers, thus bringing him to the position where he may have to adopt one of a number of reactions to their reactions. Aggressiveness toward others is a trait discovered in the only child. Social immaturity, or a passive approach toward the requirement for gregarious activity in one's life may be encountered in the personality development of the only child.

The fact that he is adult oriented, and more at ease with adults, precludes his becoming involved in depth with other children. Loneliness, breeding discontent, is the "brother" of the only child. His adult orientation causes him to fail not only in attempts, but in his knowledge of how to relate to his peers.

Intolerance of others, failure to cooperate, and impatience in human relationships are traits that exist in only children. Character disorders and neurotic symptoms have been found to occur at a higher rate among only children than among the normal childhood population.[24] It may be concluded that only children receive in their environment stresses and anxieties not encountered by other children.

SIBLING INTERACTION

As most persons who have experienced the play of young children have noted, children tend to comprehend one another. There is a communication ability existing between a three-year-old an a fourteen-month-old child. The parent who does not recognize the garbled mouthings of a very small child is told by a child not much older of the need the younger one wants fulfilled. This points to an ability for very young children to interact. Not only can they interact, but apparently they can communicate before the truly verbal stage.

Sibling interaction is that state of childhood existence in which children associate together for play and enjoyment. This is a world that is reserved for the child. It is quite impossible for the adult to effectively enter this world, and most intrusions bring about a cessation of the play. If one should enter a room where some little girls are playing dress-up, the activity tends to slow down and an embarrassment sets in, for the child readily recognizes that the adult does not understand.

Sibling interaction is important to childhood development for several reasons, but of these the main one is to insure that reality structuring occurs. All children are prone to fantasy, but in the real world of interaction with other children the fantasy world of the individual child remains reasonably structured.

Most can recall in the childhood game of cowboys and Indians, of being shot, and turning immediately and stating, "You missed me." The fact the shooting occurred at such close range as to preclude a miss was of no concern, and brought on an argument; and the ensuing "No, I didn't" and "Yes, you did" brought all of the participants out of the fantasy world and into a real world where they attempted to resolve a difference. The arguments that occur in childhood play aid in keeping children from remaining in a fantasy situation too long. Observing children at play, it may be noted there are many disagreements over role participation and the direction the make-believe should take.

These disagreements are purposeful in that they bring all the participants back to reality.

Unreal or fantasy companions are natural to children. Other children cause these imaginary personalities to be kept within the reality of nonexistence. While a young child may get away with telling the parents not to sit on a particular chair because an imaginary companion is now occupying it, other siblings will not accept that lack of reality. Childhood interaction is important because it retains reality and overcomes active imaginations.

NOTES AND REFERENCES

1. C. Ray Jeffery and Ina A. Jeffery: Prevention through the family. In William E. Amos and Charles F. Wellford (Eds.): *Delinquency Prevention*. Englewood Cliffs, N. J., Prentice-Hall, 1967, p. 78.

2. Ruth Cavan: *Juvenile Delinquency*. New York, J. B. Lippincott, 1962, pp. 43, 111.

3. Louis Kaplan: *Foundations of Human Behavior*. New York, Harper and Row, 1965, pp. 26, 80-81.

4. J. A. Book: Genetical etiology in mental illness. *Milbank Memorial Fund Quarterly*, 38:193-212, 1960.

5. J. Pfeiffer: The new biology: The role of nucleic acids in medicine, *Archives of Neurological Psychiatry*, 79:434-447, 1958.

6. Arthur Kornberg, Stanford University Nobel Prize Biochemist, in a report before the annual convention of the Clinical Congress of the American College Surgeons, as reported in *The Fresno Bee*, October 9, 1969.

7. W. H. Sheldon *et al.*: *Varities of Delinquent Youth: An Introduction to Constitutional Psychiatry*. New York, Harper and Row, 1949.

8. Sheldon and Eleanor Blueck: *Unraveling Juvenile Delinquency*. Cambridge, Harvard University Press, 1950, p. 193.

9. H. Page *et al.*: An empirical study of the relationship of four classes of body habitus to responses on the M. M. P. I. *Psychological Reports*, 5:159-167, 1955.

10. R. W. Parnell: Physique and mental breakdown in young adults, *British Medical Journal*, 1:1485-1490, 1957.

11. Ruth Cavan: *Criminology*, 3rd ed. New York, Thomas Crowell Co., 1962, pp. 694-695.

12. Sidney L. Pressey and Francis P. Robinson: *Psychology and the New Education*. New York, Harper and Brothers, 1944, p. 198.

13. M. B. Mc Farland: Relationships between young sisters as revealed in their overt responses, *Journal of Experimental Education*, 6:173-179, 1937.

14. Ralph Linton: *Culture and Mental Disorders*. Springfield, Thomas, 1956, pp. 11, 36-37.
15. G. A. Jervis: Factors in mental retardation. *Children, 1:*207-211, 1954.
16. J. Bowlby: Separation anxiety, *International Journal of Psychoanalysis,* 41:89-113, 1960.
17. L. Kanner: Problems of nosology and psychodynamics of early infantile autism, *American Journal of Orthopsychiatry, 19:*416-426, 1949.
18. J. Richmond and E. Lipton: Studies on mental health with specific implications for pediatricians. In G. Caplan (Ed.): *Prevention of mental Disorders in Children*. New York, Basic Books, 1961, pp. 95-121.
19. P. Mussen and E. Rutherford: Parent-child relations and parental personality in relation to young children's sex-role preferences. *Child Development, 34:*589-607, 1963.
20. M. L. Faegre: *The Adolescent in Your Family*. Washington, D. C., U. S. Children's Bureau Publication No. 347, 1954.
21. M. J. Radke: The relation of parental authority to childrens' behavior and attitudes. *Monographs, No. 22,* Institute of Child Welfare, University of Minnesota, 1946.
22. B. Kinmball: Case studies in educational failure during adolescence. *American Journal of Orthopsychiatry, 23:*406-412, 1953.
23. J. B. Cattell: Psychodynamics and clinical observations in a group of unmarried mothers. *American Journal of Psychiatry, 111:*337-342, 1954.
24. W. McCord: The familial genesis of psychoses. *Psychiatry,* 25:60-71, 1962.
25. C. Flammang: *The Police and the Underprotected Child*. Springfield, Thomas, 1970.
26. Vance Packard: First, last or middle child—the surprising differences, *Reader's Digest,* December, pp. 25-32, 1969.
27. J. K. Lasko: Parent-child relationships. *American Journal of Orthopsychiatry,* 22:300-304, 1952.
28. See: D. B. Hariss: Parents and war-born children. *Children, 1:*152-155, 1954.
    J. M. Toolan: Suicide and suicidal attempts in children and adolescents. *American Journal of Psychiatry, 118:*719-724, 1962.
    J. Rouman: Why they misbehave. *California Parent-Teacher, 31:*14-15, 1954.
29. B. V. Straus: The dynamics of ordinal position effects. *Quarterly Journal of Child Behavior,* 3:133-146, 1951.

Chapter Four

URBANIZATION–A COMPLEX SOCIETY

A MERICA'S urban dilemma is a concern of all. It has far-flung ramifications reaching every segment of the life of this nation. Many problems reflect planning needs, others monetary needs, while still others reflect the needs of people. A society technically advanced and capable of wondrous feats of scientific skills is the same social structure that has led its people into a seemingly cultural abyss. That few person may escape the difficulties of some phase of urban life is a fact now recognized by most. The acceptance of the unchangeable atmosphere of urbanization by the citizen points to the intense status of urban life and the hold it seems to exert upon those who are subject to it. Once encountered as a way of life, urban society seems to be capable of entangling the individual in a web of his own making. From this situation, escape is almost impossible as one is swept into the tide of urbanization and soon finds desires to the contrary, but idle dreams of the better life.

URBANIZATION–WHAT IS IT?

No examination of urbanization would be complete without a reconstruction of the noise, congestion, and isolation to which the individual is subjected. These physical and psychological forces press against the person throughout his urban experience. Overcome somewhat by the individual becoming accustomed to the ecology within which he lives, nevertheless, each person suffers from these forces to some degree.

Noise in a technological society is a problem, often ignored by those being deluged by it. It is with one constantly, incessantly, and at times, efficiently. From the ticking of one's own watch to the majestic noise of industry, all of urban society gives off its

66

own contribution to the redundancy of noise. Noise has become so much a part of urban America that those who use weekends and vacation time to escape the cities must take their noise with them into the so-called wilderness, using radios, phonographs, and even television sets as camping components.

The fan sitting in the midst of a crowded and noisy stadium viewing a football game while holding a transistor radio to his ear to catch the highlights of a baseball contest. The stillness of the crowded campsight being broken by the injection of a completely portable television. Probably the most striking example of man's inability to remove noise from his urbanized existence was experienced in a valley campsight at Yosemite National Park. The park naturalist was not scheduled for a campfire show in that campground on the occasion, but numerous people had appeared at the amphitheater expecting one. A man in a self-contained camper bus, with auxiliary generators running to maintain the electricity necessary to operate the normal accessories of kitchen appliances, television, and refrigeration units, came to the rescue of his fellow humans. Hanging a sheet over a line, he projected slides of his most recent world cruise to the sheer enjoyment of all. It is a sad commentary that such would occur in a setting where wildlife and natural wonders abound.

As accustomed to noise as modern man has become, the effects of noise upon the stability of the individual has not received the attention of a full research effort. Some studies have indicated that noise has an eroding effect upon the person. Noise tolerance is diminished through excessive exposure, and in extreme cases, severe behavioral consequences are manifested. At best, urban noise concentration is like the surf against a rock. It causes unseen wear and unmeasured weakening of the recipient.

Continual congestion can be as disconcerting. One traveling in a metropolitan area during the rush hours knows the endurance test brought upon the individual by congestion. Urban life has tended to reduce privacy and the privilege of *aloneness*. No matter where one goes, or at what hour, he encounters people. This is magnified in urban housing; refering not to ghetto tenement dwellings, but rather to the new high-rise apartment complexs and the existing tract development. Soundproofing and fencing has not reduced the goldfish-bowl aspect of city life. Even the intimate involvements of family life are subjected to the scrutiny of others. The problem is brought to its most ludicrous conclusions in the following examples.

The young lad of twelve or so, living in an eastern urban center purchased a surplus listening device for less than $15. It seems he openly exposed the gadget on his own front lawn, and sitting beside it with earphones poised, he proceeded to aim it at the direction of the homes of the various neighbors. Complaints came forth loud and clear, but there was no law or ordinance that could be found to control such actions. Finally, upon the urging of the district attorney, the father of the youngster brought the situation to a halt.

The author, during a period of educational advancement, spent part of the summer months as an impromptu guest in an apartment occupied by his nephew and several other youthful bachelors. The apartment was quite nice and very modern. It was on the third deck of a large complex. Due to the size of the place, the nonpaying guest drew the floor as a bed. One night while lying on his abdomen, the author felt a palpitation in the region of his chest. At the same time, he seemed to sense the dynamics within his ear. It took but a few seconds before he realized that what he questioned to be a physical malady was in reality the bass tone of a loud stereo being amplified in the apartment beneath.

Social isolation is the ability to exist within the proximity of large groups of people with limited attachment to their presence. It is characterized by the ability to withdraw inward from the source of a extraneous presence. Social isolation is a malady of modern urban life. It is experienced by persons who find they have no common meeting ground with others, and they know of no way to bring about a meaningful relationship with people with whom they physically associate. Isolation has become so pretentious it now warrants the concern of the behavioral scientist. At its worst, it is a scourge of the ghetto dweller. At its best, it is the devoted companion of the suburbanite. Sometimes self-imposed, and on other occasions imposed by the culture that nurtures it, isolation has become a factor in the life of the modern American.

For the reader, isolation can best be exemplified by requesting him to visualize the occupants maintaining the abodes at the four corners of the block or apartment in which the reader lives, How well is the reader acquained with any of these people? Just what would be the extent of the impact upon the reader should anyone of these persons die during the next several hours? What would the impact be upon them if the reader died? Within the context of the finality of death, one is capable of measuring the impact of isolation upon urban society.

Couple these personal ecological stresses to the broader urban problems faced by all persons and one begins to sense the enormity of the situation. All cities are faced with decay from within. They may be likened to an old and majestic home, which entered into being as the home of a person with some means, and built to the standards of its day. After some years, the family of the original owner have been raised and have left to establish homes of their own. The parents, finding age and need advising them the place is no longer suitable, sell the house. It is sold during a different era, with differing economic and social needs. Of late, the majority of such homes have found their way into the lives of families with large numbers of children. Many such families have not been financially equipped to bring about needed repair and alteration. Through the years the house has suffered from wear and make-shift repair. After some time the house is sold again, and becomes a rental, providing minimum housing for lower economic groups.

A parallel may be drawn with our cities. The inner-city has succumbed to the privations of lack of upkeep, a result of the migration of the affluent middle class to suburbia. As property decays, values fall, directly affecting an already overburdened tax base. Unless industrial or business property takes over the area, its worth as tax appraisal is reduced. Less taxes directly affect the city's ability to provide services. Accompanying the decay of private property is the decay of public property, such as public buildings, sewers, lighting, fire equipment, and quite often, schools. The overuse and normal deterioration of the public ability to provide services to the citizenry brings outcries for increased services and lessened tax burdens. Herein lies part of the reason for recent social upheaval. Property owners in many areas of the inner-city, where services and facilities need replacement or upgrading, do not live within the areas so affected. Such owners oppose increased taxation and are not concerned with the breakdown of municipal service in that area. Without the money, necessary improvements cannot take place. The persons needing the improvements cannot pay for them, nor do they control the power structure necessary to obtain such services. Frustration develops within the inner-city and spreads like ripples from a pebble dropped into a pool throughout the rest of the metropolitan area. In the meantime, decay is beginning to occur in suburbia, and a recycling of the problem may ensue.

In an oversimplified version, these factors are some of the roots of urban unrest, and are problems with which the city official must grapple constantly. Tragically, but realistically, when these problems begin affecting the American middle class in direct ways, a meaningful response will occur. Probably the first place where this will occur will be within the area of the public school system, already staggering under the strain of overburden.

URBANIZATION—CULTURAL BACKGROUND

The transition from the nostalgic life of rural America to the flamboyant existence in urban centers has brought certain alterations within the society. Many changes have been in the form of diversions of cultural limitations and standards.

All men exist within a culture. It is from this source that the incoming generation derives its socialization.[1] When a culture is stable, socialization of its youth tends to follow patterns readily identifiable and just as readily acceptable. Rural America provided a stable culture. Prior to World War II, most persons lived within the same setting that their parents, and even their grandparents, had lived. The small town provided a shelter for the customs, mores, and taboos developed as a means of social control over the actions of the individual. Even in the cities, the stability of neighborhoods that existed several generations ago provided the base from which the value system exerted pressure.

The stability of the former culture retained the values of Americanna. These values reflected the Protestant Ethic of individual initative, reward and punishment. Born of puritanical concepts and refined by the Victorian Age, the culture was bounded on all sides by a value system promulgated and understood.

Long after the alteration of the basic societal values, the fundamental values of America have been portrayed in a pitiful attempt to believe in their existence. Such is the case in the lower grade introductory readers, depicting the father, mother, brother, and sister on their way to grandmother's house for either Thanksgiving or Christmas. The grandparents' are presented as farmers, with grandmother the "saint of the kitchen," and with good tasting foodstuffs all about. Grandfather is a kindly old man who willingly shows and explains the farm animals and machinery to the wide-eyed children. The opposite side of the coin, found in modern America, reflects grandparents who, if younger, live and work in a city; and if older are confined to one of the nation's burgeoning homes for the aged.

Before World War II, most persons in this country had not been exposed to other geographical areas. They tended to live their lives, remaining within an easy distance of their birthplace and other relatives. Life was predictable, with sons turning to the occupations of their fathers or entering developed industrial factories which dotted the industrial belt of the land and supported many small towns. Daughters contented themselves with being housewives, and only occasionally ventured into a profesisonal vocation, usually either nursing or teaching. The era of the employed mother had not yet been born of wartime necessity, and what migrations occurred were depression based.

In this type of setting, the large family sphere of influence concentrated itself upon the actions of all members of the related unit. The advice of a particular uncle, or the influence of an aunt, was considered of such value as to be a determinant of behavior. This type of broad family influence was possible due to the extended longevity of close geographic association.

Neighbors and friends exerted similar behavioral restraints upon members of the community. What youngster could brave the watchful eyes of the social group, knowing that his misadventures were open to the scrutiny of a citizenry who all recognized him and were acquainted with his parents and other influential members of the larger family sphere? Prewar youth were not afforded the shelter of anonymity so readily utilized by present day youngsters.

All persons sharing the common geographical area were subject to the same social controls. It should be pointed out that these controls may have varied from area to area, but within a particular area they were universally accepted, if not adhered to completely. In addition to large numbers of people being capable of providing identification of the transgressor, a wayward youth had the assurance that his parents' would view the deed in the same value context as others.

The reward and punishment system was not only practiced, it was believed. The child was assured of the condemnation by his parents for his misdeeds. He was further assured of the punishment attached to the condemnation. It was an era when one did not want school trouble, mainly because of the reaction at home. Often, a youth found more punishment coming from the parents for a school infraction than from the school officials. The same was true for police contacts, and the police were aware of the existence of parental backing of the authoritarian figure. Police contacts were few, because if the officer were to contact the home, parental reaction to the embarrassment would result in worse judgments than official action might render.

This American culture was characterized by well-defined values, adhered to by all. These values were not challenged by the transgressor. He merely acknowledged youthful misguided conduct. No attack was made upon the validity of the standard of restraint of conduct. It was characterized by ease of identification of the perpetrator of a wrong; and those persons capable of such recognition of the individual were also persons who were influential in their relationship with the parents of the youth. The culture set forth quite clearly the actions that were to be avoided, and these were universally understood. It also set forth the decree that persons offending the value system did so on an individual responsibility, and as rewards were provided for good deeds, punishments should follow wrong doing. All of these factors set definite guides for conduct. Youth were subjected to a structured upbringing which not only reduced the opportunity for questioning standards, but also reduced the necessity.

URBANIZATION–CULTURAL EFFECTS

World War II set the need for the nation to become mobile. It caused breakdowns of the large family unit sphere. People began to move to other parts of the country and the world. They began to discover the differences inherent in new areas and that such areas afforded different, if not better, opportunities. The beginnings of the working-mother culture appeared, and as the war effort required this reversal of an old value increased.

New exposures brought about sophistications, and a more cosmopolitan attitude emerged. The decision not to return to the old life caused people to adopt other parts of the country as their homes. Postwar affluence rapidly entered the scene, and the standard of living increased. People who suffered the lack of finances of a lengthy depression, only to be followed by years of wartime rationing, were eager for the comforts of peacetime technology. Provisions for the members of the society who were less fortunate blossomed into welfare programs and subsequent attempts to eradicate poverty and misery. The nation became occupied with the meeting of these demands.

Not easily recognizable, the American culture is absent of oneness. It consists instead, of numerous subcultures, and in recent years, the contraculture. The basic concept of a universal American culture is presented through well-recognized institutions and symbols. Woven in and around these are predominent social patterns.[1] Thus, what is seen as a common culture are those universals generally not questioned by the society. It must be pointed out that recent social evolution has encountered the greatest reaction when confronting an institutionalized universal.

The American culture is not simplified. It consists of many cultural standards based upon varying ethnic, religious, geographical, occupational, and educational backgrounds and interests. From these sources emerge differing standards which have caused the socialization of others to represent a divergence from one's own. Subcultures have always existed in this country, but in the past they have been hidden in colloquialism. Their recent emergence into the mainstream of modern American life has been the result of several factors. First, there has been a reduction in the former localization of the subculture caused by a mobilized society. Second, the efforts of the liberal (or progressive) element to overcome or discard standards formerly considered universal have uncovered the existence of the divergence of acceptable values. Third, the evolution of the contracultures have focused attention upon the differences between groups within our society.

Less than twenty years ago, college classes in sociology were teaching the unity of culture, stressing the lack of cultural differences based on ethnic and racial groupings within the United States. These same classes are presently engaged in attempting to develop insight, understandings, and dialogue between subcultures.

The recognition of subcultures and differing social values has been the result of the centralization of these social patterns into urban areas where each tends to encounter the other more frequently than ever before. One subtle and major effect of the recognition of existing cultural differences within our society is the demand for tolerance and understanding of those differences by the society. This is a factor seldom discussed and to which little research attention has been directed. It calls for an increase of social tolerance; and, carrying that concept to its logical application, it calls for a new tolerance toward the behavior of others. Part of the removal of personal responsibility from the individual offender by society has been the result of this social tolerance.

Major subcultures tend to be ethnic or racial in character. These are the social classes with the most differing cultural patterns. They are also the ones who tend to congregate together in urban areas. As the areas of such congregations are usually decayed areas within the community, the ghetto image can be defined. Cultural standards of these groups, coupled with other factors, give rise to social disorganization.[2] The effects of these factors are reflected in high delinquency rates.

Generally, social disorganization is defined as a breakdown in the bonds that tie an interrelated group together, affecting the functioning of that social group or smaller segments within it.[3] The study of criminality developing as a root of social disorganization usually entails a comparison with an unaffected social group of low criminal rate. This has led to the folk society concept, wherein a colloquial grouping somewhat akin to the prewar rural American culture described before is compared to the urban disorganized culture.[4] In the folk group, there is little nonconforming behavior. Some sociologists are now utilizing the term social disorganization in a different context than before. In its newer usage, it has been applied to mean deviant behavior.[5]

Recent expressions of discontent and direct attempts to shock society have been manifested by groups forming contracultures. A *contraculture* is a group whose values tend to be the opposite of prevailing standards. Such groups have been involved in various types of activities that are socially unacceptable and given to shocking examples of criminal activity. Commonly held values on male-female relations are openly flouted. Sexual perversion and degradation of human nature is performed openly and in many instances, publicly. If motherhood is a standard of general recognition, the contraculture performs acts degrading that value. If the flag is a symbol of patriotism, it may become that target of the activity. Although the groups differ in makeup and purpose, one common thread runs through all contracultures. It is the desire to express a total disregard for the value system, to throw off restraints, and practice beliefs that are knowingly in absolute contradiction of social norms. Examples of contracultures have been the hell's angels motorcycle clubs and any number of prototypes, various racial and militant groups, and the hard-core drug cults.

For many persons, there may be an overlapping of cultures within their lives causing them to have divided loyalties and some basic concerns with terminations of values. This is exemplified in situations where a member of an ethnic subculture is also a member of a religious subculture. The new values of the ethnic group may include attempts at emergence in which the group has compromised to support liberal concepts in order to gain the return recognition of the progressives for the ethnic cause. The total liberal expression may include some areas that are contradictory to the religious teachings of the individual in question. In this situation, he must choose between supporting the ethnic group activity directed at supporting the overall liberal espousals, or he must choose to follow the teachings of his other subculture, the religious institution.

It is in this context that America finds its cultural standards. They are no longer clearly defined, structured, and easily followed. While values in this country have always differed, focus upon these differences has never been as great. There is a large grey area in which many of our values have now been placed, and situations are being judged upon the individualized merit of that time, place, and occurrence. Universal generalities are being reduced, and morality is no longer as clear-cut as it has been in the past. From this base, an examination of the effects of urbanization upon our culture and the attendant consequences on the behavior of youth will follow.

Mobility

After the war, as old communities were left behind, so were the values that restricted conduct. Not all of course, but those that the individual did not agree with or which were disagreeable to the new community. The larger family sphere was depleted, and the influence of outer fringe relatives diminished. This was true of the influence of the aunts and uncles, and even of the grandparents. In some modern families, the larger family unit is quite removed in time and space from any meaningful contact with the primary group. The *nuclear family unit* has emerged.[6] This is the immediate family, consisting of parents and children, and functioning as an independent unit.

Postwar mobility accelerated the breakdown of traditional patterns of social organization. The reduction of the communal family structure, and the transition of the family to a new area are factors that have contributed to the alteration of social values. The roots of the nuclear family unit within the community are rather superficial, and mobility is an ever increasing possibility.

Many things contribute to family mobility. Foremost is the desire for the "good life." The affluent American society is constantly presented, causing all people to be aware of the technological advancements that are available to the consumer. Opportunity is a factor in the decision to move.

Employment causes many persons to move each year. Not only does this occur for reasons of changing occupations in order to advance opportunities, but moving is built into many vocations and many employers utilize the transfer method for advancement. With more and more worldwide industrial complexes, employment with a particular concern may involve many moves to various branches of the same company.

The move from the city to the suburb, though dependent upon success, is a move that many families face. The newly developed concept in housing that occurred after the war has established the pattern to trade upward in home ownership. The small and young family will buy into an inexpensive tract home, and then as the financial security increases and the family grows, the desire to move into a larger home in a better area occurs. In our present system of moving upward in housing, it is possible to trade the old home in on the new home. This is a technique that was borrowed from the automobile industry.

Urban redevelopment deposes many families, causing them to move. Schools influence the movement of people, as does the weather. There is some evidence of movement being based upon social problems and population squeeze.

What happens when a family moves? The father, who was raised in the prewar era and in a small community with strict values, has discovered after serving in the armed forces that he no longer wishes to return to the old ways. Instead he marries a girl from another part of the country and they settle down to raise a family. They may move twice in that community in a period of eight years or less. Then, with employment alterations in that area, the family is forced to move to a new state. Now the father is several states and many years removed from the cultural standards of his youth. He has cast off those standards that he did not like, and supplanted them with values that fit the community within which he lived. But since mobility caused him to change communities and states several times, these values become less clear and cohesive. The ability of society to place restricting behavioral standards on people diminishes with increased mobility.

Children receive their basic social norms through family socialization processes. It is evident that in the event the familial values are no longer as clearly defined to the adult members of the family, they cannot be transferred to the younger members as readily as the parents had received theirs.

Social isolation occurs with every move. As the family leaves behind persons they know and trust, they find that it takes time to redevelop these same relationships in a new area. Thus, the parents will not be as supportive of the teacher's actions toward their child. They may question the validity of a strange neighbor's complaint about their child's conduct. The police officer may be seen as a stranger who is picking on the child. More and more the parents may begin to lean on the child's explanation of what occurred, rather than on the thoughts and advice of persons in authoritarian positions. Social isolation, caused in part by increased mobility of the population, contributes to juvenile problems.

It is estimated that one out of five urban families move at least once each year. With each move old friends are left behind and new ones must be made. Because of new school situations, and the fact that the schools are natural meeting grounds for a population group that have common interests and needs, it is usual for the children to begin to make acquaintances before the parents. Therefore, with each move, the children meet new youth whom their parents do not know and may have little chance of meeting. Parents who are moving about find it difficult to try to meet the parents of the friends of their own children. Quite often this is next to impossible, and even if they get the opportunity to meet, these adults may have no common ground on which to continue the acquaintanceship except for the friendship of the children.[6]

Another control is lost in that parents do not know the families of their childrens' friends as once was common. Parents do not get together to compare notes on the stories and activities of their children. Now, if a child tells his parents that his friend is allowed to do something, they seldom know if the friend is allowed to or not. The parents have lost the defense of knowledge that formerly was utilized to thwart youthful comparison attacks on the rules of the family.

With migration to urban areas, family controls disintegrate.[3] Members of the unit are drawn from the family during much of their waking hours. Fathers and mothers work, often in different parts of the community, while the children are attending schools that are fast being removed from the neighborhood. Former familial cohesiveness is reduced, and the American nuclear family no longer functions toward attaining common ends.[1]

A unique aspect of social migration in America is the loss of controlling values, without the benefit of replacement. In most instances, urbanization brings about a reduction in the number of social restraints retained by the members of the family, hence the community. Patterns of isolation tend to insulate individuals from each other, thus reducing the opportunity for the social members of the urban society to develop replacement controls that will become meaningful. While each individual has values, and to some extent these values are utilized within the proximity of family life, such controlling devices are not promulgated throughout the community. The consequences of this phenomenon are a "do as one pleases and leave me alone" attitude, and some degree of confusion in social consciousness.

From all indications, urbanization will continue to be felt in this country, and the migratory nature of the social groupings will continue to polarize in urban areas. Further research is needed to determine the effects of urbanization and mobility upon the values of the individual, and to develop methods of assisting such social groups in reestablishing value controls within their new setting.

Affluence

The prosperity attained in this nation during the past several decades has surpassed the grandest dreams of the builders of civilizations. Recoiling from depression and war, the nation entered a period of a sustained and growing standard of living. Technology, honed by the necessities of war, turned toward providing the consumer demands of a period of peace. Interrupted by the Korean conflict and several minor recessions, the structure of the economy grew, reaching new heights. The years of supporting armed intervention in various parts of the world, while delving into the probing of space, seems to have been incapable of doing anything to reduce the prosperous growth of the nation. If anything was to effect the national standard of living from these two sources, the technological advancements resulting from those efforts being placed at the disposal of the American consumer would be the main result.

Not only has the nation become urbanized and child-centered, but the affluence of the society has increased by astounding proportions. As an example, in the early thirties a political sampling was first attempted. The procedure was a telephone survey of persons supporting the Hoover presidential candidacy. It was discovered that a majority of the persons sampled were in favor of the Hoover administration. The facts were later refuted at the polls when Roosevelt attained victory by a clear margin. It was then that the statisticians discovered their error. The telephone was a higher income bracket device. That income group would most naturally accept the Hoover administration. The fact that affluence had not occurred to the extent that a majority of homes would have telephones, presenting a true random sampling, led the pollsters astray.

In modern America, it is considered inconceivable that a person would not have access to the telephone. Economic status is no longer measured by the availability of a phone in the home, although admittedly it might be measured by the *number* of such devices. In many homes, the children are granted their own telephones. These are not just extensions of the family phone, but are systems of their own, at the sole disposal of the child.

Other indications of affluence may be exemplified in the following situations. The author recalls desiring a football in his youth. One day his older brother came home with the leather cover of such a ball in which the bladder had been destroyed. The discarded item had been found in a vacant lot. It is still within the memory of the author, how the older brother, himself only age ten, stuffed the leather bag with rags, laced it, and made a football. It may be said that such a ball develops a good kicking foot and passing arm, for playing with one must be associated with playing with a medicine ball. But, to the children of that day, it was a football. The author also recalls, some years later, being approached by his own young son who wanted to know where *any* of his footballs were located. This is the result of affluence. The child with more than one item identical to the type the parent was denied at the same age, and the son not knowing the whereabouts of at least one. The author remembers the day that the family got a radio, and he came in from his play to sit in front of it and listen to such shows as "Jack Armstrong"; dramatic incidents forcing the child to conjure up the details of the story out of his own imagination. Contrast that situation to the child of today, many of whom not only have access to their family television, but may also have a set of their own.

The author recalls working as a social caseworker during the time that television was first becoming a part of the American scene. He experienced the transition from the point where the television set for the welfare client was viewed as an excess, to where it was officially accepted as a family recreational need. The same is true of the bicycle, the credit card, and the inevitable automobile. All such items have crept into the life of the youthful American. Just recently, some stores in various urban areas have offered to open credit accounts for teenagers, *without their needing an adult signature.*

Affluence has developed a whole new market—the youth market. Because our children have so much money to spend, business has recognized their buying power. There are numerous magazines on the market for teenagers. The cosmetics industry has really had an outlet via the juvenile. The same is true of the clothing industry and the retail outlets. Few clothing stores are without their youth section aimed at the teenage group. This has not been good enough, and so the preteen group was invented. Preteen catering has even included girdles and bras for teenyboppers. What ten or twelve year old girl is in real need of a girdle? Only part of that group would be in need of a bra. It is possible that the muscle tone of the teenage girl might be improved if the girdle were not introduced at such an early age.

Some years ago, the author and another couple went out to

dinner. It was an occasion, as all were young people struggling to raise families and to make ends meet. Entering one of the nicer restaurants in the area, these adults chose their food according to price, passing up the choice steak dinners that were offered. While they sat at their table enjoying the relaxation of good company and good food, two young teenage couples walked into the establishment. To the astonishment of the adult witnesses, the teenagers ordered selected steaks with the deft of gourmets. It was quite obvious that they had been in the restaurant before, as their bearing betrayed their affluence. A mute question arose. If this was the way the youths were experiencing teenage life, what would be left for them as adults? It struck home that youths were being exposed to adult behavior, actions, and rights much too soon. Was there any wonder that youth were in need of *kicks?*

Affluence has reached such proportions that, protests to the contrary, *the poor are not as poor.* There are degrees to everything, and all is relative. Poverty in modern America does not reach, much less exceed, the proportions of previously experienced poverty in this country. This is a fact that is hard for many youthful detractors to realize. But, as in situations of protest and demonstration against various institutions of society to do something about the conditions of the poor, in previous eras, the people who now turn out for such gatherings would have been too involved in attempting to survive to have appeared. Many of the older generation, who considered themselves middle class in previous periods, would be classed as *poor* in affluent America. Thus, the modern poor of this affluent nation are no longer concerned with the basic items of food, shelter, and survival; but rather, through their exposure to the consumer products offered this nation, "want a piece of the action." The poor want expensive homes, newer cars, colored televisions, personalized medical care, and the various needs of an affluent society which were formerly considered luxuries.

The sight of high school students in vehicles of varying values, cruising the neighborhoods of schools, has provoked humorous comments relative to student's cars being better than the ones driven by their teachers. This condition is no longer as humorous as it once was, as the need for expanded parking facilities is a real issue at most high schools. Certainly, future planning for school plants will have to consider such facilities.

Affluence has reached such proportions that many children are virtually subjected to a life of quasi-bribery, in that their parents shower them with material objects as signs of affection. Better stated, *in lieu of affection;* of that real affection that the parents no longer have the time to give.

Youths no longer are in a position to obtain the part-time and summer employment that was so common several decades ago. Restrictive child labor laws, increasingly difficult insurance regulations, and general affluence have combined to remove younger persons from the labor market. With some few exceptions, children are no longer exposed to the experience of working for someone else in a more than informal atmosphere. The inability of youth to procure jobs, coupled with the funds made available to them from their families, all join to present an unrealistic view of the monetary system. It is difficult to obtain meaningful perspective and develop realistic financial values when one spends his formative years free from any financial or vocational responsibility.

This nation's total consumer advertising effort is aimed at promoting desires for material effects and pleasurable experiences. This is only natural, but the advertising network is tremendous and reaches the public in subtle, as well as obvious ways. Consequently, the total population is constantly subjected to the calculated efforts of the industry to cause purchase or spending. No one is isolated from this effort. No group of people has ever been persuaded more effectively. The result has been the dissemination of the knowledge of the "good life" to everyone, with the attendant response of their desire for these items and pleasures. This exposure has built desire in many who are unable to afford these "necessary luxuries." Affluence, then, has its own built-in system of fomenting unrest and dissatisfaction.

The concept that if one cannot afford an object, "buy now and pay later" is being twisted into "buy now and someone will pay later." This is partially the result of parent-child financial relationships, and partly the effect of an extremely generous and complex welfare system. It has culminated in a situation that is presently becoming a concern of sociologists and other behavioral scientists, for this concept has produced the *subsidized marriage.* A subsidized marriage is one that is supported all or in part by the parents of those who have gotten married. It began shortly after World War II and the system has continued to increase in usage. There are many persons, whose children are getting ready to graduate from high school, who are still being assisted in sizable fashion by the *grandparents of the graduates.* Many of these people are ready to endow the following generations with the same assistance.

Youthful marriages, coupled with unrealistic desires for material comforts, *cause* the subsidy of the marriage to be a necessity. With the coming of the first child, the grandparents will intervene, if not before. The young married couple's parents are usually in a better financial state than ever before, and their generosity toward their children has become a way of life. The notable thing is that the very youth who proclaim their maturity and wisdom are incapable of providing themselves with their concepts of the marriage needs. Nothing closes the *generation gap* as quickly as a youthful marriage.

Increase in the Body of Knowledge

A knowledge explosion has occurred. The body of knowledge refers to all the information that is known to man. It embraces all fields of knowledge and all that man has acquired or developed through the use of his intellect. Since 1900, the increase in the amount and variety of information known to man has expanded at a rate that is difficult to comprehend. Basically and simplified, the body of knowledge doubled between 1900 and 1940. Since then, it has again doubled several times. On each occasion, the time lapse between these tremendous leaps in knowledge has shortened. Thus, not only is the body of knowledge expanding, it is doing so at a rapid rate that continues to increase in velocity.

The impact of such increases has been felt in several ways, related to problems of youth. First, there has been an upsurge in the holding power of the school. To begin with, education is a basic part of the American scene, and due to the system of public education this nation has developed a great respect for the necessity of educational preparation. Education is seen as a panacea for many of the ills of the nation. It is viewed as the keystone necessary for personal success. It is an opportunity that has become an established right.

Despite the dropout situation, the educational community's holding power on the individual has increased, and will continue to do so as the answer to meeting the needs of a technological age. By holding power is meant the ability of the educational system to retain the student for a number of years, or until he is fully prepared to enter the mainstream of community life and be a contributing factor. This holding power has been, and is being extended.

Many of the state colleges and universities of this country are descendants of the Normal School, familiar as teacher preparatory institutions at the turn of the century. At that time, two years of college were enough to obtain a teaching certificate in most areas. Today, five years of college has become almost a universal standard. And, that is merely a minimum of the preparation necessary for a career in the field of education.

Not too many years ago, a young person entering college had but several opportunities. He could prepare for a profession, such as medicine, law, or the clergy. He could study agriculture or business. Or, he could prepare to become a teacher. For most persons, high school was enough education to more than make one's way in life. Still others found that less than high school was an adequate background and did not severely deprive the individual of the necessities of life.

All this has changed, and the change has been quite rapid. Today, almost anyone will admit that a high school education is virtually a mandatory goal for every person. In addition, many occupations are now requiring two years of education beyond the high school period. Community colleges, an outgrowth of the old junior college concept, have sprung up throughout the land, and now exist in areas where the need for a college was unheard of as late as a decade ago.

Curriculum has been developed in all types of technical, vocational, and paraprofessional fields. One may study such foreign sounding occupations as dental assistant, ferrier, engineering technician, reprographics, inhalation therapy, police science, data processing, and building technology to name but a few. All listed require either two years of college or *less*.

On the four year level, the opportunities for education have also expanded. In the field of education alone, a person may now major in teaching at one of several levels of instruction, as well as to specialize in pupil personnel, counselling and guidance, or administration. More and more, intradisciplinary developments are taking place. These programs are evidenced in schools of urban affairs, social work, and even to some degree, in criminology.

As the society becomes more complex, so does the educational system, and as these events occur the need for education increases. For most children presently attending elementary school, two or more years of formal education beyond the high school level will be a necessity. To be able to earn an adequate living, advanced educational preparation is well on its way to becoming mandatory.

The team approach in various professions has become a reality. By this is meant the concept of having persons with various skill levels perform functions within the profession that were formerly performed by the professional only. As examples, the following are interesting.

Several institutions and at least one state have developed programs or enacted legislation providing for a medical assistant. This person would receive from four to five years of college instruction in the medical field. He would not be a doctor, but would be more skilled than a nurse. The job would involve the assistant performing routine medical services, under the supervision of a physician, that would release the physician for the more extensive work of a doctor. The assistant is seen as the answer to a growing shortage of physicians, and would take his place among an already well-developed paramedical team.

Even in the field of criminology, the team approach is becoming evident. Already there exist correctional technology programs preparing persons to assist probation and parole officers with routine tasks, releasing those professionals for more exhaustive case work. In the police field, the concept of a team approach was first extended by the President's Crime Commission in the police agent, police officer, and police administrator hierarchy.

In the area of psychiatric services, the team approach consisting of the psychiatrist, the psychologist, and the psychiatric social worker has long been held to be a successful approach to mental health.

It may be expected that expansion of the concept of teams within professions and vocations will continue. With each new development, the need for specialized training increases. This training will become a part of the educational system. The holding power of the schools will become more entrenched.

The second impact, and a direct result of the first, is the lengthened period of financial dependency that is placed on youth. In former years, children were an economic asset, as they quickly grew into contributors to the family income. This was very true on the farm, but it was also true in the preurban sprawl days of family unity. This has now changed. The alteration has been the effect of the holding power of the school. Youth must be dependent, at least in part, upon the family for many years, often extending into the early and middle twenties.

For families, children have become an economic liability. They are born with the assurance of dependency until they are about eighteen, and very often much longer. This not only places a burden on the family, but it also creates difficult adjustment problems within our youth.

As the individual grows older, the drive for emancipation becomes greater, but so do the demands for preparation for life's work. The young person is caught between the drives of nature and the demands of a complex social system. Frustration can only occur. If the youth goes on toward educational goals, immediate and immature goals may be subdued; but the individual's ability to become a meaningful contributor to himself or society has been impaired if he does not get trained.

Such a dilemma is difficult to cope with, and for those youngsters whose choice is to continue their educational pursuits, many frustrations will be endured. It is more than coincidental that at the same time student militancy has emerged, these frustrations have begun to exist. Some scholars have turned their attention toward possible correlative factors that may interact in the formation of this social phenomenon.

In view of the fact that the dropout rate among high school students has become a serious factor in recent years, the importance of the holding power of the school is magnified. Problems related directly to education and employment become readily apparent when consideration is given to the increased necessity of educational preparation for vocational endeavors. Unless present trends are reversed, one-third of the 25 million who will enter the labor market during the coming decade, will do so without the benefit of a high school education. Finding employment for these educationally handicapped will be a monumental task. It is estimated that for persons under 21 years, unemployment is over twice as high as within the general population.[7] There are 50 percent more school dropouts than there are new jobs for unskilled workers at the present time. The educationally unprepared cannot hope to compete within the needed labor market.

Increased antisocial behavior is an offshoot of the seriousness of the situation affecting the uneducated. While their material desires are equal to those of the rest of society, their lack of skills places them in a category from which it is quite difficult to emerge. As time goes on, the ability to be educated as an adult will decrease. The reasons are very clear. Education is fast becoming a series of highly specialized presentations. All require basic reading and language skills. It has been discovered in various programs for the disadvantaged that these persons are not gifted with patience. As a result, the very remedial programs they need to bolster their otherwise inadequate academic backgrounds extend their educational life beyond the point where the institution can retain their interest and motivation. Therefore, either the school is required to reduce standards to the point where preparation is questionable or those students lose their interest in continuing a program especially designed for them. For a dropout who has been lured back into a academic setting, a second failure to adjust is often the loss of that person's educational desire for the remainder of his life.

While academic difficulties are certainly the plague of the poor, such problems are by no means economically based. The fact is many of our youth are so lacking in the basic tools of education by the time they enter high school competition is virtually impossible. Continued failure coupled with exposure to what the student feels is unnecessary subject matter contributes to the inability of the school to succeed with these people. It is apparent that the field of education must exercise a diligent effort to overcome the problems encountered in teaching the basic skills during the early years of educational preparation.

Breakdown of the Family Unit

Many persons think in terms of death or divorce when they are exposed to concepts of broken homes. It should be pointed out that while the foregoing severances of family unity certainly are perplexing social problems there do exist other manifestations of reductions in family solidarity that are more subtle and often go unnoticed.

The complexities of modern life have brought about serious threats to normal family existence. The cohesiveness of the unit is under attack constantly, and in most cases the members are willing contributors to disunity.

Employment requirements, taking the father and sometimes the mother out of the home, are continuing problems encountered in an affluent society. Not only are the normal working hours given to removal from the home, but many after hours are spent attending business or contact meetings, directly or indirectly related to the employment.

The reasons for the absence of the parent may be quite valid, but the effects will be the same when continued for long periods of time. For many children, one meal a week that is experienced with the total family membership in attendance is near maximum. The children themselves contribute to the breakdown. More and more, children are engaged in activities that require them to be gone from the home. These often begin at an early age, sometimes prior to beginning formal education.

The dance and music lessons, various athletic endeavors, organizational memberships, and even church group affiliation all play a role in attacking the unity of the modern family. It is not unusual for any parent to find an almost impossible schedule of transportation facing him, due to the various activities of the children. One child might have to be at a certain ball park for a little league game, while another child is due at a recital during the fifth inning. At home, one may be awaiting transportation to a birthday party and has begun fussing because of the fear of being late.

The author recalls talking with a father a number of years ago. The man had brought his teenage son to the law enforcement agency in desperation, as the boy was felt to be incorrigible. The father recounted that the boy, now fifteen, had always attended church, but that lately no amount of cajoling could get the boy interested. As the father lamented this obvious sign of change, he was questioned regarding his own church attendance. He quickly stated that he was not a religious man, and that he had always had a foursome on the local golf links that met on Sunday mornings. The man was astonished when he was advised to take his son golfing. It was pointed out that the father had spent years showing the boy that church attendance was for kids, and that golfing was for men. Why, at that point in the boy's life, should the youngster not feel that he was entitled to the pursuits of the adults? Why should church attendance have any continued meaning? This example also points up the extremes to which parents will go in order to expose their children to what the parent thinks is good for the child; while the parent pursues activities that deplete the limited unity within the family. Is there any wonder that the child begins to exhibit traits and behavior that the parent no longer understands? The parent has not held a meaningful relationship with the child for a period of time prior to the youth's development of alien interests.

Accompanying the breakdown of the influential and communal pattern of the larger family sphere is an increase in the severity of the effects on the child of the disruptive forces that lead to disunity within the modern family unit. In former years, the loss of one member of the family was not the drastic shock to the equilibrium of the family that is now experienced. Other members of the larger family sphere were present to step in and take over. The child of the modern family has few persons in whom to turn. It evolves that for the most part the child has but the remaining parent. In many cases, such as death or divorce, the remaining parent is not in the position to aid and comfort the child in a manner that will assist effectively in overcoming problems and developing understanding.[8]

Upwards of 15 percent of the children in this country are living with either one or no parents. The number of broken homes caused by divorce or separation has been increasing steadily during the past few years.[6] Many children are faced with developing in an incomplete environment.

The working mother has contributed to the breakdown in the family. Mothers entering the labor market have tripled since World War II.[9] It is true that not all children of working mothers suffer ill effects, but those that do not fail to be harmed because of the extensive effort and intelligent planning on the part of the parent. Unfortunately, this is often not the case. Many times, a mother who is required to work out of the home and tries to retain the vocation of motherhood at the same time is so fragmented that she is ineffectual at one or both. Children in these situations suffer from feelings of rejection, as they encounter many instances of need for parental guidance that do not occur.[10] The child who has just succeeded in something and needs the attention and encouragement at that time finds the emptiness of the home detracting from the spirit of the moment.

As was earlier pointed out, a broken home can exist when both parents are together in the household. In this context, one finds the old concepts of a home broken by the absence of one or both parents not nearly as valid as once was believed.

While broken homes have been blamed as sources of delinquency, former studies must be discounted, as few made any attempt to compare delinquent and nondelinquent groups. Some errors were made by grouping various types of broken homes together. In such studies, the differing psychological difficulties accompanying each type of broken home were not taken into account. Still other studies failed to reckon with the nature of the cultural, social, or ethnic attitudes toward such homes.[3]

Recent studies have attempted to determine the ramifications of the different types of broken homes upon the personality development of the child involved. Contradicting popular assumptions, more than half of the delinquents studied lived with their own parents.[11] It should be noted that in many instances where a youth has been identified as being delinquent and coming from a broken home there are other siblings in that home who are not delinquent.

Broken homes are important considerations in the effect of the severance of the parent-child relationship on the development of the personality of the child. Thus, where the stronger or more loving parent is retained the effects of the broken home may not be nearly as severe as in the case where the surviving parent is a rejecting, nonloving, or weak parental image. As an example, one comprehensive study of parent-child relationships in delinquent and nondelinquent children discovered that neglecting mothers were most likely to have an adult criminal son, while only about half of the passive, cruel, or absent mothers had a criminal son. The same study concluded that the home that was quarrelsome, in which discipline was lax and the parents were neglecting, had the greatest potential for producing an adult criminal.[12]

In another important study, it was discovered that delinquent boys expressed close emotional attachments to their mother, while at the same time relating the feeling that the mothers did not have a deep concern for the well-being of the offspring.[13]

It may be concluded from studies such as the ones mentioned that a home in which the parents exhibit love and affection, and are at the same time good models for the children to pattern their lives after, are least likely to produce children with severe antisocial behavior. The reader must be cautioned that such a conclusion is a broad generalization meant to point up the need for both affection and a model. Further conclusions should be reserved until the reader has appraised himself of the totality of the studies, which have only been lightly touched upon herein.

In conclusion, the broken home may have to be reexamined in order to include those situations where both parents are in the home, but neither are performing adequate parenthood. While a broken home cannot be said to be a cause of delinquency, such situations in the totality of the use of the term herein must be seen as adding to the stress of living. It may be a serious factor in the difficulties of adjustment experienced by youngsters in such situations.[14]

Population Increase

The term *population explosion* has become a part of the vocabulary. It carries various connotations when considered from differing perspectives and varying meanings for different individuals. Within the context of youth problems, population increase is an important consideration. It is important in respect to sheer numbers, if for no other reason.

An increase in the birthrate is only part of the explanation of the increase in the population. Other factors are just as significant. For one thing, the extention of longevity presents unique problems accompanying the population increase brought about by a longer life expectancy. Questions concerning retirement and leisure time, health care for the aged, and utilization of the pool of human resource contained within the older group all are a part of geriatrical considerations.

The development of the rest home business as the place of care for the older and more infirm members of society has evolved as a partial answer to a perplexing problem. Admittedly, it has tended to be a more commercial than a social venture, but the increase in the number of aged persons needing such services has brought about a boom in that business. One may query how the rest home contributes to the problems of youth. It does so in respect to the *why* of the evolvement of that service. One must not discount the fact that many persons who have been confined to a rest home are in effect being discarded. Not all of the patients in a home for the aged are incapable of living outside of that type of institution. Many are there because they have outlived their generation.

The facts of urbanization and its influence upon the American family in the areas of familial ties and the physical, economic, and social ecology of the nuclear family have contributed to the impossibility of retaining the older generation in the homes of younger America. As the days of the meaningful family relationships extending outward to encompass the larger related sphere have ceased, so has the willingness and ability to shelter the aged within the family.

House size, working adults and children who are engaged in numerous activities beyond the home, as well as the totality of the social setting tend to preclude the nuclear family from taking and retaining the aged person within the home. The fact that more and more acquaintances are found who have an elderly relative in a rest home situation increases the ease by which other members of the younger generations may decide upon the same action. As in most social activity, acceptance tends to be in proportion to the extent of the performance of the activity.

The effect of the life and activity of the aged upon youth has not been measured, but it may be safely stated that certain assumptions can be drawn. What does the younger teenager feel when he sees grandmother enter a rest home, and expriences the lessening of the frequency of the family visits? What are the effects of witnessing a previously productive person dwindle into a retirement oblivion? What connotation may a youth place upon the actions or lack of actions of his parents toward their parents? Is it not possible that another dual standard has arisen, when youth witness the care of the aged by the children of the aged; by the same persons who are expounding general respect for adults and the honoring of parents? And, what about youthful conceptions of what will be in store for them? It is not uncommon to hear the statement that one does not wish to live to attain old age. Yet, this is not a denial of the desire for survival, but rather the recognition of the problems of longevity.

At the other end of the spectrum, medical science, technology, and affluence have all combined to reduce infant mortality. While this nation ranks thirteenth in infant mortality, the low ranking reflects society's failure to insure the same services to certain isolated minority groups and lower economic families, which are considered to exist universally. However, for the average American there is little concern about a child's opportunity to survive to age 21. In the preurban period, many children died before attaining majority. This is no longer a truism. Survival of the fittest is being replaced by survival of even the weakest. The reduction in infant mortality has been a considerable factor upon the increase in the population.

Conservative estimates indicate that the nation is reaching the point where 25 percent of the population will be under 25 years of age. This percentage is expected to increase quite rapidly within the next decade. It may be noted, that without any increase in delinquency rates, the mere increase in the number of youth within the population will place an extreme burden upon those agencies and services with the mission of dealing with the detection and control of delinquency. The police officer of tomorrow will be in greater need of an adequate understanding of youth and their problems than any of his predecessors. If the control of delinquency remains as a police function, ultimately a majority of the police effort will be expended with juveniles, just as a majority of that effort is presently being directed toward the young adult. Unless preparation is made at this time, police and community resources for coping with juvenile problems will be drastically strained.

An additional thought needs to be hypothesized. In the event many of the youth survive infant mortality due to the technology of the society, is it not possible that there are more potential misfits attaining adulthood? During a period of congested urbanization, with the development of a complex society and the increase in tensions and anxieties experienced in daily life, it is important to consider the nature of the input into that ecology. The weaker individual is bound to succumb to the difficulties experienced in an urban nation, and the manifestations of the failure to adjust may take any number of avenues. While this is not a call for selective breeding, certainly it is a call for research effort in the area of the weakening of the species, and for the development of resources to effectively cope with the burdens that antisocial behavior may place upon the social order in the future.

NOTES AND REFERENCES

1. Louis Kaplan: *Foundations of Human Behavior.* New York, Harper and Row, 1965, pp. 97, 99.
2. Ruth Cavan: *Juvenile Delinquency.* Philadelphia, J. B. Lippincott, 1962, pp. 67, 69, 116.
3. Don C. Gibbons: *Society, Crime, and Criminal Careers.* Englewood Cliffs, N. J., Prentice-Hall, 1968, p. 182.

 4. Robert Redfield: The folk society. *American Journal of Sociology, 52:* 293-308, 1947.
 5. Reece McGee: *Social Disorganization in America.* San Francisco, Chandler Publishing Co., 1962.
 6. Interdepartmental Committee on Children and Youth, *Children in a Changing World,* White House Conference on Children and Youth, 1960.
 7. James B. Conant, quoted in *U. S. News and World Report,* October 26, 1964, p. 104.
 8. J. J. Honigmann: *Culture and Personality.* New York, Harper and Row, 1954, p. 289.
 9. W. T. Vaughan: Children in crisis. *Mental Hygiene,* 45:354-359, 1961.
10. L. W. Hoffman: Effects of maternal employment on the child. *Child Development,* 32:187-197, 1961.
11. Clifford Shaw and Henry D. McKay: *Social Factors in Juvenile Delinquency.* The National Commission on Law Observance and Enforcement, No. 13, Vol. 2, U. S. Government Printing Office, Washington, D. C., 1931, pp. 261-284.
    William Healy and Augusta Brenner: *New Light on Delinquency and its Treatment.* New Haven, Yale University Press, 1936.
12. William and Jean McCord: *Origins of Crime.* New York, Columbia University Press, 1959.
13. Sheldon and Eleanor Glueck: *Unraveling Juvenile Delinquency.* Cambridge, Harvard University Press, 1950.
14. E. H. Bernet: Demographic trends and implications. *The Nation's Children, 1: The Family and Social Change.* New York, Columbia University Press, 1960, pp. 24-49.

Chapter Five

ENVIRONMENT AND BEHAVIOR

I N law enforcement circles, much criticism is leveled at the concept that delinquency and crime are rooted within the social environment. Many professional police personnel interpret this as a denial of the responsibility of the individual. Instead, it should be recognized as an attempt to *understand* causation, and not the failure to require accountability.

Admittedly, there are instances within every discipline where the concept has been distorted. Examples may be found within the courts, the correctional system, and among social welfare practitioners. Erroneous application of a concept, however, does not invalidate the principle. It should be stressed that no matter how valid the theory of personal responsibility seems, it is also true that "no man is an island." Just as the actions of an individual affect others; the actions of others, and the setting in which one finds himself will influence an individual's behavior.

Few persons would deny that the physical environment has important effects upon the individual; and that as a result of those circumstances, certain adaptions must be made in order to cope with the alteration of environmental conditions. The physical disruption of the ecology and the effects upon the individual are well-documented scientifically.[1]

Accepting the fact that an individual's physical surroundings, e.g. weather, will cause certain reactions and even behavioral alteration, why must the argument relating to the effect of the totality of the ecology continue to exist? There are several answers. First, as indicated previously, many opponents of the societal effects upon behavior are in opposition not to that concept, but to the distortion of the theory through application. Secondly, to admit that social factors affect the individual's actions tend to cause the first criticism to materialize through the introduction of mitigation. Third, social environment is so complex, to include it as a serious consideration in determining the motivation of the individual introduces such a variety of ramifications as to appear bewildering. Finally, for some the American ethic of individual responsibility is so strong that it brings about a natural recoiling from the possibility of the original premise.

Interpretation of behavioral motivation is an extremely complex task, and much remains to be accomplished in such areas. Certain facts are known, pertaining to responses to external stimuli. It is apparent that compensation to extreme ecologies depends in large measure upon the nature of the stress encountered and the individual's repertoire of mechanisms allowing him to cope with the adverse or hostile input.[2]

Physiological reactions to social stress have long been identified.[3] These changes in biological functioning have been experienced by all. Examples are increased pulmonary activity brought on by a stress situation, or increased adrenal flow accompanying fright. Studies of peptic ulcers have indicated that such disturbances are related to social isolation. Physiological equilibrium is disrupted by the absence of meaningful interpersonal relationships. This may be one reason why service men who were not committed to battle were found to have a higher incidence of ulcers than combat troops, or even prisoners of war.[4] The comradeship of experiencing a similar stress situation grouped the participants into meaningful, supportive relationships reducing tensions and overcoming the strain of the input.

Emotions responding to external stimuli may bring about increased metabolistic reactions providing excess energy. At the same time, skilled actions may suffer from the body's mobilization to react to danger, as small muscle coordination is affected under stress.[5] The opposite, a depressed emotional state, drains the individual's energy, leaving him in a state of fatigue when he needs all of his biological prowess to overcome the emotional burden.[6]

This is not to say that stress is harmful per se, but rather to indicate extremes. Moderate stress is necessary in order to bring about the motivation that will lead to achievement. Controlled emotional response is needed to bring about an aggressive and competitive life style. Uncontrolled emotional response is a mobilization of the body's forces to cope with a particular situation. In doing so, other areas of behavioral functioning are foregone.

MECHANISMS UTILIZED TO COPE WITH STRESS

Just as the biological organism reacts to stress, the psychological nature of the human being is affected by the anxieties to which it is subjected. The term *defense mechanism,* also known as mechanisms of adjustment, is familiar to most. Some persons react to the term with disdain, feeling that it implies a malady or weakness. In reality, all persons employ such mechanisms throughout their lives. It is not the existence of the mechanism that indicates trouble, but rather the debilitating utilization of the adjustment process.

An external social factor can cause such an extent of stress that tolerance of the anxiety for any length of time would be impairing. The fact that the origin of the stress may not be readily recognized indicates that the ability to correct the situation is not always present. It is under this type of stress that the person will employ a defense mechanism.

Utilizing one source's classification of these devices, the following terms shall be employed:[3]

1. *Mechanisms of deception.* These devices are used by the individual to reduce his perception of the threat. They include reationalization, repression, suppression, projection, and displacement.

2. *Mechanisms of substitution.* Using these devices, the person replaces the tension-bearing goals with more attainable ends. The devices include sublimation, reaction formation, compensation, and substitution.

3. *Mechanisms of avoidance.* Here, the individual removes himself, psychologically speaking, from the situation. These devices are identified as fantasy, regression, identification, and negativism.

A certain amount of the use of such devices occurs in everyone's life. It is when the use of the device causes the person to be incapable of consciously coping with anxieties that problems are encountered. When one begins to rely upon the device as the answer to life's problems, severe limitations on personal capacities may be recognized.

ENVIRONMENTAL THREATS TO SECURITY

Every individual encounters threats to his well-being. Generally, these threats will be environmental circumstances. These stresses tend to be external in origin, and when encountered the individual's security or safety will be viewed as being in a state of jeopardy. His reactions to the threat may set off a chain of events that result in behavior subject to police action. Youth itself will increase the chance that the chosen action to overcome the stress will be unacceptable behavior. This is because of the normal indiscretions of youth, coupled with lack of experience.

Experience plays an important part in threat interpretation, and in the foundation for the reactions to the threat stimuli. Actually, a threat is a pain-fear conditioned response. It is the attempt to avoid that which may bring harm.

It is important to recognize that it is not the threat-object which is feared. Rather, it is the *symbol* of the threat-object. In other words, the anxiety is brought on by the symbol of what may cause the harm. In many cases, the true threat-object, if immediately faced, would bring about responses that would tend to reduce the immediate condition. Instead, the symbol of the threat-object is initially recognized. The individual's powers are mobilized to cope with the anxiety aroused by the symbol, and not the actual threat.

Persons voicing anxiety over violence, including war, are not as concerned about violence as they are anxious about the pain, suffering, or death that the violence may bring. As an example, one would not be concerned when they were about to be struck, if they knew in advance that they would not feel the blow. This is the basic reason men are not generally afraid of being hit by a woman. This act of being struck is still a violent act, but the symbol of the threat-object (pain or fear) does not exist.

A person who goes swimming often may not be eager to assist a drowning victim. The water, when the victim is in difficulty, becomes a symbol of a threat-object to the would be rescuer.

Yet, the latter person may have just gotten out of the same water. Experience gives one understanding. It has a tendency to allow the individual to overcome the fear of the symbol, and to concentrate upon the reality of the threat-object. Under these circumstances, the threat-object may be handled on a more rational basis.

In dealing with juveniles, it is important to remember that all symbols of threats are not coupled to physical outcomes. The fact a youth has been restricted from seeing the moment's object of affection may cause that youngster to believe that the affair will end and romance will vanish, never to return. The juvenile's reaction in the face of this symbol may be most anything, but there will be a reaction. A bad mark in school may become the symbol of a negative action being taken by the parents. The juvenile's actions may be because of *his* preconceptions of the parents' reactions to the poor grade. Damage to the family automobile may be viewed by the youth as the symbol of the threat of familial retribution. It may come as the final straw in a sequence of events. The youngster's interpretations of the seriousness of the threat may far exceed the reality of the threat. It is within these types of situations that juvenile reactions to environmental threats are likely to bring about over reactions that worsen the incident.

Many juvenile offenses are subject to "snowballing." One perceived threat causes a reaction, which brings about another threat, and the snowball effect begins to occur. When the threat symbols are *over-read* by the juvenile, he increases the velocity of the buildup through his inappropriate reactions.

This is easily seen in the *chicken syndrome*. Having his courage and willingness to participate challenged by the group brings a threat symbol of peer group rejection. Bravado sets in, and is utilized as a manifestation of confidence. The act ensues. The moment the act takes place, the youth has neutralized the threat symbol of peer rejection. However, the act has produced a new threat symbol, the reality of which may only be determined by the nature and the severity of the act. In the majority of instances and contrary to common conceptions, the juvenile will be ill-informed on the nature of the act and the various reactions to its performance. He will be in a position of not being able to make clear judgments relating to his act. As the new threat symbol becomes stronger, the juvenile will have to take action to reduce the stress it has caused. Since he has misread the reality of the threat symbol, his reaction to reduce its significance will probably exceed the reality of the threat.

Just as the concept is difficult to describe, it is more difficult to attempt to discriminate between symbolic and real threats. It is the symbolic threat that brings on the anxiety and the need for activity to reduce the stress. Due to the perceptional difficulties involved, some drastic behavioral effects may be the result of the individual's interpreation of an environmental threat. Many actions of behavior are the result of indiscriminate acts of an individual when faced with what he views to be a threatening environment. The greater the ecological stress, the more desperate the behavioral response. The threat does not need to be physical in nature. It may be anything that is perceived to be an attack upon the individual's security. The motivation to perform a particular act may be based solely upon the individual's recognition of a threat symbol.

ADDITIONAL FACTORS AFFECTING YOUTHFUL BEHAVIOR

Analyzing behavior is a complicated process. Individual differences, cultural backgrounds, family conditions, and social environment are all important variables that are a part of the complicated scheme. It would be impractical to attempt to present the totality of the circumstances that tend to affect the behavior of an individual. Instead, a discussion of several of the more obvious youthful behavioral influences will be undertaken. It is intended that by this means the more common factors affecting behavior will be identified, thereby creating in the reader a positive understanding of the nature of youthful behavior.

Social Tolerance

Preceeding sections have indicated the importance of culture in relationship to behavior. The cultural basis of the group in which an individual finds himself determines the norms or values that guide the behavior of the members of the group. Thus, in a highly matriarchial society certain norms revolving around womanhood will be a dominant behavioral control. In another group where values are less clearly defined, more liberal behavior may be expected. Behavior, although individually manifested, is not an individual entity. Rather, it is the sum total of many factors, including cultural values and the individual's response to them.

The concept of social tolerance is basic to the functioning of any social group. It is from the implementation of this concept that rules and laws governing the behavior of the members of that group emerge.

All societies develop standards of behavioral expectations for various positions within the social group. Traditionally, certain ones are universally applied to related positions within any society. As an example, courage is demanded of military personnel, no matter what society is being studied. Wisdom is expected of the leaders of society. Men are expected to behave differently under stress than women. For centuries, children have been granted a wider tolerance than adults.

In modern society, the tolerance of the public toward the behavior of persons in different classifications or roles is an important part in determining inadequate or antisocial behavior. The question is not so much what is intrinsically good or bad, but rather how tolerant the group will be in the observation of the behavior of one of the members.

Instead of viewing behavior of youth as either delinquent or nondelinquent, it should be visualized as running along a continuum that closely approximates the normal curve.[7] To aid in this visualizing, suppose the reader draws a bell curve. Divide the curve into seven components, with each segment given equal distance along the horizontal line at the bottom of the curve and using vertical lines to separate each segment within the curve. Upon completion, it is obvious that as progression is made from the center segment outward in either direction the area within each segment decreases. The largest area remains within the center segment.

By drawing a vertical dotted line that bisects the actual center of the bell curve, it becomes apparent that the large center segment extends one-half on each side of the actual center line.

This means that *average* behavior, or that which may be performed without any degree of adverse reaction, incorporates both behavior that is tending to be bad and behavior that tends to be good as the outer limits (left and right of center) of the segment are reached. Conversely, very little behavior would fall at the actual bell curve center.

Moving outward in each direction, and into the segments directly to the right and left of the center section, it is first noticed that the total area of either of these two segments is smaller than the total area of the center segment. Behavior falling into these segments tends to be good or not so bad, as the behavior is found to be situated near the segment boundary closest to the center. As the opposite occurs, the behavior becomes either quite good, or becoming bad, depending upon the segment chosen.

Therefore, in the center three segments, behavior tends to be tolerated by society. The actions of individuals performing in these areas seldom result in anything more adverse than personal criticism.

But, as the behavior begins to fall into the two segments that are next found on either side of the center of the bell curve, then some sanctions are imposed by society, disapproving of the behavior as being either bad or good. Behavior that falls into those segments that are found at the extreme ends of the bell curve draw the severest forms of social intolerance. For the negative behavior the punishments appear severe, but that is because they are more noticeable. The extremely positive behavior may result in social responses that are as severe, but which are more subtle.

In other words, it is just as possible to be too good as it is possible to be too bad. This is a concept that the majority of persons never realize. But the truth is that in modern society there is no place for the "goody two-shoes." Among youthful peers these persons are called "sissies" and other terms that denote dissatisfaction with the individual's behavior. It is important to understand that behavior does extend along this continuum from extremely good to extremely bad, and that the further the behavior is toward either extreme the greater the opportunity for societal disapproval and reaction.

One other point needs to be made. Behavior is relative. It is relative in time, place, and circumstances. On the continuum of the normal bell curve, the younger or older the individual, the greater leeway from the actual center his behavior is given through social tolerance. We would not condemn a child of tender years for actions that we would condemn a young adult for performing. Nor would the individual past 70 be sanctioned adversely for actions that would have been censored during his middle years.

In dealing with juveniles and youth, it is necessary to not only recognize the meaning of social tolerance, but also important to bring the concept to the attention of the youth in question. A child, who while quite young used certain swear words at which people laughed, may find it difficult to understand why the tolerance has diminished after entering school. The same is true of the child who has always been the center of attraction within the family. His attention-gaining antics are usually found wanting in peer group or other adult situations. The same parallels may be drawn between the same delinquent act being performed by a preschool child and a high school student. Society is going to be more lenient with the former, and more severe with the latter. It is too bad, but a truism, that many modern parents are not aware of the concept of social tolerance themselves. Thus, they not only fail to direct their children with the concept in mind, but find it hard to understand why social reaction has altered toward the actions of their offspring.

Permissiveness

Just as many terms become placed into general usage to describe persons or situations that tend to be viewed from polarized positions, the term *permissive* has gone through a period of emotional reaction. For persons who are at one extreme, it symbolizes the fault finding that explains or gives a semblance of understanding to situations and actions that are otherwise unfathomable. Persons at the other extreme deny the existence of the meaning underlying the word, claiming instead that others are utilizing semantics as a basic for an otherwise illogical argument.

The act of being permissive may be defined as *habitually or characteristically permitting or tolerating behavior that others might disapprove or forbid.*[8]

The key in the above definition is the concept of tolerating behavior; and the full statement defines one of the elemental behavioral nuances of the so-called *liberal* or *progressive*. In order to fall into the latter category, tolerance toward or understanding of unusual behavior is necessary. For many individuals, these feelings are real. For others, they are merely meaningless verbal expressions never acted upon, but which give to the individual mouthing the utterances a feeling of sophistication or intellectualism, both pseudo in reality. For many young people, these feelings, and even when translated into actions, are actually the result of two independent factors that have been joined by an unidentified catalyst.

The first factor is youth. As already noted, the very process of growth and maturation requires that youth seek emancipation. This has been a normal pattern of youth. It cannot be ignored. Youth have always and will always strive for their own identification at the expense of the accepted and expected.

The second factor is the existence of immediate and universal news coverage of the actions of a few. The fact that this exists at this time is historical and uncontrollable. The fact that the news media, especially television, as well as those in the creative arts who are quick to utilize a new theme, emphasizes the importance of unusual behavior as newsworthy seems to be partly legitimate and partly economically based.

The catalyst that has brought the two together, blending these factors beyond proportions previously known and molding them into a social cataclysm, is the philosophical school known as *existentialism*. This philosophy has made great strides in the past twenty years, and has recently surmounted *pragmatism* as the most prevalent and dynamic educational philosophy.

There is no room for these two philosophical disciplines to be discussed herein. It is more important to identify the fact that existentialism has crept into our society, and that it is very important in the development of the basic attitudes of college youth. These in turn bring poorly conceived interpretations of the philosophy into the society, often putting the theories into practice. Misled application of existentialist conceptualizations gives the desired effect: shock. It is this quality, the shock of the sensibilities of others, that appeals to the normal youthful drives toward emancipation.

That youthful desires to establish a self-image could be coupled with the technical development of a means of producing news almost instantaneously with its occurrence would coexist at a time when the most independent of all philosophical thought emerged, could not be foreseen. The fact that the influence of this philosophy upon the other two factors has not been generally recognized emphasizes the subtly of that influence.

A Permissive Society

Much has been said about the permissive nature of the modern society. There are many pros and cons involved in this topic. Yet, one cannot but ponder certain facts that do point to the existence of permissiveness as a social dictum.

The present generation of youthful Americans are the product of child-rearing practices that tended to be based upon the thoughts and writings of the well-known pediatrician.[9] That he promulgated a permissive attitude can be established from the fact that such an attitude is a necessary ingredient of liberalism. His actions of a social nature in the past several years certainly earn him a liberal designation.[10]

Keeping in mind the element of tolerance toward behavior that is not condoned by others as the key to understanding the nature of permissiveness, examples may be readily discovered within recent social action. Some examples will be unofficial social action, while others will be the official response of government to the permissiveness within society. In the latter case, one must understand that when a social attitude or posture affects the national policy, it is a certain sign of its significant existence.

Permissiveness began to be indicated within the social order in the early fifties. Law enforcement was affected by numerous and increasingly more frequent restrictive court decisions. It was about this time that the first public movements to do away with capital punishment were noted. As the decade passed, the proponents of the attack on the supreme penalty became more vocal, and in some states their efforts were rewarding. Since that emergence, even in those states maintaining the punishment within the body of law, executions have dwindled to a standstill.

It is not the purpose of this book to discuss the merits of the death penalty, but rather to use it to illustrate the effect of permissiveness upon the official nature of society's actions.

In the celebrated Chessman case in California, the then governor, Edmund Brown, an outspoken opponent of the death penalty absented himself from the scene during the final hours when he was being sought for a stay of execution. Chessman was executed after having spent the longest time-period of any person in this country on death row. Within two weeks, the same government official granted stays for two condemned men who had killed two Los Angeles police officers. This was without fanfare.

It is interesting to note that in the Chessman case the defendent had never killed anyone. True, he was a habitual criminal, but he had been convicted under California's Little Lindburg Law, and had received the death penalty. The Chessman case had reached extreme public proportions. The executive authority of the state could not make a decision that would not have brought a response from some segment of the public. The answer was to make no decision at all, and none was made. The other case had never received such notoriety. Stays of execution given in that situation would result in no public outcry from any significant quarter. The official response of government in the latter case was contradictory when compared with the official response in the Chessman case, but it was permissive when compared to the two sides of the question of the death penalty.

In the late fifties, a young boy and his early teenaged girl friend went on a killing spree covering several states.[11] Among those slain were the parents of the girl. The two were captured in Nebraska, a state which no longer had the death penalty. Their crimes had horrified the nation, and that effect had been multiplied in the states in which the murders had occurred. Under such circumstances, the permissive attitude that had brought about a change in the official government response in one state to capital punishment would inhibit the conviction and execution of either of the suspects.

The answer was quite simple. Extradition. That is what occurred. Although Nebraska could have assumed jurisdiction, the extent of the crimes caused a public outcry, affecting the official response to allow the suspects to be extradited to a neighboring state where the male suspect was later executed and his teenage female companion was sentenced to a long term of imprisonment. It is interesting to note that she is now in the process of seeking her freedom, and she will probably succeed.

In 1945 the National Forensic League set a resolution to be debated throughout the country and the question was *should eighteen-year-olds be allowed to vote?* Some 24 years later, the same question was debated nationally on the college level. The concept had come full circle. In 1970 Congress granted the vote to eighteen-year-olds. The same year politicians of all levels began to woo the youthful voter.

This action is quite important, for if the youth are more liberal than their older counterparts, then they are more permissive. A significant increase in the numbers of youthful voters, caused by the Voting Rights Act of 1970, could have the effect of increasing the success of liberal candidates and causes. Hence, permissiveness would have a greater opportunity of becoming the official national policy. Led by the "intelligensia," given impetus by self-serving politicians, and publicly supported by a large youthful power group, permissiveness may become the voice of America.

It seems incongruous that the same groups who support granting the vote to youth on the basis of an assigned wisdom to the youth, also support legislation that is designed to protect the same youth from the effects of their bad decisions. Thus, in most states a youth coming into conflict with the law as a juvenile may have his record expunged after a given period. In California, the ability to have criminal records expunged has been extended to offenses occuring until the individual is 21 years old. This is true for either felonies or misdemeanors.

The effect of such protective legislation is to extend the period when an individual may be considered a *first offender*. As an example, if a youth commits five serious burglaries between twelve and eighteen years of age, he may have them removed from his record after turning eighteen. Later, he commits another burglary and is taken into adult court for the first time. He is now a *first offender* again. Now, if he is involved in several other burglaries before reaching 21 years, he may have those removed from his record, and after 21 on his ninth or tenth burglary, he may again appear before the court as a *first offender*.

To the author it seems contradictory that the same youth, endowed by others with being well-informed and full of wisdom, should be granted the decision-making power of the vote on the one hand, while being protected from the effects of his poor decisions on the other, with both being official governmental policy as reflected by statute.

Prior to the recent increase in drug abuse among the youthful population, the national policy left no doubt that drug sales or use were criminal violations. Yet, when society was faced with a *numerical* increase in drug use, the official governmental response was to tolerate behavior that was formerly condemned. Not only has Congress lessened the penalties for use, but there is now a good chance that some jurisdictions will begin to allow juveniles to seek aid *without* parental knowledge. This is already a fact in the fight against venereal disease. California has enacted legislation permitting the treatment of juveniles for such an infection *without having to notify the parents* of the infection or the treatment.

The President's Commission on Obscenity and Pornography officially found that it would not limit either for consenting adults.[12] It did indicate that it would advise limitations upon youthful utilization of such material. The Commission's findings were rejected by both the presidential office and the Congress, but the fact that such a blue ribbon committee would issue those results is indicative of the permissive reaction prevalent in the society.

Other examples may be found in situations of violence and disorder within our communities and on college campuses, and the official response to such actions. Examples of permissiveness may be discovered as a part of the clogged court calenders, open defiance and even extreme violence in the courtroom, and dismal results from the correctional experiments. Others are evidenced in official verbal license being granted to militant activists, some of whom have been convicted of crimes and are awaiting appeal at the time of their dialogues, under the guise of freedom of speech.

Official permissive response is seen in the reaction of government to the increasing numbers of militant exiles who often cease their self-imposed removal only to come back to the country and utilize the very system they seek to destroy in order to gain their freedom by means of courtroom antics and legal technicalities. All of this occurs on the premise of the worth of the individual and individual freedom and rights.

Yet, when faced with a decision of whether to grant asylum to one crew member from a Soviet ship who jumped aboard a Coast Guard cutter as the two ships were side by side during fishing rights negotiations, the official governmental response was that the request for freedom should be turned down.[13] The seaman was returned to the Russian ship, and the reason was stated to be that the request of one individual for asylum had to be weighed against the ability to culminate a fishing treaty successfully. Apparently, the rights of the individual *can* be superseded by the needs of the state.

This is the difficult thing about liberalism and permissiveness in our society. It is always easy to be liberal *until* the situation becomes uncomfortable.

Movements are underway to give legal social sanction to homosexuality. Recent state and national actions in the area of firearms control have resulted in meaningless restrictions being placed upon persons who would normally utilize such weapons rationally. There has been no attempt to require courts to issue mandatory sentences of a severe nature in cases where weapons and extreme violence have been the instruments of the crime.

Social permissiveness can be likened to an individual who

refuses to take a stand. With each new and liberal conceptualization, the society withdraws from an open confrontation. Social tolerance increases on the premise that morality cannot be legislated and that what an individual does is of no consequence as long as it does not hurt others. While it is true that morals cannot be absolutely legislated, certainly society cannot abdicate its responsibility for making moral judgments. Such judgments are necessary for the socialization of incoming generations, a primary responsibility of society. Social moral judgments must be promulgated, and the means for doing that are either through official policy or by statute.

In answer to those individuals and groups who claim that a human act is devoid of morality as long as it does not harm or affect others, experience has demonstrated that few acts are committed by one human that do not affect another. This is exceptionally true in a modern society.

The land of individual freedom without full responsibility for the rights of others is an unattainable utopia. A complex society without legal and moral order is a self-destructing mechanism. Just as reactionary extremism is harmful, so is extended liberalism.

That permissiveness exists within our society can be identified in the words of one of the world's foremost religious leaders, who actually made that statement to a group of youths in Australia while on a world tour.[14] He was speaking out not as a religious leader, but with a shared concern for the modern social order.

Permissiveness Within the Family

The primary socializing group is the family. Many authorities in police circles believe that much delinquency and crime is rooted within that unit. Most social observers have been concerned for the American family unit for a long time. Certainly, the impact of the family upon the future behavior of the child cannot be ignored.

Parental permissiveness permeates the child-rearing practices of this society. Its evidence is noted during the child's tender years, and continues to be observable throughout the major portion of the individual's maturation. The most difficult element of parental permissiveness is its quality of sincerity. Most parents actually believe they are acting in the best interests of the child. Most are imbued with the attitude that to do otherwise will be harmful. It is important for the professional practioner who is dealing with youth problems to be mindful of this quality. It is the existence of honest sincerity that makes treatment of youthful offenders a very difficult task.

Examples of parental permissiveness exist all around us and in every segment of the community. Permissiveness should not be confused with indulgence. The reader should keep the two concepts clearly separated.

Permissiveness is seen in the act of a preschool child entering a room where the parents are visiting with other adults and stating that it is time to go home, with the parents responding to the wishes of the child. It exists in the situation where one or both parents made an earlier rule that their child would not be able to have a bicycle or automobile until reaching a certain age, only to relax their convictions when faced with the fact that their child is riding another's bicycle or driving another's vehicle.

The author encountered an excellent example of permissiveness while dining in an expensive restaurant not long ago. A couple with a girl about three years of age were seated at a nearby table. The little girl kept getting up from the table and going throughout the room. The parents, talking to another couple at a table closeby, indicated that they allowed her to do this at home. They proceeded to expound their thoughts on not requiring a child of that age to perform certain functions. They ended the conversation on the note that at home, during dinner hours, their girl was allowed to leave the table and return at will. She was allowed to eat standing up, and on many occasions would leave for awhile, go to her room, and watch television on her own colored set! The parents liberally sprinkled their conversation with comments about harsh actions toward children, the thwarting of development, and the fact that such permissiveness did not affect anyone else.

It certainly did! The author, as well as many others in the

restaurant were not intentionally desiring a nervous dinner situation while wondering what the little darling was going to do next. The thoughtlessness could be attributed to the parents, but more concerning were the projections that could be applied to this child's uncontrolled actions after reaching puberty, adolescence, and even adulthood.

When a parent of a twelve-year-old pregnant girl states that she often thought she should have looked into her daughter's bedroom, but could not bring herself to turn the knob on a closed door as it would violate the child's privacy, something is amiss. In the case in question, the girl was going out the bedroom window to meet a nineteen-year-old boy who eventually became the father of her child.

What type of a social system develops parents who are being caught off guard in relation to their child's actions, on the basis of a *child's right to privacy?* It happens, and quite often. The girl who gets into trouble at school for carrying weapons or contraband in her purse, often for her boyfriend. The boy whose car is a moving arsenal, all carried for months without the parents ever having looked into the vehicle. It seems that many parents attribute to their children wisdom and sophistication that just does not exist. In other situations, the parents practice permissiveness as a means of avoiding conflict through confrontation with their children.

The author has experienced the parent who argued with his child, after the youth admitted committing an offense, trying to have the youth tell him that it did not happen. In many of these situations, the parent having been convinced by his own child of the latter's involvement with the offense, would then begin to rationalize the actions. Many of these rationalizations could be summed up in the attitude that "boys will be boys."

Thus, many permissive parents attribute both wisdom and rights to their children that exceed the child's capabilities, until something negative results. At that time the same parents will demand that others view their child as a well-meaning youth who has used poor judgment or misused a privilege, with either acting as the reason for excusing the action.

Permissiveness exists in any society in which parents have

ceased to react with a sense of shock when told by an outside source that their daughter is expecting an illegitimate child. This does not mean that the parents should not stand behind the girl. It does not mean that they should condemn her. But it does mean that there is something noticeably wrong when they can hear the news with little initial adverse effect.

The more disconcerting results of parental permissiveness involves the personality development of the child. Childhood should be a developmental stage during which time certain lessons necessary to the life task are learned. This learning process should be slow and deliberate, so that the individual will reach the end of adolescence with the preparedness for moving onward toward young adulthood.

In order for this process to occur, the child must endure situations that will strengthen his will and develop his character. He must learn to overcome the adversities of life, and to seek fulfillment through the positive formation of his personality and effective planning for life tasks.

Permissiveness has altered the necessity to face disappointment. It has caused the need to develop patience, and for understanding to wane. It has created the impression that one is free to act in any manner that he desires, with only superficial regard for the person and rights of others.

The "hippie" cult and other contracultures have resulted from the permissive habits of many homes. Few youths are emotionally prepared for the realities of adulthood. They are not economically independent, and continued educations, military service, or marriage require sacrifices that they are unwilling to make since they have few experiences where they were required to perform.

Growing older is a reality that many youth can no longer face. The fact they have created the youth image as being anti-everything that represents the older generations has also placed the present generation in the position of having to remain forever youthful, or enter the same arena where they will have to compete with the *establishment*. Only the next few years will expose how well this can be done. The haunting question remains: *What becomes of an old hippie?*

The whole discussion of permissiveness may possibly be best described in the line of a little jingle from bygone years.

Little Willie choked his sister
She was dead before they missed her
Willie's always up to tricks
Ain't he cute and only six?

THE INFLUENCE OF THE AUTOMOBILE

No discussion of environmental influences upon youthful behavior would be complete without the mention of the impact of the automobile. Its contribution to youthful problems can be classified under several of the automobile's attributes. These are (a) status, (b) mobility, and (c) lack of supervision.

The importance of automobile status among youth exceeds its developers wildest expectations. With few exceptions, having the use of a vehicle is in the forefront of youthful aspirations. It is this factor that serves as the motivation for the largest single group of auto theft offenses: joy riding.

The automobile has been used by both parents and children as a means of barter in an attempt to gain performance. Parents have reached for it as a reward, while youth have made promises of better actions based upon its reception.

Ownership seems not to be too important. What is important is vehicular availability. A youth who may use the family car receives as much attention as one who has the complete control of his own.

Some facts known by insurance companies go unnoticed in the manipulations that occur between child and parent for the attainment of the vehicle goal. One is the high risk involved in youthful driving, evidenced by increased insurance costs for the younger age group. The second is the higher academic failure rate among teenage drivers as opposed to nondrivers. Almost three times as many nondrivers are honor students. These facts are reflected in special low rate insurance plans for youths with high academic averages.

If a youth has a car, he must drive it to gain the desired satisfaction. One cannot study while dragging the main.

With the inclusion of the vehicle into the life style of a youth, he begins to encounter new peer acquaintanceships. Many of these are "hangers-on" who are attempting to gain some desired goal of their own. Not all of the increased peer group will be desirable individuals, but the peer group influence will still persist. It takes a strong individual to withstand the suggestions for just one more spin, or to "see how fast she'll go."

The vehicle provides mobility. It allows the youth to be in another town in a short period of time, a period that might match a trip to the library. It serves as a mobile gathering place. Its mobility gives a false sense of security for indulging in practices and actions that might otherwise be quite impractical. For a large number of youthful offenses, the automobile is a necessary ingredient. Fights, drinking bouts, sexual activity, and drug abuse are quite common offenses involved with the use of the automobile. Car clouts or the theft of car accessories is another crime category that centers around youthful utilization of the vehicle.

Once behind the wheel, there is no supervision over the youth. Almost every teenage driver would have to admit to an occasion where the car was used for a purpose unknown to the parents. This element of lack of supervision is a singular difficulty to overcome.

Many parents feel that they must trust their children, extending the term trust to almost challenge. In many instances, they have allowed their children unlimited use of the car, never making the normal checks of their child's activity that a prudent person would consider necessary as a means of providing supervision and guidance.

When the child approaches the earliest legal driving ages, the rationalizations of parents begin to be heard. One of the more popular reasons for allowing the youth to drive is the assistance that his driving will offer the family. The fact that the unit has gotten along without the added driver for a sizeable period does not seem to dim the logic of the statement.

Some jurisdictions have restricted the issuance of drivers licences to persons under eighteen year of age, unless the individual has successfully passed a driver's training course. This is not as worthy a piece of legislation as it may appear on the surface.

First, to *pass* means only not to fail. Thus, a youth who has performed only superficially while taking the course of instruction is eligible for the license. Second, in those areas of a state where there are large rural populations, often necessitating farm equipment operation at an early age, many times there are no drivers training courses offered in the school system. This situation requires special legislation exempting farm equipment operation, circumventing the original intent. Third, most traffic convictions result in a fine. For youth, that means the parent will pay the fine, either directly or indirectly. This offsets the penalty as it applies to the youthful offender. Fourth, many parents will allow their child to drive without a license. This opens a whole new topic, which is that of the example set when parents allow a youth to knowingly flaunt a statutory regulation.

The automobile is a basic part of modern society. It should be recognized for what it is, a means of transportation. Regulations relating to youthful operation of the motor vehicle should be based upon consideration of the effect of the vehicle upon youthful behavior, youthful driving statistics, and the restriction of the privilege in cases involving persons who have failed to demonstrate the ability to utilize the automobile for the purposes for which it is intended.

NOTES AND REFERENCES

1. H. Seyle: The general adaption syndrome and the diseases of adaption. *Journal of Clinical Endocrinology,* 6:117, 1946.
   W. B. Cannon: *Bodily Changes in Pain, Hunger, Fear, and Rage,* 2nd ed. New York, Appleton Century Co., 1936.
2. George Ruff: Adaption under extreme environmental conditions, *Annals of the American Academy of Political and Social Science,* 389:23, 1970.
3. Louis Kaplan: *Foundations of Human Behavior.* New York, Harper and Row, 1965, pp. 37, 225.
4. M. Pflanz *et al.*: Socio-psychological aspects of peptic ulcer. *Journal of Psychosomatic Research,* 1:68-74, 1956.
5. D. H. Funkenstien: The physiology of fear and anger. *Scientific America,* 192:74-80, 1955.
6. D. C. Wilson: Dynamics and psychotherapy of depression. *Journal of the American Medical Association,* 158:151-153, 1955.
7. Ruth Cavan: *Juvenile Delinquency.* New York, J. B. Lippincott, 1962, pp. 18-20.

8. Jess Stein (Ed.): *The Random House Dictionary of the English Language.* New York, Random House, 1967, p. 1073.
9. Benjamin O. Spock, M. D.
10. Doctor Spock's antiwar activities and physical participation in public acts of protest during the decade of the sixties.
11. Charles Starkweather was executed in Colorado for murders committed within that state. His girlfriend was imprisoned.
12. Charles H. Keating, Jr.: The report that shocked the nation. *Reader's Digest,* January, 1971, pp. 37-41.
13. Fishing rights negotiations between U. S. and Russian representatives, held onboard the Coast Guard Cutter *Vigilant* and in American Territorial Waters on Monday, November 23, 1970 were interrupted when a Lithuanian seaman defected from the vessel and sought asylum upon the American ship. Coast Guard officials after contacting the State Department, allowed Russian seaman to board the U.S. ship and forceably remove the sailor, utilizing a U.S. launch to return the seaman to the Soviet vessel.
14. Pope Paul VI in a speech during his Asian tour, December 3, 1970.

PART II

Chapter Six

THE JUVENILE COURT SYSTEM

A NY attempt to work with juveniles involves a need to understand the juvenile court and the corrections system, both of which have evolved as a means of coping with juvenile problems. The failure of general officers to be exposed to the system has led many to develop negative reactions toward what can be done for a youthful offender. This attitude has caused some police officers to evade working with juveniles, while others have indicated an openly hostile attitude toward these segments of the criminal justice system.

Juvenile court law varies from jurisdication to jurisdiction. Rather than attempt to present such a variance, attention will be focused upon those universals found within the system. Both the juvenile court and the correctional services will be discussed, offering the reader the opportunity to determine the roles, capabilities, and limitations which these institutions and agencies possess.

HISTORY AND DEVELOPMENT OF THE JUVENILE COURT

Law in the United States can be traced to its English roots, and juvenile court law seems to be no exception. The English system of criminal justice began late in the ninth century during the rule of King Alfred. It was strengthened and improved by the Normans, beginning with William the Conqueror in 1066.[1] During the reign of Henry III, about 1250, certain identifications of inequities were made from the recognition that various groups, such as the aged, the infirm, and some classes of youth needed special protections.

This gave rise to the Court of Chancery.[2] This court became the place where issues involving the special classes of persons were adjudicated, upon *petition* from a local court. The Court of Chancery was based upon the legal concept *parens patriae*. This concept stated that the king had a responsibility to insure the welfare of those subjects who were incapable of attending effectively to their own needs.

Parens patriae was brought to this country from England. Instead of the King's concern for his subjects, it has been translated into the state's inherent right to protect the welfare of those classes of citizens who cannot otherwise assist themselves. In its application to juvenile court law, the doctrine of *parens patriae* is the basis for the society to intervene in the parent-child relationship. Without that doctrine, parental rights could not be abridged.

It is the legal and philosophical basis for the juvenile court. The philosophy behind the doctrine placed emphasis upon the treatment rather than the manifested behavior of the child. The juvenile court system is founded upon the assumption that age alone is a factor for specialized consideration.

With the enactment of the first Juvenile Court Law in Illinois in 1899, there has been a recognition of the immaturity of the child; and as a consequence, the logic of the demand that each child be dealt with as an individual within an individual set of circumstances.[2]

While the concept of *parens patriae* existed within the common law brought from England, considerable time elapsed before the beginnings of the juvenile court law in Illinois. By 1903, California had adopted its first such law, and Wyoming was the last of the continential 48 states to enact the legislation in 1945.[3] Both Alaska and Hawaii had juvenile statutes upon attaining statehood. It is apparent that this specialized legislation did not come easily. The many existing differences in juvenile statues from state to state is further indication of the failure to attain a level of agreement on even the basic issues, such as what constitutes a juvenile.[2]

Yet most persons living in this country have been directly affected by the application of the doctrine of *parens patriae*, but few realize this experience. It is, however, the basis for compulsory school attendance laws. In other words, the state, acting under *parens patriae*, may not only demand a child's educational attendance for a prescribed period, but may also enforce the requirement upon parents or guardians. This is the most universal example of the utilization of the doctrine.

In order to further explain the basis of the juvenile court law, the terminology that it exists to act *in behalf* of the child probably does the most by way of clarification. Therefore, juvenile court actions are to protect the child, even if this means to protect him from himself.

THE JUVENILE COURT

The juvenile court is a combination of legalistic procedures and socially oriented rehabilitative efforts.[4] In any locality the jurisdiction of the court is fixed by state statute and allows for the control of the court over only those persons legally defined by that state as juveniles. In addition to those laws that control the adult citizen's actions, the individual juvenile court law of any state may prescribe other situations extending the court's control over juveniles. Examples of these latter areas are instances of truancy, runaways, and the broad sphere of control that relates to the term *incorrigibility.*

Questions relating to what court level should preside over the juvenile court are not universal. While many states follow the example of Illinois, California, and Colorado in which the jurist comes from the highest trial court bench, other states utilize systems extending from the family court concept to lower court responsibility.[5]

Original Jurisdiction

Among the many universals identifiable within the juvenile court system in the United States, the concept of *original jurisdiction* is primary.[6] As the court has an upper age limitation regarding jurisdiction, after which it ceases to maintain control, the court does have original jurisdiction over those persons who have not yet attained the upper limit of age. Until that upper limit is reached the juvenile court maintains original jurisdiction, which is to say that no court action can supersede the child's appearance before the juvenile court. The youth must appear before the juvenile court first.

A Finding of Unfitness

Exceptions to the original jurisdiction concept do exist, but they are easily identifiable. Traffic cases involving juveniles are often heard by local traffic and inferior courts. This is due to volume and is actually a necessary convenience. In such situations, the lower courts are restricted in the amount of sentence they may impose.[7] There are also situations involving special and serious circumstances wherein the juvenile may be found to be *unfit to be handled as a juvenile*. This does not infringe upon the juvenile court's original jurisdiction, as the unfit finding must be by the juvenile bench. Upon such a finding by the juvenile court, the youth is *remanded* to the normal adult proceedings.

The declaring of a youth to be unfit to be handled as a juvenile is controlled by statute in the sense that it cannot occur before the youth has reached a specified age.[8] While it may be done for a long record of serious acts, it usually occurs in association with the crime of homicide.

Concurrent Jurisdiction

In many areas the juvenile court has *concurrent jurisdiction* with the adult criminal system for a specified period after the youth has exceeded the upper age limit requiring a juvenile classification. In California for instance, the individual ceases to be a juvenile after attaining his eighteenth birthday. The juvenile court retains concurrent jurisdiction with the adult court until the youth reaches the age of majority. In practice, the juvenile court in that state does not normally accept actions involving youths over eighteen, unless there is a question of maturity that rightfully demands a juvenile action. There are times, however, when defense attorneys take a eighteen- or nineteen-year-old into adult court and request that the adult proceedings be suspended and that the case be remanded to the juvenile court. With no objections from the People, the remanding will usually occur. In these cases the juvenile court will hear the matter, but little effective action will follow as neither the court nor the probation service are prepared to deal with these older youths.

Those officers working in jurisdictions such as California would be well-advised to insure that the police agency is represented at the initial arraignment of these older youths in order to serve as the Peoples' advocate in making recommendations to the adult court regarding the remanding. Seldom will the prosecutor's office be present during an arraignment, but officers may be assured that the defense counsel will be in court.

The Petition

Juvenile court proceedings are initiated by means of a legal document called a *petition*. A petition is a written instrument setting forth the allegations surrounding the incident. In an adult situation its counterpart is an accusatory pleading, which is utilized to institute a criminal proceeding.[9]

Who may *file* a petition is another variable. In California any interested party may *request* a petition, but only the probation officer, the clerk of the juvenile court, or the juvenile court judge may file one. In Tennessee and Pennsylvania any adult citizen, who is an interested party to the action, may do the filing.

One may easily determine that in California the probation officer usually acts in the capacity of the district attorney, in that he performs the same decision-making function as the prosecutor's office does in adult cases. It is the probation officer to whom most requests for petitions are made, and it is he who makes the decision whether to file or not to file. This decision may be appealed to the court, but usually is not. For the most part, the decision is based upon the sufficiency of the evidence to sustain the petition, but occasionally other reasons are the underlying factors for a refusal to file. These include an extremely heavy caseload, the probation officer's subjective bias regarding the type of act, and even the existence of influential parents.

In the face of these weaknesses, the author supports the California system, as it provides for all petitions to be known to the probation officer, thus establishing a control on the juvenile caseload within the community.

THE JUVENILE COURT HEARING

The proceedings in a juvenile court were nonadversary and were considered to be civil in nature. In recent years, however, the system is being forced into proceedings that more readily resemble normal adult criminal processes.

These changes are coming about due to the recognition that the capability for severely limiting personal freedom and restricting movement of the individual can occur after a finding in juvenile court. Therefore, it is reasoned that the same guarantees to insure the rights of the individual must also exist in the juvenile court.[10]

Still, the juvenile court hearing is informal, and attempts continue to be nonadversary even in the face of more defense counsel appearances before the court. In some areas, such as California, all juvenile court proceedings must be transcribed. This is a good requirement, and it safeguards the public as well as the youth.

A juvenile court hearing is closed, and only those persons necessary to the case, or allowed to be present by the bench, are admitted. This is to protect the child from undue publicity. This latter statement opens an old area of controversy. Let us digress to pursue the question of publication of the names of juvenile offenders. To begin with, many areas have no laws restricting news media from making the names known, but the media itself has adopted the policy. Certainly, there are crimes and instances where the public has a right to know for its own protection. But, in all jurisdictions the findings of the juvenile court are confidential and may be obtained only by court order or the approval of the juvenile bench. Now suppose a newspaper printed that a particular youth had been arrested and charged for a burglary. Later, the petition was not sustained in the juvenile court. The paper would have no right to view the record of the fact that the youth was acquitted of the charge, and no retraction could take place. In addition, many times the publication of the name would not benefit, but rather would hamper any attempt at rehabilitation. There are considerations regarding the other children in the family, who may also suffer from undue publicity.

The following example is probably the best argument against the publication of juvenile offenders names on a continuous basis. At age fourteen a youth was apprehended as an indecent exposer.

Not only did he have a brother who was a student in one of the nation's military academies, but his father was a high school counselor having to deal with all types of youth who could have used the arrest information to undermine the father's professional effectiveness. Later, the suspect became an outstanding athlete and an honor student. He may soon be a member of the professional ranks. His problem was experimental, and he soon outgrew it. Publicity in this case would have brought severe repercussions in the lives of many persons and for years to come, especially if the offender does become nationally known as a sports figure. Those who desire pure punishment may take note of his failure to be accepted at the military academy due to his juvenile record.

In the hearing the juvenile must be advised of his rights by the court.[11] In the past, evidence need only support the fact in issue *to a preponderance of the evidence,* as in civil cases. On March 31, 1970, in *Winship v. New York,* the United States Supreme Court reversed the former criteria regarding evidence and instituted the requirement that proof of fact be established *beyond a reasonable doubt and to a moral certainty.* With Winship the essential nature of the juvenile court proceedings were altered toward criminal adversary procedural structures.

Basically, the juvenile court hearing is two hearings in one. The first portion deals with determining that the facts exist giving the court jurisdiction over the minor. The second part provides for the adjudication of the case in the best interest of the youth involved.

Unknown to most persons, a juvenile automatically comes under the jurisdiction of the juvenile court *when that youth commits an act bringing him under the court's control.* These acts are enumerated by statute. Thus, whether or not the juvenile ever appears before the court, the court still had legal jurisdiction beginning with the moment that the youth committed the act. It is this concept that allows many jurisdictions to make an arrest of a juvenile either with or without a warrant, on a misdemeanor or a felony, whether committed in the officer's presence or not. It is also on the basis of this concept that law enforcement agencies have the right to institute their juvenile procedural methods regardless of the personal desires of the parents or guardians of the youth involved. Police agencies that perform otherwise are not carrying out the police juvenile mission and are in error.

Findings of the Juvenile Court

In consideration of a petition, the juvenile court may either *sustain* (uphold or find guilty), or *deny* (acquittal) the allegations. It is important for the reader to grasp these terms. The words are positive symbols for the guilty or not guilty findings of an adult criminal action. These terms are additional evidence of society's attempts to mitigate the actions of juveniles on the basis of age. Connotations of guilt or innocence are disguised from view by means of the vocabulary choice.

Whenever a youth appears before the juvenile court and the petition is sustained, the court is in the position to adjudge the individual a *ward of the juvenile court*. Court wardship provides the court with continuing jurisdiction over the youth, with a specified maximum limit as set forth by statute. In effect, this action provides the probation officer with supervisory powers, acting as an arm of the court.

Once a court ward, the youth is subject to the control of the court. He may be called upon to answer for any actions that violate the conditions originally imposed by the court. New offenses may bring the youth back before the court on the basis of a violation of the wardship. Court wardship, then, is an extremely powerful tool in the effort to combat delinquency. Whether it is being utilized effectively is another question.

PROVISIONS FOR PROTECTING THE RIGHTS OF THE JUVENILE

In addition to the requirements for advising the youth of his rights under the court decisions of Miranda and via Gualt, most juvenile court law has built-in provisions for the protection of the juvenile from being taken into custody unnecessarily or without probable cause.

The first of these is the requirement that a probation officer or some other official designated by the court must make an immediate investigation into the facts surrounding the youth being taken into custody. This is usually done by means of a review of the police record, questioning of the offender, and interviewing the parents.

In complicated situations, it may even be necessary to consult with the arresting or investigating officers.

During the period of this investigation, a petition may or may not be required to be on file depending upon the state law. In Florida and Tennessee, petitions must accompany the physical incarceration of a juvenile, while in California a period of 48 hours (excluding noncourt days, such as weekends and holidays) exists before the petition must be filed.

In jurisdictions requiring the petition to be on file, the question to be determined during the course of the investigation is whether or not to detain the youth pending the Juvenile Court hearing. In the California situation, not only does the detention question have to be considered, but also the question of whether or not the incident warrants the filing of a petition.

In any case, once the juvenile has been placed in custody, and the probation officer's investigation reveals there are statutory reasons for the continuation of detention, the matter is calendered for a *detention hearing* in the juvenile court. Sometimes referred to as a *custody hearing*, it amounts to an opportunity for the court to review and reaffirm or alter the decision made by the probation officer to hold the youth pending the juvenile court hearing.

In California, the juvenile who is placed in custody will undergo a probation intake investigation. From the moment the police take the youth into custody, the 48-hour period commences. At the end of that period of time, the youth must either be released or a petition must be filed.

It should be noted that the California system allows for the offender to be released, even though a petition has been filed.

In the event the youth is detained, the detention hearing must occur within 24 hours (excluding noncourt days) of the filing of the petition.

Illinois law provides a similar situation as in California, however, there are two distinct differences. First, any adult person may file a petition; and second, the time period for incarceration prior to a petition being on file is 36 hours. The same time period exists for the detention hearing.

The system of investigation, petition, and detention hearing removes the necessity for a youth to post bail. The safeguards necessary to insure that one will not be illegally detained have been built into most juvenile court statutes.

What is important for the student of juvenile procedures is to insure his understanding of the petitioning process, time limits, and custodial procedures in his own jurisdiction.

CUSTODY vs. ARREST

Most juvenile court law refers to the taking of the juvenile into *custody*. For working police officers, custody is synonomous with arrest in those instances requiring physical incarceration. It is important, though, for law enforcement personnel to grasp and utilize the custodial terminology and concept. The reason this is important is that the juvenile court statutes of most jurisdictions do not mention or otherwise recognize the existence of the arrest of a juvenile. It is a misnomer for officers to utilize the term arrest in conjunction with the physical custody of a juvenile.

An almost universal requirement of the juvenile court law with respect to taking a minor into custody is the requirement placed upon the officer to *notify the parent*. Most jurisdictions refer to the need to immediately take steps to make the notification. The notification does not have to be in person. If local, it may be accomplished by means of a telephone call, a note, or having another unit dispatched for that purpose. If beyond the area serviced, the usual procedure is to either make a telephone contact with the parent, or contact the local law enforcement agency in that area and request that they make notification. The time of the attempts and the final notification should become a permanent part of the police record, to establish compliance with the law.

PROBATION AND PAROLE

The field of corrections is of paramount importance in any effort to control delinquency. No attempt will be made to present the totality of that enterprise in this writing. Rather, some concepts dealing with that segment of the corrections function that is normally encountered by others involved in juvenile work will be the theme.

Probation

Usually viewed as an arm of the juvenile court, probation services range from full intake powers, through actual court presentation, to the generally perceived task of field supervision. The duties and powers of the probation officer will vary from jurisdiction to jurisdiction.

Generally, probation personnel are county employees.[12] In most areas, the probation office is a county agency. The chief probation officer is selected without regard to political ramifications. The selection procedure often is performed by the judges in the local jurisdiction. More and more, probation officers are college trained, with specialization in social work, corrections, or allied fields.

In larger jurisdictions, probation personnel are assigned specific duties either in adult work or juvenile endeavors. The major portion of the juvenile probation effort is aimed at supervision of individual offenders; however, the quality of the supervision is often affected by the mechanics involved. For instance, many probation officers are assigned intolerable caseloads. Alterations in officer-youth relations occur regularly caused by worker turnover, district changes, or increased workloads.

Many probation officers complain about the extensive paper work involved in court reports and case recording.

Experienced juvenile police officers are familiar with instances of contact with youthful probationers *who have never seen their probation officer.* Such instances occur with disconcerting regularity.

Probation officers working in the field with probationers tend to develop tremendous amounts of information relating to the individual, his family, and his associates. This represents an invaluable source of investigative information. It is important for working law enforcement officers to become personally acquainted with the probation officer in their area. This is true, whether the police officer is assigned to juvenile specialization or is a member of the patrol unit.

In theory, the probation officer is charged with the obligation of developing a plan for the correction of the offender. His supervision effort should parallel that plan. But, for reasons already stated, in practice the probation officer finds this activity limited by other professional requirements.

One authority has identified five general areas of performance for an individual probation officer.[2] The probation officer is seen to have a role as an officer of the court. He certainly has duties as a social worker, although these may be more correctionally oriented than social welfare. He must be capable of functioning in the area of social diagnosis, in that he must identify causation factors and recommend rehabilitative solutions. The more familiar aspect of his function may be noted in the supervision activities in which he must engage, leading the offender to the point where the youth will begin to see the need to control his own life. Finally, all of the first four functions should cause the probation officer to fulfill his role as a vehicle of change.

Many police personnel become frustrated in their dealings with probation representatives. In part, this is due to the lack of understanding on the part of the police of the limitation inherent to probation services. The probation officer acts to carry out the desires and commands of the court. In juvenile work, the probation role is well defined by statute. Both the court's direction and the statutory requirements limit the authority and scope of the probation activity.

The differing philosophies encountered between the probation enterprise and the police effort should not become barriers to mutual cooperation. The police should strive to develop effective relations with local probation services. This can best be accomplished by focusing upon the desired outcomes of such relations, rather than the existing differences in basic philosophy.

Parole

Parole agents are usually members of the state department of corrections. In juvenile work their efforts tend to be identified with the supervision of offenders in the field. In fact, parole services are quite extensive, but since the supervision role is the one in which parole agents are most often encountered by other members of the criminal justice field, this examination will be limited to that portion of their work.

Parole agents are assigned the supervision of juvenile offenders who have been in custody in a state institution, and who have subsequently been released under parole conditions. In this capacity, the parole agent has far more authority over the offender than does a probation officer. Ultimately, the parole agent is capable of sending the offender back to the institution for failure to comply with supervision.

The inherent problems found in probation also exist in parole. There are both budget and manpower limitations, as well as the limitations created by job mechanics, that all tend to reduce the effectiveness of the parole effort.

One of the more intensive programs of the parole effort in juvenile corrections may be noted within the California Youth Authority. Seen as a model by many jurisdictions, the C. Y. A. has become the leading force in the philosophical and legal development of the California Juvenile Court system.

As an example, during the sixties, the agency discovered that the state's institutions for juveniles were bulging at the seams. Either more institutions would have to be built, or the tide of incoming offenders would have to be stemmed. Since a building program would be extremely expensive, and would also conflict with basic correctional philosophy, the second alternative was considered more practical. Offense rates predicted that the trend of institutional intake would not subside. Another method had to be developed.

Through an intensive educational effort, expounding the need for rehabilitation on the local level, coupled with a financial subsidy, the C.Y.A. was able to dramatically reduce the number of offenders referred to it for custodial care. The system employed was to pay each county a maximum of $4,000 per year for each eligible offender who was *not* sent to a state institution. This state subsidy has enabled many jurisdictions to establish intensive supervision units within local probation offices, and even build local units of incarceration and treatment. More importantly, the program has resulted in the convincing of the majority of juvenile court judges of the worth of local treatment. It also demonstrates the capacity that the Youth Authority has in dealing with the legislature on fiscal matters.

Police relations with parole agents tend to be better than with probation personnel. This is due, in part, to the added authority over the offender that is enjoyed by the parole agent. As is the case with probation officers, police personnel would be well advised to become quite familiar with the parole agents operating in their jurisdictions.

THE SYSTEM—PERCEIVED BY THE DELINQUENT

Much attention has been paid to the system. Many studies have been aimed at determining how well the system operates and its effects upon the ultimate socialization of the delinquent youth. Few efforts have been directed toward determining the manner in which the delinquent *himself* views the various segments comprising the criminal justice process. This section has been included for two reasons: (a) to present the findings of one study dealing with how the delinquent perceives the system into which he is placed; and, (b) to illustrate the need for further research into this area.

The strongest social sanction given to an adolescent behavioral problem is a commitment to an institution.[13] Although limited in number, the significance of the incarcerated group cannot be overlooked in any meaningful assessment of delinquency prevention and control. This group represents the *failure* of the preinstitutional efforts of the society. Within this group, the majority of its members may present life-long antisocial behavioral patterns.

In an attempt to determine the way in which the *newly* committed delinquent sees the various entities within the criminal justice system, a study was undertaken in Massachusetts that not only provides significant insight, but also will tend to summarize the material within this chapter.[14] Utilizing sophisticated social research methodology, the study dealt with the views of first offender commitments to a juvenile institution. These youths had been exposed to certain parts of the system (the police, the court, etc.), but had not fully experienced contact with other portions (probation, the institution, etc.).

For the purposes of this writing, all of the categories of perceptions will not be related. Instead, perceptions dealing with the police, the judge and the court, and probation officers will be summarized.

Quite contrary to some popular beliefs, the youths studied indicated a perception of the *judge* as a person with little interest in the individual offender. They saw him as a man who acted quite impersonally, serving in the role of an authority figure. They could associate his relationship to the law as serving the law. In general, they ascribed very few positive characteristics to him. These perceptions, however, were *not* hostile; but rather tended to be neutral.

On the other hand, when viewing the *court* as an institution, the delinquent did not make the normal equated relationship between the institution and the man. Therefore, findings in relation to the court were quite hostile. The court experience seems to have been unpleasant, and when interpreted by the delinquent had one reoccurring thread interwoven: personal fear. It appears from the findings that the juvenile court experience for the first offender is a frightening situation. This latter finding should not be confused with unfairness, as few indications were received that would support the conclusion that the delinquents felt they had been treated unfairly. If the concept of the court as an institution is that of presenting the law in an awe inspiring manner, then it would appear that the court procedure is fulfilling that function.

The *policeman* and the *police juvenile officer* were seen in different light by the group of delinquents studied. For the police in general, as well as the police agency, responses were quite equal in appearance. Extremely negative findings were not noted, and it must be assumed on the basis of the data that the relationship between the police/police agency and the delinquent is not always hostile or negative.

The attitudes expressed toward the police juvenile officer were generally more favorable than those encountered relative to the general police service. In fact, the positive relationship existing between the police juvenile officer and the delinquent was an unexpected finding. The youth tended to see the juvenile officer as helpful and friendly. They presented feelings that indicated they felt the juvenile officer treated them as persons and with some respect for their feelings.

The one area in which youth expressed negative attitudes most often was the complaint that the juvenile officer was inconsistent. It appears that the juvenile assigns a trustworthy quality to the juvenile officer and quickly recognizes any deviation from this perception. This is of extreme importance to the police juvenile practitioner. It is a lesson that was verbalized to the author many years ago, upon first entering the area of juvenile specialization. Do not perform in such a manner as to be labeled a *phony*. This admonition was the most singularly valuable advice the author ever received during his police tenure.[15]

The study revealed two concerns relating to probation. One was the view of *probation as a service*, while the other dealt with the *probation officer as a person.*

Probation officers tended to be viewed in a personal context that was quite positive. They were seen as being interested and helpful. They were also perceived as being lenient. In some respects, the probation officer's role was related to that of a teacher.

In contrast, the probation service was generally regarded unfavorably. As a group, the delinquents studied did not see the act of probation as being very helpful to them, and almost totally lacked any perception of its constructive role. This lead the researchers to believe that more effort should be expended in the systematic presentation of the probation function to persons first coming into contact with it.

SUMMARY

The easiest manner by which the juvenile court system can be summarized is by dissection. It is, therefore, a special system, utilizing special law for a special group to perform a special function. Any attempt to apply adult criminal standards to the system in their entirety would be a misnomer. It is within this last area that most general police personnel make their biggest errors.

Once the specialized nature of the juvenile court system and its ultimate objective is determined, many of the frustrations and improper tactics of the police will be overcome.

NOTES AND REFERENCES

1. *Municipal Police Administration*, 5th ed. Chicago, International City Managers' Association, 1961, p. 2.
2. Edward Eldefonso: *Law Enforcement and the Youthful Offender.* New York, John Wiley and Sons, 1967, pp. 140-147, 159, 161, and Appendix A.
   California Welfare and Institutions Code, Sections 502 and 503 for a statement of philosophy of juvenile court law.
3. *California Welfare and Institutions Code*, 1903. Revised, 1961.
4. Ruth Cavan:*Juvenile Delinquency.* New York, J. B. Lippincott, 1962, p. 267.
5. *California*: The juvenile court is a Department of the Superior Court of the particular county. *New York*: The juvenile court is the Family court of the State of New York. *Tennessee*: The juvenile court may be a minor court, a city court, or a special juvenile court.
6. For more on the subject of universal aspects of Juvenile Courts see, *Standard Family Court Act.* New York, National Probation-Parole Association, 1959.
   Standard Juvenile Court Act, 6th ed. New York, National Council on Crime and Delinquency, 1959.
   Standards for Specialized Courts Dealing With Children. Washington, D. C., Department of Health, Education, and Welfare, 1954.
7. As an example, California provides for lower court magistrates to serve as Traffic Hearing Officers, but these officials are severly limited as to the amount of sentence. If a penalty in excess of statutory restrictions is to be imposed, the case must be remanded to the juvenile court for a hearing.
8. *California*: The juvenile court may waive jurisdiction when the juvenile is between 16 and 18 years of age. *Illinois*: The juvenile court may waive jurisdiction in any case. *Pennsylvania*: The juvenile court may waive jurisdiction in cases amounting to a felony if the child is over 14 years of age. *Tennessee*: Committed delinquents, later found to be dangerous or incorrigible may be remanded to adult court, if still of juvenile court age. Offenses punishable by death or life imprisonment are excepted from the jurisdiction of most juvenile courts in Tennessee.
9. Accusatory pleadings are complaints, informations, or indictments.
10. C. J. Flammang: An attempt to clarify some areas of police juvenile procedures, *Police, 15* (3):20-22, 1971.
11. *In re Gualt* (1967) 387 U. S. 1, 13.

12. In *Tennessee,* probation and parole services are combined at the state level as a part of the Departments of Corrections, similar to the federal government. There may be local probation officers appointed under other statutes, but the general system is state personnel.

13. Martha Baum and Stanton Wheeler: Becoming an inmate. In S. Wheeler (Ed.): *Controlling Delinquents.* New York, John Wiley and Sons, 1966, Chapter 7.

14. Brenden Maher with Ellen Stein: The delinquent's perception of the law and the community, In S. Wheeler (Ed.): *Controlling Delinquents.* New York, John Wiley and Sons, 1966, Chapter 8.

15. Admonition to the author by Lt. E. Haley, Commander, Juvenile Division, Fresno County (California) Sheriff's Department.

Chapter Seven

THE POLICE JUVENILE ENTERPRISE

THE law enforcement arm of the criminal justice process has been involved with the juvenile offender long before youths were generally labeled by that term. Historically, adults have utilized the officer along a continuum representing the spectrum of the retribution that would befall an erring child at the one extreme, to the image of the kindly public servant to whom the child could turn in the event of difficulty at the other extreme. That the police have been historically involved with youth in trouble is a fact that cannot be erased. That the police have a mission to continue their efforts in this regard should be a recognized consideration of police administrators and practitioners.

The complexities surrounding juvenile enforcement have increased since the bygone era when Officer Clancy controlled the youth on his walking beat through a combination of size, demeanor, curbside court, and parental reaction to police contact. Some of these complexities are the result of changing police procedures, others have come about due to legislation and court decisions, while still others relate to an altering cultural environment and the demands of a complex society.

The result has been the need for police specialization in the area of juvenile enforcement. This need permeates the totality of the range of police agencies, from the very largest to the smallest. It remains that police personnel must exceed the generalist sphere if they are to become truly effective in coping with juvenile problems. This does not mean that there is not a role for the generalist to play in the police juvenile enterprise. Quite the contrary. But it does mean that the police effort in the area of juvenile work will be only as good as the individual officer's ability to act as a social diagnostician. This ability can

141

only be built upon certain basic knowledge and skills, including insight into the basics of human behavior, a sound background in the areas of general criminal law and juvenile statutes, an awareness of alternative solutions, a familiarity with community resources, and a cognizance of the objectives of juvenile enforcement. The preceding requisites have not alluded to the need for the officer to be knowledgeable in police procedures, as well as being an adequate investigator, interrogator, and interviewer.

The evolution of police juvenile specialization has been the result of external demands and changes, more so than internal need identification. This process is still going on in many departments throughout the country. The recent emphasis upon law enforcement in this country has given impetus to the continuing process of recognition for the need for juvenile specialization that is being reflected in the number of newly created juvenile units that are springing to life in many police agencies.

THE SPECIALIZATION CONTROVERSY

Two definite schools of thought have emerged regarding police specialization in general. Juvenile specialization has not been ommitted from the arguments for and against developing a narrow expertise within one area of law enforcement. Important considerations face the police administrator in making a decision relating to juvenile specialization.

First, there is the question of whether the special enforcement is necessary, and if so, will its adoption create other problems? To what extent should the specialization occur? What areas of responsibility will be assigned to the specialist, and what areas will remain within the scope of the generalist? Each police executive must make the decision to specialize or not, based on the answers to these questions and after careful study of other considerations.

Arguments Against Specialization

Probably the most significant danger involved in any type of police specialization relates to the nonspecialist officer utilizing the specialist as a crutch.[1] This can be especially harmful in juvenile matters, as so much of an officer's working life will be spent dealing with juveniles. If controls are not such that there exists ample opportunity for all officers to engage in a certain portion of the juvenile enforcement caseload, then the nonspecializing officers will tend to view juvenile enforcement as the sole responsibility of the specialist. If nothing else, the attitude of sloughing juvenile matters off will tend to prevail among generalist officers. This type of situation is greatly disconcerting, as no enforcement effort in the juvenile area can hope to be adequate if the total department does not perceive its role in the control and prevention of delinquency.

The concept of total generalist police officers capable of handling any type of police matter is prevalent in the thinking of some police administrators. The difficulty arises in the fact that in certain areas, e.g. vice, intelligence, and often investigations, specialization does occur. This is because the administrator has recognized these areas as more important, and has created an investigative oriented agency. Of course, the opposite may happen, and the agency is patrol oriented. In either case, the generalist becomes a specialist in his own right, and *specialization by assignment* generally follows. In that type of situation, supervisors begin making specialized assignments in areas that they feel a particular officer demonstrates capability. This amounts to officer specialization, although it may not find its way to the departmental organization chart.

Specialization may give rise to the police executive becoming dependent upon the opinion of the specialist in policy matters relating to that area of the police mission. Policy-making is an administrative task and while the executive should rely on the use of all sources of information for this function, the *de facto* delegation of the function to a specialist would be erroneous.

Arguments Favoring Specialization

This is an age of specialization. Almost every field of endeavor has been forced to develop special areas of emphasis. The increase in the body of knowledge has been one motivating factor. Complexities within the field and within the society account for other influences in the direction of specialization. Police work does not differ greatly from the needs found in other disciplines.

In fact, the very breadth of police functions has caused many to recognize that it is impossible for one officer to be highly skilled in all facets of the police enterprise.

Some amount of juvenile specialization is necessary. To begin with, an officer working a juvenile matter to its conclusion must be able to involve himself with the case for a long time period. At times, this would require the exclusion of other assignments. The total juvenile enforcement and court process is so complex, as to require a considerable time element for the successful handling of cases.

For every juvenile contacted there is at least one parent or guardian who must be brought into the picture. This causes the juvenile case to be more *visible* to the public than many other police matters. It also opens the door for criticism, justified or not. Much of the criticism is aimed at perfectly correct police procedures that are misunderstood by the parent. Officers who are not fully aware of the many ramifications of juvenile work would be hard pressed to successfully forestall situations of an unusual nature.

Altering child rearing practices, changing mores, revised statutes, and even new youthful fads all may affect the handling of a juvenile matter. It is important that these factors be recognized and articulated into the actions of the police in dealing with youthful offenders. This cannot happen without specialization.

Specialization will develop a cadre of interested persons who will pursue new approaches and techniques, or develop new programs. Innovation is sorely needed in the juvenile field, and may be lost if generalist officers are the only ones involved. To begin a new approach requires extra effort which the generalist may not be willing to provide.

The challenge of effective juvenile enforcement lends itself to specialization in this area. In major departments, the juvenile specialists may even be in a separate division. In small agencies, the specialization may take a part-time form, with the officer performing other duties. In this modern age, with an emphasis upon police-community relations, the juvenile officer in the small department is a natural person to assume the duties of the community relations officer.[2]

A Handicap to Specialization

Recently it has become vogue to rotate officers throughout a department, having them work in all areas a given length of time. For the majority of police efforts this is a sensible approach as a supplement to training. However, the complexities of the successful juvenile operation, coupled with the length of time necessary for the officer to truly develop as an effective juvenile specialist, precludes the rotation approach being a positive aid to the juvenile enforcement program. On the contrary, the skills and knowledge necessary for effective juvenile work demand a singularly long tenure in the specialized section. The specialist will then develop a backlog of knowledge relating to individuals. He will be able to recognize trends and changes occurring within the youthful population of the community. Possibly more important than all the other reasons, the community will be provided with personnel in whom its members may place confidence.

Benefits of Juvenile Specialization

One authority, writing a well reasoned plea for the institution of specialized juvenile services within police agencies, provided a critique of the benefits that agencies, youth, and the community have derived from police juvenile officers.[3] It is important that these benefits be repeated.

Police juvenile officers have almost single-handedly brought the nonpunitive concept to the law enforcement field. They have been pioneers within the field in the introduction of the concepts of the behavioral sciences into the police effort to control and prevent delinquent behavior. They have aided in the implementation of central juvenile files, available to social and correctional as well as police agencies.

On the basis of their experience and expertise, juvenile police officers have contributed to the exposure of poor or inadequate juvenile detention facilities. Their specialization has given rise to increased data relating to delinquency, much of which has been incorporated into accurate statistical accounting. Many juvenile problems have been identified as the result of the specialized police efforts, and a considerable amount of what is known about delinquency is related to that endeavor. Even the existence of community resources is often the outgrowth of the juvenile specialists identifying social needs.

Within the police agency itself, the juvenile specialists have been found to be a valuable training resource for in-service personnel. They have represented the police agency well in their numerous public speaking engagements throughout the community. What is known about the techniques utilized for preventive patrol are the result of the combined experience of police juvenile officers.

In many departments throughout the country the only officers with a firm grasp of the need for what is now termed police-community relations were the juvenile officers. They have had a fuller view of the need for true police *service* within their communities, and they have shouldered police leadership responsibilities long before it was popular to think in terms of the *totality of the community*. Communities and police agencies alike owe a debt of gratitude to this group of dedicated police officers.

POLICE RESPONSIBILITIES IN JUVENILE ENFORCEMENT

The police have been involved with youth since the inception of the service. Youth work is a part of the police mission. This raises the question relative to what the police mission actually involves. Discussions of the function of the police are many.[4]

It is indeed important for law enforcement personnel to be aware of the identified functional areas of the police. For the purposes of this writing, the police function is only related as it pertains to juvenile enforcement. Due to this limitation, the responsibilities of the police in carrying out their mission of dealing with youthful offenders and the members of the community involved with youth will be explored.

One should be cautiously aware of the fact that these are *responsibilities* the police have inherited as a part of their function in relation to youth. In order for a police agency to be professionally involved in the totality of police service to the youth of the jurisdiction, it must be capable of performing *each* responsibility. It is not enough to do well in one area at the expense or exclusion of another.

All police juvenile efforts may be categorized as coming under one or more of the following police juvenile responsibilities:

1. Discovery of delinquency.
2. The investigation of delinquency.
3. Case disposition.
4. The protection of the juvenile.
5. Delinquency prevention.[5]

Each responsibility represents a single facet of the juvenile enterprise. An examination of each will provide insight into the extent of the police involvement necessary to comply with the requirements of these responsibilities.

Discovery of Delinquency

This area of responsibility is of primary importance to any delinquency control program. Youthful problems cannot be controlled unless they have been identified. In any community where problems exist, but are arbitrarily denied to exist by official sources, no action can take place to attempt to cope with or alter the trouble.

Juveniles are very fluid. Their dress, mannerisms, and concepts are subject to rapid change. Successful police juvenile operations will keep current. At the same time, there are elements within any community that are constantly ready to prey upon youth, especially because of youth's economic potential. The opening of a new pool hall, drive-in, or other amusement business is of concern to the modern enforcement operation.

In every community are parents who not only expound an extremely permissive attitude toward their own children, but who are also compelled through some attitude of misguided self-righteousness, to extend their liberalism to the children of others. Very often, these parents open their homes to a multitude of youth and youthful escapades. Situations of this nature are difficult to deal with, but the failure of the police to know of their existence is a sign of law enforcement's failure to perform.

Any police juvenile officer or unit must actively seek out information regarding youthful problems and delinquency breeding grounds within the community. This is a major task, and cannot be performed by the juvenile specialist alone. It requires the active effort of the total department, most certainly the patrol operation.

The regular patrol force is in a unique position to discover vital juvenile information and pass that knowledge on to the juvenile personnel. It is incumbent upon the juvenile specialist or unit to insure an atmosphere of cooperation that will cause patrol officers to become motivated to act in this capacity.

Juvenile police personnel must cultivate reliable sources of information. In addition to departmental personnel, the juvenile officer should become well-acquainted within the community in order to establish the recognition of the capability of the police in juvenile matters. The best single method of developing broad sources of information is by creating a climate of confidence within the potential group who possesses the information desired. The juvenile specialist role is uniquely equipped to build such confidence throughout a large segment of the community, because of the breadth and variety of the police juvenile contacts.

The most effective sources of reliable juvenile information within a community, in an accessed order of importance, are as follows:

1. *The police agency personnel.* The department represents one of the best sources of information, if properly handled. This must be through democratic processes of persuasion and intended development. It will be doomed to failure if the program is based upon autocratic administrative directives. The normal resistance of line personnel to juvenile matters cannot be overcome by command alone. This must be the outcome of a recognized effort by the juvenile personnel.

2. *The schools.* One of the most effective and cooperative juvenile resources within the community, the schools represent an institution that is capable of providing a constant source of information. Its role in the total police juvenile enterprise cannot be overstated.[6]

The responsibility to develop effective relations between the police and educational community rests squarely upon the police. Within the police agency, the one group most fitted to carry out the development of a meaningful relationship is the juvenile unit.

3. *Correctional, casework, and welfare agencies.* Included in

this group are both public and private agencies offering services to families or children. The probation and parole units dealing with juveniles have already been discussed in a previous chapter. It is worthwhile to reiterate that these agencies have a wealth of information that they will share with the police. They represent a valuable resource for the juvenile specialist.

In addition, every community has agencies that deal with family situations or youthful problems. More are being instituted constantly. The police juvenile personnel should not only be familiar with the groups by name, but should know individual members personally. Officers should be familiar with the rules and regulations of the agencies, and with the limitations of the various groups. The police must be aware of the need to work with these agencies in the scope of the particular group's legal or administrative limits. No group or agency should be neglected as a possible resource on the basis of a differing agency goal or philosophy.

4. *Religious institutions.* Area churches and their clergy are constantly encountering juvenile problems. That these institutions do not normally refer these matters to the police stands as mute testimony to the failure of the police to generate the confidence necessary for the institutions to possess before being willing to refer many of the matters. Therefore, least there be condemnation of church groups, let the police look inward. Effective police juvenile efforts will overcome the resistance of many of the institutions and their representatives, and police juvenile enforcement will benefit. The "who needs them" attitude can no longer suffice. To continue in that direction would be a denial of the principles of the modern police juvenile effort.

5. *The Public.* Included in this grouping are both private individuals and business and service persons within the community who do not normally come forward to offer information to the police. This is the area of the telephone lineman, reporting an incident he noted while working on a high line. It is the T. V. repairman, offering information on the conditions of children in a home that had utilized his services. The corner grocer, advising officers of the grocery purchasing habits of parents who are neglecting their children. It is the anonymous caller who not want-

ing to get involved still feels compelled to pass information to the police.

6. *Clubs and organizations.* The circuit, as the public speaking grind many juvenile officers find themselves involved in is affectionately called, offers a tremendous opportunity to develop informational sources. It also provides a chance for the police to become involved in real community leadership by guiding such groups into the selection of identified youth community needs as club projects.

7. *Parents.* Probably the worst and most unreliable group of juvenile informants are parents. There are several reasons for this statement. First, many parental reports are vindictive attempts to get back at other persons, both juveniles and adults. Second, much of their information is unreliable or old. Third, they have often discussed their intended reports with their children, or the parents of other children, negating to some extent the value of the information. Of course, in cases where the police have dealt productively with their child's problems in the past, and they have developed a sense of both obligation and confidence, their information may be quite legitimate. As a group, however, the concerned parent should be viewed critically.

One group intentionally left out of the list are other law enforcement agencies. Due to long standing jealousies and differing opinions on the importance of juvenile work and the directions it should take, other police agencies cannot be categorized, but must be dealt with on an individual basis. Some will be capable of providing effective information, where others will be so oriented that they even fail to retain the information for themselves. If it is a professionally oriented department, it will have information it is willing to share.

Among the many informational areas that should be brought to the attention of the police juvenile specialist are those community hazards that may be harmful to children. These include empty or abandoned houses, waterways, culverts, improperly supervised recreational areas, and railroad yards. Juvenile personnel should attempt to discover the background examination techniques or licensing regulations utilized by various agencies for the procurement of personnel who will normally be working with youth. These groups include recreational personnel, foster parents, and others coming into direct contact with youth in situations where adverse or illegal influences may occur. If such background checks are not made, or poorly handled, the police should strive to cause the procedures to be remedied.

Investigation of Delinquency

Many police officers differentiate between the requirements of an adult investigation as opposed to a juvenile investigation. This is an overt error. There is basically little difference between the investigative procedures required in the two situations. Investigative techniques do not alter because of the age of the suspect or the age of the victim. Alterations in the employment of investigative skills and procedures are related to the typology of the offense.[7]

Either category of investigation must be accurate, thorough, and with the rights of accused protected.[8] The change in the requirements for evidence necessary to establish the fact in Juvenile Court has gone a long way in dispelling the general officers' concepts toward the investigation requirements for a juvenile case.[9] In the past, the Juvenile Court matter was decided on the basis of a *perponderance of the evidence,* similar to civil cases. The requirement has been changed to comply with the rules applied in adult criminal matters, that the evidence be *beyond a reasonable doubt.*

Police personnel must understand that a juvenile case is of no less an investigative problem than the same incident would be if performed by an adult. If anything, the juvenile case would be somewhat more complex. There are several reasons for this. First, juveniles do not establish set patterns of *modus operandi.* This is due to their age and rate of growth and maturation. What may appear to be an M. O. at one period of the juvenile's offense committing stage often will not be applicable several months later. As his interests alter, so will his M. O. It is for this reason that the author has been in disagreement with many police agencies in California utilizing the practice of sending Crime Reports (for M. O. purposes) to the California Bureau of Criminal Identification and Investigation in matters pertaining to juveniles. All that process has truly accomplished is to fill that agency's files with superfluous information.

Second, juvenile police investigations tend to be quite complex, if properly pursued. This is due to the peer group involvement. It is also attributable to the juvenile's lack of an interest span necessary to hold his attention. It is not unusual to find five or six involved in one offense on a given night, and then to discover that four of the original group, plus one or two new youths became involved in an unrelated violation the following evening.

Not only the large numbers and the variety of individuals that may be included in a juvenile offense, but the chain of events often is confusing. Youth will begin one type of offense, and as the situations snowballs it will lead to one or more violations that seem unrelated to the first. The author recalls five boys and one girl who were brought to the attention of the juvenile unit on a charge of theft. The item stolen was one watermelon. On the surface, it appeared to be a routine situation calling for a reprimand. A thorough investigation revealed that the watermelon theft was incidental to a sex orgy that was taking place in the field where the fruit was grown. The promiscuity of the girl led to the arrest and conviction of several adult males, in addition to the Juvenile Court adjudications.

Third, a juvenile investigation requires good interrogation. Most investigations of youthful offenders must be based upon the interrogative process. This has been made no easier by the decision of the case of Miranda, but remains a fact. The variety of offenses, the number of persons involved, and the manner in which juveniles tend to range geographically, all combine to reduce the possibility of obtaining effective physical evidence. Interrogation is necessary to work backwards to determine other crime partners and to clear other offenses committed by the same youth. It is necessary to recover stolen property, as juveniles are notorious for widely distributing loot, often with no recompense to themselves. One matter that should never be allowed is for the juvenile to sense a *gain* from a theft. That juveniles are often either not incarcerated or are released shortly after such incarceration, demands that the police work rapidly to recover the loot. In order to do that, interrogation is usually necessary.

Fourth, the police juvenile investigator must proceed one step beyond that of the adult investigator. It is necessary in a juvenile matter to attempt to discover the *why* of the act. This requirement should be pursued in order to comly with the screening obligation of the police. A juvenile case must have a disposition beyond a case closure. Once the offense has been cleared by the apprehension of the juvenile, the matter of what action to take with the youth for his benefit becomes paramount. On the surface, this may appear easy, but reliable police juvenile officers will support the contention that this is one of the more difficult tasks to perform.

A word of caution in relation to juvenile investigations. It is not unusual for youth to fabricate a story indicating that they are victims of an offense in order to cover some activity that may or may not be a violation. Their motivation for false reporting of offenses may range from fear of parental rebukes to concern over terms of probation or parole. Furthermore, it has long been known that juveniles may admit all but one minor and significant part of an offense during an interrogation. In relation to questions about that portion of the incident, the youth may continually lie, to the point of exasperation. The officer should realize that the youth is afraid to admit the fact because of his anxiety over what others have told him, or what his own life experience has demonstrated. It usually has nothing to do with the police or officer. He feels that if he tells this one fact it will be the cause of parental anger, or it is viewed as the one thing that will cause the authorities to take severe action with him. It is at times such as this that the police juvenile officer must use patience and understanding in order to lead the youth to the place where the juvenile can admit this part of the violation activity. To get mad at him in an attempt to try to short cut the interrogation, will merely reinforce the subject's anxiety. He will read the police reaction to mean that it really must be bad, and he will become more resolved not to tell.

In a juvenile investigation, the police must bear in mind that they have certain responsibilities to the parents of the offender.

One of these is to include them in the situation as soon as is practicable. This does not mean that parents should be brought in at the outset of the investigation, for this may cause severe interference. Rather, it refers to the need to advise them, within reason, of the nature of the investigation and to inform them of the facts as soon as those facts are discovered. It would be difficult to expect the youth to admit acts in the presence of his parents upon first contact. This is placing the youth into a position that few adults could adjust to adequately. If an officer is going to question a youth in the presence of his parents, expect that juvenile to cover his actions. Later, however, when a juvenile has admitted his part in an offense to the officer, the officer should attempt to encourage the youth to handle the admission to the parents himself. This should be with the officer present, of course.

In an offense where adult and juvenile suspects have been coparticipants, the juvenile matter should be pursued *whether or not the adult case proceeds,* assuming there is evidence to support a petition. This may be the only opportunity for society to help this youth prior to his becoming an adult.

The police have the responsibility to investigate all matters in which a juvenile is either a *suspect* or a *victim;* and, these investigations deserve the same attention, effort, and skill as any other.

Case Disposition

As previously mentioned, this area of the police juvenile responsibility is extremely important. It places an added burden upon the police, but to fail to perform in this area is to shirk a duty. Because of the difficulty involved in carrying out this mission, police juvenile specialists should be assigned to perform the dispositional function.

The best course of action for the juvenile will vary immensely, but that action should be the outcome desired. What will best suit this individual in this matter in the long run? Only experience in juvenile enforcement will provide the officer with the tools necessary to adequately supply the answer to that question.

One of the reasons for the importance of the case disposition is the need to screen juvenile court referrals. To begin with, the caseload at that level is already suffering from expansion. Secondly, not all cases warrant juvenile court action, which could explain some officers' frustrations with juvenile court outcomes, when in fact the officers are referring situations that should be otherwise handled.

The following two areas of case disposition are of concern:

1. *The preliminary action.* What does the officer do with the juvenile when encountered on the street? What does the patrol or detective do with a youth?

2. *The final action.* If not referred to the juvenile court, what then? Should the juvenile specialist be involved in all case dispositions? Should all members of the department dispose of cases at their own discretion?

To begin with, an examination of the criteria for incarceration of the juvenile offender is warranted. A youth should be placed into custody in the following situations:

1. If the offense is of such a serious nature, so as to demand incarceration immediately. Offenses of this nature would include so-called infamous crimes (murder, forcible rape and certain other sex offenses, true arson, robbery, serious crimes of violence) and some serious thefts and burglaries.

2. If the youth represents a clear danger to the community or if some segment of the community is a threat to his person (such as an irate parent of the victim of a child molest).

3. When it appears that the youth is a danger to himself, in the sense of a possible suicide as a result of the apprehension by the police.

4. When there is reason to believe that the juvenile will flee the jurisdiction of the court.

5. In cases in which large amounts of property are still outstanding, and there are other suspects involved who have not been apprehended. In similar situations in which recovery of property is an issue, and it is felt that the suspect will destroy or hide the loot, if released.

Unless the situation amounts to one of these criterion, the suspect should *not* be placed into custody. This admonition includes situations in which there are other suspects who have not been apprehended, and the officer feels that the youth will inform his partners that the police are looking for them. This is just one of those added burdens upon the police, for the juvenile suspect should not suffer incarceration anymore than the police have the ability to retain an adult in custody without bail for the same reason. Generally speaking, police officers should employ the least restriction of the juvenile's freedom under the circumstances of the case.

The police, as much as possible, should develop and employ the *citation* system to be utilized at the preliminary disposition stage. This procedure allows the field officer to cite the juvenile, with one or both parents, to the police juvenile specialist or unit. It is a citation in lieu of placing the youth into custody. Normally, it would be given to the youth who would have the obligation to notify the parents himself. Naturally, there are isolated instances of failure to appear, but these are easily handled by the juvenile specialist.

This method not only assists in reducing the number of bookings, but it also insures that the parents are notified of a pending police action. It places the burden of notification upon the offender himself, in most instances. The parents are then required to make the effort to appear at the police station several days hence, at which time the juvenile officer takes over, using the original citing officer's report as a basis for a continuation of the investigation.

Most often, minor offenses can be handled with the suspect being reprimanded and released back to his parents for action within the family setting. This does *not* mean that the youth is on probation to the police, and this fact must be fully explained to both the offender and the parents. Rather, it is an official case disposition in which the police advise the youth and the parents of the nature of the law governing the infraction, and return the child to the parents providing them with full freedom in relation to what action should be taken.

Police officers are not correctional personnel. Neither general officers nor juvenile specialists have time to attempt long range supervision of cases. Members of the correctional discipline, as well as others, would tend to state that officers do not have the necessary training for rehabilitative therapy.[10] Be that as it may, the fact is that police personnel should not become involved in having juveniles report to them in aftercare situations.

Upon citation to the juvenile specialist and his review or investigation, should the matter appear to require referral to another agency, community resources, or the juvenile court, that action should occur. A full explanation of the ramifications of the referral should be made to both the juvenile and the parents. This should include the facts relating to any restriction upon the freedom or movements of the offender pending the referral and based upon legal statutes or court order providing the police with the power to set such restrictions. If none exist, then the youth and the parents should be advised that the offender is under no restrictions from the police agency.

In carrying out the responsibility of case disposition, the police would be well-advised to consider the following:

1. What can the officer do for the juvenile?
2. What can the police agency do for the juvenile?
3. What can another agency do for the juvenile?
4. What can the community do for the juvenile?[11]

The utilization of the citation system tends to eliminate the use of "curb side court" by regular field personnel. The system of reprimanding a youth on the street and releasing him usually results in no record of the encounter. Seldom will the offender tell his parents about the situation, and more often than not he will gain stature among his peers by bragging about the manner in which he got off. This will occur more than in juvenile court encounters in which the youth has been subjected to an apprehensive situation in the presence of his parents. The same is true if the street corner release is compared to an appearance with the parents at the police station.

A word of caution. Police officers should not rush the decision to place a youth into custody, nor to refer him to the juvenile court. If there is probable cause, this action can always be taken; but, if taken too quickly the youth has then been exposed to the one institution in the society that he has not had contact with before and which may have a deterrent effect upon his behavior. Once he has been to court and survived, the deterrence diminishes.

Officers should not attempt to elicit promises of good future behavior from youth. If the officer is going to give the youth a break, that is a free choice within the discretion of the police function. To begin gaining promises of a meaningless nature serves to make the officer appear foolish.

The Protection of the Juvenile

Many officers perceive the juvenile as an offender, but police personnel should bear in mind that the youth of this country are exposed to many situations in which they are victims. Probably more children are numbered among victims of crimes perpetrated against them than are the impressive numbers of juvenile offenders.

The police have a responsibility to protect youth from themselves and others. They have a responsibility to protect juveniles from harmful objects and situations. This includes crimes of neglect and abuse, which are manifested in the home and at an early period in the child's life.[6] Sex offenses, committed by members of the child's family, friends, neighbors, or strangers. Child stealing situations, in which the children are being utilized by estranged parents as pawns in a divorce. Self-appointed youth leaders or youth workers, no matter how well intentioned, should be a police concern. Dubious merchants and other business persons who intend to prey upon the follies of youth. The "sensationalists," be they educationally or church oriented, or a local radio station disc jockey. And the police themselves—the obligation to protect youth from those officers who are so cynical or maladjusted as to represent a true threat to the police juvenile enforcement contact.

As an example of the sensationalist and the police response to such individuals, the following situation may be of value. Early in the sixties and before the drug abuse problem among teenagers had grown to its recent proportions, the author's department began receiving calls from numerous citizens desiring the truth about the local drug problem among youth. The callers were telling about the ability to make a buy on the main street of town at high noon, and at every school area.

The truth was that during that period, teenage hard drug use was a rarity with the exception of major urban areas. In attempting to discover what had precipitated this sudden outburst, the investigation led to a brochure that described a young woman who had been a delinquent and drug user while in her early teens in Canada. According to the biographical sketch, she had numerous encounters with Canadian law enforcement, and finally came to the United States. It went on to describe how she had been a gang member in several Eastern cities.

As the brochure's story unfolded, the woman had been incarcerated in a correctional school for girls near Elmira, New York. During the period of her confinement, she had undergone a religious transformation that altered her life. From that moment on she was dedicated to helping delinquent youth.

The brochure was the publicity for her speaking engagements. It had been based upon an interview by a female news reporter in a Northern California community. The subject's speaking appearances were church sponsored, but not confined to any one denomination. Within the author's jurisdiction she had made a number of speeches in a very short period of time, and she was in great demand.

Her talks were based upon sensationalism. The material was pointed at the listener's shock threshold, and was intended to excite an emotional response to the evils of wholesale drug abuse that the speaker indicated was existent among the teenagers of the area.

She did not condemn law enforcement, but rather indicated that the police were unable to obtain the same information that she could get, due to her ability to work with gangs. The woman was well received and the response coming to the department's attention dramatically conveyed that reception.

The department's position was against the unreliable information that the speaker was providing. Her religious message was not the issue. A quiet beckground investigation began.

The only information available was from the brochure. It provided a name and a Province in Canada. It also included the town in New York, near where the correctional institution was alleged to be located. There was a reference to a private farm for delinquents that the speaker had started near Carlise, Pennsylvania.

A records check was attempted, with negative results. The Pennsylvania State Police were the first group to provide an answer. It was merely that the farm had been closed after a short duration, by health authorities. This indicated that the woman was using her correct name, a fact that had not been established until then.

The U. S. Border Patrol furnished information relating to her entry into the United States. She had come to this country when she was in her early twenties, and had been sponsored by a single female government employee in Washington, D. C. On her application for a visa, the woman had denied that she was or had ever been a drug user, a statement required under the Immigration Laws. This information coincided with the negative records checks from both the United States and Canada.

A letter to the New York State Police describing the so-called correctional school near Elmira obtained an important source of information. The woman had been to a school in that area, but not a correctional institution. It was a legitimate Bible College operated by a recognized religious denomination. Her enrollment was as a regular student and she had attended the school for about one year. She was no problem. Information from the school provided necessary family background.

The Royal Canadian Mounted Police were contacted and made the final assessment. They discovered that she had been born and raised in a small, remote village in Northern Ontario. Here she had completed high school. The report said she had never been in any trouble, and added that the particular community had never known a serious crime problem, let alone a narcotics situation. One other fact was added. The woman had been considered a lesbian by the hometown people.

On the basis of the information obtained, the department developed an official communiqué describing the background of the individual. This was directed to the local council of churches. Presumably it was effective, as the subject ceased coming to the area, and the community's emotional reaction stopped abruptly.

This incident demonstrates the ability of one person to create problems for a community. It also demonstrates the ease by which community polarization can be attained. It was not necessary for the local police agency to become involved in the situation. It's involvement was by choice. The decision to attempt to verify the validity of the speaker's background was based upon the realization of the need for such a determination, the fact that the department was best suited to make the investigation, and that the agency had a responsibility to the community.

The Prevention of Delinquency

After a career exposure to the problem of juvenile delinquency that spans almost two decades, the author still encounters disciplines, agencies, and individuals who make reference to a particular prevention program or activity. If it is from a poorly informed source, the activity will revolve around the need for more outlets for youthful recreational needs. More informed sources make reference to newly developed programs or experimental innovations. Even police officials utilize the term, delinquency prevention.

The fact is there are few, if any delinquency prevention programs in existence anywhere in the United States. There are, however, many delinquency *repression* programs. Let us examine the difference.

Prevention implies not only the mechanical forestalling of a delinquent or criminal act, but also the forestalling of the planned conceptualization of the act by the individual. It is quite possible to forestall or repress the illegal acts committed by members of the society. In fact, the more repression of the individual liberties of the members, the greater the ability to forestall the undersirable acts performed by the members. Of course, this method is not what is desired. Therefore, what is left is a void between those procedures and programs that will serve to repress illegal action within the limits of a free society, and the need to create an anticrime climate that permeates that society.

While much reference is made to prevention, it remains the least developed area of the criminal justice system. There is little meaningful theory involved, and what research does occur tends to be in situations that do not actually produce effective results.[12]

There exists a difficulty in defining terms employed in prevention, and this has a spill-over effect upon the conceptualization of the meaning of prevention. The confusion surrounding the whole area of prevention has resulted in a lack of knowledge about the subject.

As an example, much diverse response may be generated within various groups with the mention of punitive prevention practices. In this type of prevention, the threat of punishment is utilized to overcome the individual's planned conceptualization of committing an offense. Many will argue that this is not prevention, but it is very closely related to the true meaning of prevention. It demands a certainty of retribution, a fact that has not existed within our criminal justice for a long time, if ever. That it may not have been employed effectively does not negate its existence as a preventative technique, although it is seldom thought of in that light.

Causes of crime and delinquency have not been isolated. Certain *factors* have been identified that tend to be discovered as existing within the backgrounds of many delinquents. These factors have been given much attention, but in themselves cannot be attributed the luxury of being termed causes. There are many delinquents who came from low economic backgrounds. At the same time, there are many nondelinquents who also come from the same backgrounds; some in fact are found within the same family group. Many delinquents are poor academic achievers, but so are many nondelinquents. Many delinquents come from minority group ethnic backgrounds, and yet certain minority ethnic groups are well known for the lack of delinquency among their children.

The broken home is highly represented among delinquents. At the same time, with the divorce rate reaching 1 out of every 2½ marriages are not many of our youth also faced with the broken home? Is the broken home the cause of the youth's delinquency, or could it be that his delinquency is the cause of the broken home? Could not the broken home be but a chance situation—it just happened to occur in the particular instance and not be related to the delinquency?

In order to prevent an occurrence, one must know the cause

of the incident or outcome. Since there has been no effective isolation of causes, how can there be effective prevention? The whole area of prevention is a tremendous problem, touching upon all segments of our social, economic, and political system. It calls for the reexamination of national and local goals. It demands the recognition of the need for the society to perform the function of the socialization of the incoming generation, and to perform that function well. Predictable measuring devices that will detect delinquency at an early age need to be developed.[13] There must be programs that will be capable of reducing the influence of the factors that have already been identified. These and many other problems must be solved before delinquency prevention can be a reality.

One area that needs immediate attention is the problem of *early detection*. One of the favorite topics for many correctional personnel, sociologists, and educators; the early detection concept is a myth. Many parents and others have spent much effort running from pillar to post attempting to obtain assistance for their child in a situation that they have recognized as a sign of delinquent tendencies. The fact remains that few communities are capable of dealing with predelinquents. Probation agencies do not wish to handle the problem, as there has been no violation. Since the child has not been involved in a clear-cut violation, he does not come under the jurisdiction of the Juvenile Court. Public social agencies and mental health programs are too involved with the more serious cases of manifested behavioral problems to be able to take the child; and psychiatric or psychological assistance on a private basis is out of the question for most families.[14] The end result is the frustration of the parents until the child has in fact become clearly delinquent. At that point, he may then enter the mill of the criminal justice system.

The only public agency that might assist, within the scope of its apparent limitations, would be the police. Police juvenile officer quasi-counselling, often condemned, may be the only present answer to this obvious need. In many instances, it has been effective. That the official social disciplines are aware of failures that have occurred does not negate the police attempt

164   *Police Juvenile Enforcement*

to hold the line while these same disciplines are in the process of discovering that "talk is cheap."

NOTES AND REFERENCES

1. Edward Eldefonso: *Law Enforcement and the Youthful Offender.* New York, John Wiley and Sons, 1967, p. 105.
2. Frank Manella, Associate Professor, Police Training Institute, University of Illinois in a presentation during a Police-Community Relations Workshop, Western Springs, Ill., May 5, 1971.
3. George H. Shepard: The juvenile specialist in community relations. *Police Chief,* January, 1970, pp. 3-6.
4. *Municipal Police Administration,* 5th ed. Chicago, International City Managers' Association, 1961, pp. 7-8.
5. For a different perspective, see,
   John P. Kenney and Dan G. Pursuit: *Police Work With Juveniles,* 3rd ed. Springfield, 1967, p. 75.
6. C. J. Flammang: *The Police and the Underprotected Child.* Springfield, Thomas, 1970 pp. 53-55.
   William E. Amos: Prevention through the school. In William E. Amos and Charles F. Wellford (Ed.): *Delinquency Prevention.* Englewood Cliffs, N. J., Prentice-Hall, 1967, pp. 128-149.
7. C. F. Flammang: An attempt to clarify some areas of police juvenile procedures. *Police, 15* (3): 20-22, 1971.
8. *In re Gualt* (1967) 387 U. S. 1, 13.
9. On March 31, 1970, in *Winship v. New York,* the U. S. Supreme Court set the criteria for establishing the truth of a fact in Juvenile Court proceedings to be *beyond a reasonable doubt.*
10. Jesse R. James and George H. Shephard: Police work with children. *Municipal Police Administration.* Chicago, International City Managers Association, 1969, pp. 148-157.
11. C. J. Flammang: Juvenile procedures. An unpublished study prepared for the Division of Vocational Education, Berkeley, University of California, July 30, 1967, p. 44.
12. Peter P. Lejins: The field of prevention, In William E. Amos and Charles F. Wellford (Eds.): *Delinquency Prevention.* Englewood Cliffs, N. J., Prentice-Hall, 1967, p. 1.
13. For an interesting appraisal of predictors, see,
    Sheldon and Eleanor Glueck: *Unraveling Juvenile Delinquency.* Cambridge, Mass., Harvard University Press, 1950, pp. 101-113, 127-129, 193.
    Sheldon and Eleanor Glueck: *Delinquents in the Making.* New York, Harper and Row, 1952, pp. 165-166.

Sheldon and Eleanor Glueck: *Family Environment and Delinquency.* Boston, Houghton Mifflin Co., 1962.

Maude M. Craig and Selma J. Glick: *A Manual of Procedures for Application of the Glueck Prediction Table.* New York City Youth Board, 1964.

C. Ray and Ina A. Jeffery: Prevention through the family. In William E. Amos and Charles F. Wellford (Eds.): *Delinquency Prevention.* Englewood Cliffs, N. J., Prentice-Hall, 1967, pp. 89-91.

14. Brandt Steele, M. D., Psychiatrist, Universtiy of Colorado Medical Center, in a workshop on the Battered Child Syndrome, Denver, March, 1969.

Chapter Eight

THE POLICE JUVENILE UNIT

A S a result of the specialization of police officers in the area of juvenile enforcement, the concept of a number of specialists grouped together in common design of purpose and assignment has emerged. The police juvenile unit, known by several other designations eg. juvenile bureau, juvenile division, youth services, is a method of organization that attempts to bring the police mission in youth work under a controlled management setting.

There is no standard design for such specialized groups. No doubt, the manner of organizing more than one juvenile officer into a productive functional unit is a subject which if pursued could elicit an extensive controversy. It is important to understand that while such units often are quite varied in their organizational and functional designs, these variances do not reflect actual standards. Rather, the differences in the fundamental nature of the numerous types of units that have been developed, reflect local administrative attitudinal sets, local attempts to identify needs, local resources, and in some instances, community demands.

The fact that there exists such a variance between the manner of forming these groups implies one of two things. Either there is no standard basis for forming the group that is capable of being identified, or the enforcement needs for the juvenile police responsibilities are so varied as to defy the development of basic standardization of group formation. The author rejects both of the implied conclusions. Instead, it may be assumed that in the area of juvenile enforcement practices, the same patterns of police management techniques have been employed that are used as the basis for the totality of police operation. This assumption alludes

166

to the resistance of police administrators to move from their traditional police posture or to examine the current concepts of effective management. The poor record of police management efforts leads to this conclusion, as police executive endeavors are not supported by the base of knowledge presently available to persons engaged in the field of administrative management.

ADMINISTRATION

Few police executives have received the necessary tools to perform their basic tasks of management.[1] Fewer are capable of isolating their management role from their police role identification. Ineffective police management is easily identified within police agencies across the country.[2]

In order to determine the manner in which a group should be formed, it is first necessary to gather certain data and to formulate the foundations for perspectives. What are the objectives of the group? What functional requirements are placed upon the group in order to meet the stated objectives? Who comprises the clientele with which the group must work? What dynamics are involved between the group and the clientele? What is the nature of the clientele population? These and other questions must be subjected to scrutiny and the answers developed should become the basis for the necessary planning for the group formation. Planning is a prerequisite to insure the development of proper direction and thrust of a newly created organization.

Planning is a managerial task. It cannot be delegated. The responsibility for the task of planning resides with the chief administrative officer of the agency. He may use the efforts of others to develop the background information necessary for the act of planning, but the evaluation of the data, its utilization for purposes of implementation, and the decision-making involved, all remains the task of the executive.

The police executive, either with an established juvenile unit, or contemplating the development of juvenile services, should recognize the following:

1. He must recognize the fundamental objectives of the societal response to juvenile delinquency, and the application of those objectives to the juvenile enforcement enterprise. This re-

quires a departure from the traditional police orientation of identification, apprehension, and adjudication. The desire of the society to intervene in the socialization process of the incoming generation by removing or diminishing the predisposition toward deviant behavior is a necessary part of the police juvenile rule perception.

2. In order to achieve the objectives of the demands of the society, the police must gear their juvenile efforts toward the more expanded scheme that comprises societal intervention as a response to delinquency. The functional requirements of a specialized police juvenile unit will exceed the requirements of a purely investigative branch of the police service. This raises a question that will be more fully discussed under the heading Organization; that of the location of the unit within the police agency. The functions of the juvenile unit should reflect community needs, as delimited within the executive management planning task.

3. On first appraisal, it would appear that the clientele to be served could be conveniently labeled juveniles or juvenile delinquents. To forestall such an oversimplification, an examination of the clientele is in order. Delimiting the client group to juveniles requires a definition that is statutory in nature. Thus, depending upon the statutory definition of a given jurisdiction a child of three years may or may not be included within the client group. It is certainly clear that children of that age must be subject to the concern of a specialized juvenile police unit, as victims if for no other reason.

In some states, the upper limits of the legally defined juvenile age differs according to sex. This differentation is a matter of legislative action, and fails to account for the peer group activity that is evident in delinquent behavior. It would be a serious fragmentation of police effort to cause part of a case to be handled by one police entity while the other part is handled by the juvenile officer. Some attention must be given to the problems involved in the client group as it reaches the upper limits of the juvenile age.

The predelinquent cannot be ignored. The police must be capable of dealing with problems arising in this sensitive area.

This is extremely evident in the lower middle and lower socio-economic groups, as the predelinquency encountered within such subgroupings may lead to a serious life-style set in the future.

The child who comprises the basic client group for police juvenile officers is represented by a parent. Parents or guardians are *de facto* a part of the client group. Not only are there statutory requirements that affect the functional police juvenile operation, but there should also be managerial policy decisions relating to various police actions. Such policy would include the manner in which juveniles are contacted, taken into custody, transported, interviewed or interrogated, and confined. Policy must be developed relating to fingerprinting juveniles, handcuffing youth, and in relation to the use of reasonable force in juvenile matters. How, when, and to what extent the parent is to be involved in the police action should be governed by general administrative policy.

Other agencies that are involved with juveniles must also be considered as a part of the juvenile unit's clientele. The unit has certain obligations within its relationships wth the schools, welfare and social services, correctional services, and the Juvenile Court.

Police planning must include decisions relating to the mechanics of establishing and maintaining necessary relationships, and meeting the police obligations to these agencies and institutions. Policy must include the delegation of the authority and responsibility for these police-client relationships to the juvenile unit.

4. After the client group has been determined, the administrative task of defining the nature of the group, and the various subgroups that make up the client group, should be examined. The factors that are isolated as a result, are all part of the information necessary in making judgments relating to the dynamics involved within the client group and its various components. These dynamics are varying and changing, and have a direct influence upon the possible outcomes of the juvenile police effort.

This cannot be a superficial effort, but must involve an active appraisal system, that in some instances will require the utilization of persons external to the police agency. Without the appraisal of the nature of the client population the relationships that are beneficial to the police juvenile operation cannot be perceived, and the operation will falter.

It is apparent that the process of administrative development of a police juvenile unit exceeds the superficiality of designating certain individuals as juvenile officers and placing the unit in a convenient position within the organizational flow chart. In departments of moderate size, the management obligations and functions that should precede the establishment of juvenile services (or the reevaluation of present services) would require a time period that might encompass as much as one year. The justification for such an administrative effort would be measureable in effective results.

As one of the most crucial segments of the total police operation, the police juvenile involvement should be of major concern to the police manager. The police are constantly involved with youth, and youth account for a disproportionate amount of crime and deviant behavior. If for no other reasons, these facts would justify the efforts of police management in the area of delinquency prevention and control.

ORGANIZATION

Without effective planning at the developmental stage, the juvenile unit's placement within the departmental structure is an arbitrary factor. This placement may be of singular importance to the functional operations of the unit.

It has been the practice of many departments of moderate size to place the juvenile unit within the organizational structure that comprises the investigative services. As a part of the larger group, the juvenile unit is assigned a commander who is of a lower rank than the overall investigative service commander. In effect, the commander of the detective division has both administrative and functional authority over the commander of the juvenile unit, and hence the unit itself.

That a detective commander is fully oriented toward the investigation of criminal activity may not be in conflict with the investigatory functions of the juvenile unit; but, certainly the emphasis that the detective commander places upon feloneous crimes and prosecutions and convictions is an orientation that may run counter to the productive efforts of a juvenile operation. Traditional police orientation and effective juvenile operations represent conflicts, both in philosophy and function. The placement of the juvenile unit within an existing detective operation may result in some disturbing outcomes.

First, the juvenile unit may suffer from the perception of its worth by the detective commander and other detectives. If this occurs, the assignment of selected personnel to the juvenile unit may also suffer, with the juvenile operation becoming the deposit point for ineffective detectives. In place of the efficient police officer who is needed, the juvenile unit may be comprised of persons who are inadequate to respond to the demands of juvenile service.

The opposite may be postulated, indicating that the location of the juvenile unit within a detective division would not subvert the assignment of qualified personnel because of the administrative efforts to avoid inadequate manpower selection. While this may be true in some instances, there is another hazard that should be evaluated. After making effective personnel assignments, the commander of the detective division may be prone to dip into the juvenile unit's manpower resources to provide bolstering of the general investigative force, as he deems necessary. The more the juvenile officer functions effectively for the general investigative program, the more frequently the detective commander will turn toward the juvenile unit as a source of reliable manpower. Eventually, there may ensue reassignments of personnel that would amount to a situation that would resemble the one described under the first criticism.

The same type of criticisms can be directed toward the allocation of equipment within the investigative unit. The juvenile officers may discover that their efforts must be carried out minus the equipment that might increase their ability to achieve objectives. The diverting of funds and equipment from one operation to another is a natural outcome of the need to establish priorities. When the juvenile unit is combined within a larger detective force, the function of setting the priorities is assigned to the officer in charge of the larger unit.

It is interesting to note that most police agencies will locate their vice and intelligence units in a direct relationship with the chief executive officer, while at the same time failing to notice the significant effects that a juvenile unit may influence (either positive or negative) throughout the department, with other agencies, and within the community. It would be recommended that in police agencies of moderate size, the juvenile unit be organized as a separate entity, and that the unit's commander report directly to the chief executive of the department. The same principles can be utilized in the small department, with the only alteration being the use of one member of the agency, rather than a number of officers. In the larger police agencies, the juvenile service should be a division in its own right, and its commander should be of the same rank as other division superiors.

Much of the effort of the juvenile operation will exceed traditional police practices. It is imperative that the chief executive be in the position to be appraised of situations that require actions which transcend routine police procedures. In many instances, commanders of juvenile units are frustrated in their attempts to be more effective by superiors who have other priority interests and who stand between the juvenile unit and the head of the agency. Innovation, as well as flexibility, is required in a modern police juvenile operation. These cannot develop freely without the support of the department executive officer. The organization of the juvenile unit must insure the means of bringing these exceptional matters to the attention of the executive manager, who is the person who should make the decision of whether or not to proceed. As a consequence of the positioning of the juvenile unit within the organization, the matter may never reach the executive for his consideration. This type of organizational stupidity is not only unfortunate, it is unnecessary.

Organization Within the Police Juvenile Unit

The concept of organization for management purposes is not an end in itself, but rather is merely the vehicle by which individuals are grouped together in order to perform related functions under the direction of a person with the responsibility for the direction, supervision, and coordination of the activities. Organization is not static, but is subject to change. It should be constantly evaluated to insure that the grouping of the unit, and its relationship to other groups within the total institution is actually an asset to the operational function of the unit itself and the agency as a whole.[3]

It is not enough to isolate personnel by grouping them into a juvenile unit. Each individual juvenile officer will have certain strengths and weaknesses that must be evaluated. The commander of the juvenile unit should then base his assignment decisions, as well as his future manpower need assessments on the basis of the evaluation.

It may develop that additional specialization should occur within the juvenile unit itself. This should be encouraged by the commander of the unit. While manpower limitations almost certainly require that all juvenile officers be able to perform adequately in all areas of the juvenile enforcement function, there will be strengths that do develop in certain areas for each officer. As these are noted, or as needs arise, the officer in charge of the juvenile effort should attempt to develop the individual's further expertise through additional assignments in that area, and by providing the officer with training opportunities in the subspeciality.

As examples of the specialization concept just described, consider the following:

1. An individual officer demonstrates ability in the area of crimes against property, such as burglary and vandalism. The juvenile unit commander should attempt to assign the more serious cases of property loss to that officer, allowing other personnel to handle minor crimes against property. Attempts should be made to provide the officer with the opportunity to attend training conferences covering that type of offense pattern, and the officer should be encouraged to become an active member of any law enforcement groups specializing in the investigation of such crimes.

2. When an enforcement problem occurs in such a unique manner as to indicate special action, the commander of the juvenile unit should seek to develop an individual officer's ability to cope with the problem as a specialty in addition to the general specialization in the area of juvenile work.

With the increase in the incidence of drug abuse among youth, many juvenile units found that there were no members who had any real knowledge of the subject. In situations of that type, the assignment of one officer to become a drug and narcotics specialist should occur, regardless of the existence of other officers in the police agency who may have more expertise or by reason of their assignment to a narcotics unit are more directly involved in narcotics investigation.

The juvenile narcotic specialist would work with the regular narcotics details in drug matters in which juveniles were involved. His additional specialization would allow him to speak intelligently on matters of drug abuse with the parental population, the educational system, the juvenile court, and the youth community. The juvenile specialist in narcotics would serve in a liasion capacity to the total narcotics enforcement area, the judicial process, and the community as those categories pertained to juveniles. This would reduce the requirement of the regular narcotic force to extend its efforts beyond the investigatory stage of the juvenile caseload. It would also insure that departmental policy and legal requirements regarding juvenile contacts be maintained throughout the investigation.

The examples are merely indicators of the need for further specialization within the juvenile unit. This will occur unofficially in any event. That fact precipitates the recommendation that such specialization be recognized, encouraged, and become an official part of the organizational process. The responsibility for the development of further specialization rests with commander of the juvenile unit.

In major departments, police juvenile officers should be on duty during the majority of the 24-hour period, but in medium-sized agencies and the very small department, manpower limitations will normally preclude around the clock juvenile services.

Instead of depleting the work force and assigning a few officers to work under the functional control of supervisors of other units on a regular basis, it would be beneficial to consider retaining the integrity of the juvenile unit and utilizing other means to extend service to additional shifts.

One effective method is to insure that the function of the juvenile unit includes the training of patrol personnel to handle routine juvenile matters, with referral to the specialist at the follow-up point of contact. The employment of the citation system provides a natural mechanism for extending routine juvenile capability to the patrol division.

A second method that may be incorporated with the insurance of adequate training to other departmental units is the use of a "standby" service emanating from the juvenile unit. This method places an extra burden upon the juvenile unit's personnel, but the burden is subject to various means of compensation and also to policy control that would delimit the amount of calls required.

A third means of providing juvenile services to other shifts is to reassign juvenile personnel under the direct control of their commander to work during evening or night periods in situations of a unique nature. Halloween evening would be a good example of a problem situation requiring the reassignment of juvenile officers' hours.

The act of permanently assigning part of the juvenile staff to work as an attachment to another division, under another commander, and during separate time periods, leads to the eventual misuse of the specialist. It serves to negate the supervisory control the juvenile commander must maintain over his personnel, and eliminates his ability to evaluate the performance of his officers. Coordination of the juvenile effort is thwarted, and the eventual outcome is the unofficial integration of the juvenile officer into the operational functions of the unit to which he has been assigned. The police juvenile effort is not assisted by having a juvenile officer become a patrolman.

For all but the major sized agencies, it would be recommended that juvenile officers work a unified shift, under their own commander, with provisions for extending the service to the other shifts as required. This insures the continuity and overall effectiveness of the juvenile specialization.

SUPERVISION

The tasks of coordinating, directing, and controlling the operations of a police juvenile unit are significant in relationship to the overall effectiveness of the program. These tasks are the basis for supervision. They do not alter because of the specialized nature of the work to be performed.[4] The principles of supervision are the same for a normal line operation and specialized operations.[5] The nature of the juvenile police enterprise demands a departure from the traditional role of law enforcement. This element of the juvenile operation causes the role of the unit supervisor to be somewhat more demanding than normal line requirements. It is essential for the police executive to be aware of this difference, as it represents the only differential between the supervision activities.

The dynamics of the relationship between the juvenile unit and the rest of the internal organization of the police agency, and the relationship between the juvenile unit and the community are quite sophisticated. The day to day contacts with the various segments of the police juvenile unit's clientele need excellence in supervision. It is imperative that the selection of the juvenile unit's commanding officer be made with diligence. This is a position to be filled with an individual who is a dedicated police officer who has a full grasp of the ramifications of the juvenile operation, a sense of responsibility to the community, the willingness to cooperate with other agencies, inherent foresight, and who believes in the processes that are involved in protecting and rehabilitating the juvenile.

Educationally it would be hoped that the selected supervisor has some amount of advanced academic preparation, with a background in the behavioral sciences. This cannot be a hard and fast rule, as there are individuals who would be capable of functioning well without advanced academics. By and large, however, the officer in charge of a juvenile unit will be able to develop and direct a more productive program if he is college educated in addition to other background preparation.

It would be a tragic disservice to the community and the police service to select a juvenile supervisor on the basis of anything but the highest standards. These standards should not only be reflected in the individual's professional background, but also in the actions of his private life and his personal ethics, as personified in his moral conscience. Youth are quick to identify hypocrisy and dual standards. Nowhere in police work is the importance of a high degree of ethical integrity in such demand as in the role of the juvenile officer. To orient and train incoming juvenile officers, as well as to control those officers already a part of the unit, requires the highest professional standards on the part of the supervisor. Nothing would alter the complexion of the juvenile operation more severely than the personnel being led into a reduction of high standards through the words and actions of their superior. Nothing would be held more contemptible by the citizenry at large than a scandal within the juvenile unit. In dealing with the youth of the community, the people demand excellence. This excellence will only be achieved and maintained if the supervision is sound.

Probably the worst system that may be employed by a department in relation to the overall effectiveness of the juvenile operation is the systematic rotation of personnel into the juvenile unit. This personnel practice is based on the concept that all officers will become familiar with the operation, and because of this exposure will somehow become proficient in carrying out that function. Police managers have not discovered that there is no correlation between *ability* and functional *proficiency* and *exposure* to an operation. This is a false perception in actual line functions, but it is more of a fallacy within the specialized juvenile effort. To extend this procedure to encompass the supervision aspects of the juvenile enterprise is pure folly. Each supervisor will make certain alterations in the operation and the direction of the unit to fit his own personal predispositions toward juvenile enforcement. As these changes occur, the unit will suffer internally, but more objectionable will be the external effects. Other agencies, the youth, and the community will be faced with a never ending succession of policies and procedures affecting the application of the juvenile court statutes and the general function of the juvenile unit in its response to the youth problems encountered. These constant fluctuations will serve to render the unit functionally inoperable relative to the true juvenile police mission. The eventual result will be the evolution of a juvenile unit that is either an extension of the patrol or detective function, neither of which is desired or necessary. Careful selection of the juvenile commander should bring into the unit a supervisor capable of developing a program with a lasting impact upon the community. Rotation of tenure in the command position limits this objective.

Tasks of the Juvenile Supervisor

While the principles of supervision are the same in any operation, there do exist some special tasks of supervision that should be deemed very important to the juvenile function. These tasks place responsibilities upon the juvenile unit supervisor that exceed the degree of like responsibilities of other commanders within the police agency. In some instances, the additional burdens pose unique problems for the juvenile supervisor, and require his constant attention and energies in order to fulfill his obligations to accountability.

The Juvenile Supervisory Training Function

Training must be applied in its broadest sense when the juvenile operation is being considered. To exemplify the variety of responsibilities that may be found to exist within the general category of training, the following areas of that function have been identified as each relates to the police juvenile mission:

1. *The training of incoming personnel.* A primary obligation of the juvenile unit commander is to insure the initial training of newly assigned personnel. Because of the demanding job requirements, the extent of the knowledge necessary to adequately perform in the juvenile enforcement area is extreme. Officers must not only be good policemen, they must have an above average working knowledge of all statutes pertaining to offenses that may be committed by or against a juvenile. They should be familiar with custody laws, and they have the additional burden of being acquainted with the procedural laws related to the handling of juvenile cases.

In addition to their knowledge of law and procedures, the practical application of these within the policy and program setting of the individual police agency and juvenile unit has to become second nature. This includes report writing techniques that exceed the mechanics of deciding which form to use at what time.

New personnel must be oriented to the various relationships

that exist between the juvenile unit and the other segments of the community. Any special problems pertaining to procedures that are utilized in dealing with other agencies have to be made clear. The general area of community resources is not a topic that many new officers will have fully developed prior to entering juvenile work.

Due to the follow-up function of the juvenile operation, the new officer will usually need to develop advanced investigative skills, with a major emphasis upon interviewing and interrogation. A general orientation period under the direction of the juvenile supervisor should occur. During this period, the supervisor is actually performing selected juvenile enforcement tasks, with the new officer in an observation role. This increases the burdens of the supervisor, as he must not only perform his routine tasks of supervision, but must also perform in the field with the new officer. After a reasonable period of orientation, the new officer should be assigned to a qualified officer who is experienced, and further on-the-job training should occur.

The supervisor should receive regular reports from the training vehicle on the progress of the newer officer. Strict evaluation of the new personnel's reports should be performed by the supervisor. Periodic meetings with the neophite should be held, and these should consist of an honest evaluation and critique of the officer's progress.

This portion of the training function of the supervisor should gradually taper off until the integration of the new officer into the unit actually occurs, and he is capable of performing the tasks of the juvenile operation without continual guidance. The training of incoming personnel is an individual situation, dependent upon the many variables that will exist between the new officer and his new assignment. The point to be considered is that the juvenile supervisor cannot shirk this responsibility, nor can he perform this function without first analyzing its many facets and developing an effective training procedure. Once such a procedure has been established it should be adhered to with periodic evaluation and modification.

2. *The continuous training of personnel.* The supervisor is responsible for the development of the unit to attain its full

potential. This requires the recognition of the need to continue the training function in relation to the on-going operation of the unit. Included within the area of this training would be found items pertaining to new procedures, not only of the unit, but within the total police agency and other agencies directly involved in the juvenile operation. Alteration in police procedures, as affected by court decisions should be made known immediately upon the ruling of the court. A three or four month time lag may prove to be disatrous. New legislation affecting youth must be brought to the attention of the personnel, and the manner in which such statute alterations or additions affect the juvenile and the police enforcement process should be fully explained.

The need to provide formal training services for selected personnel is very important. There are many schools, institutes, and workshops that would be beneficial to the juvenile police effort, if the officers were exposed to the training.[6] It is incumbent upon the juvenile supervisor to encourage attendance, directed both to the administration and the officers. As a part of the supervisor's identification of training needs is the budgeting of funds for attending training programs. This must evoke long range planning efforts on the part of the supervisor, and it will be doomed to failure if it is just another item included in an annual budget formulation. The identification of training needs within the unit is closely associated with the supervisor's task of developing individual officer expertise or subspecialization.

3. *Departmental in-service training.* While it is not necessary for the juvenile supervisor to actually perform the training, it is his obligation to insure that all departmental personnel are trained in the basic procedures involved in a juvenile case. Other units need to be familiar with those portions of the juvenile court law that relate to the role of the police. Line officers need to know what matters should be referred to the juvenile unit. They should be appraised of when to call for the juvenile unit to assist or to take over a field situation.

All line units should be aware of the policies and procedures that the department has developed for the processing of juvenile cases and governing police encounters with youth. Most certainly, line personnel in other units need to be informed of the types of dispositions given to cases that are referred to the juvenile unit, and they should be appraised of the limitations placed upon the unit or that are inherent to it.

Information of this nature cannot be promulgated on a purely informal basis. Much of the confusion and annimosity that exists in many police agency line units in relation to the juvenile specialty could be avoided or controlled by means of effective in-service training. This training responsibility rests with the juvenile supervisor. This is true even in situations where there is no other formal in-service training, or where the need is not perceived by the police executive manager. It is incumbent upon the juvenile supervisor to strive to install or develop effective juvenile training for all police personnel.

4. *Public education relating to juvenile enforcement.* Formerly identified as a part of police public relations, and more recently incorporated under the pseudonym of community relations, the education of the public in matters pertaining to juvenile enforcement is a function that should be performed as a part of the juvenile unit's operation. Because of this alignment, public education in juvenile matters falls under the command responsibilities of the supervisor of the juvenile unit. This does not mean that he must make all the presentation, but it does place the accountability for the department's efforts to educate the public in this area within the many tasks of the juvenile commander. To initiate a public education program calls for the utilization of all means of communication. Limiting the program to a few speeches before groups that use speakers as a regular part of their programs is only scratching the surface. The supervisor should develop an actual program, utilizing other resources within the police agency, and coordinating the police efforts with those of other agencies that have such programs. Naturally, the efforts of the supervisor should fall under the general direction of the agency executive.

Assignment of Work

One of the more obvious areas of the supervisory task is that of assignment of work. This is a difficult supervisoral task, and for the most part it is poorly performed in the total police function.

One reason why it is not well done is the failure to assign work both on an *equitable* basis and at the same time to insure *quality* of performance. Invariably, quantity becomes a major criteria, and this emphasis is greatly influenced by constant increases in workload, with disproportionate increases in police personnel, especially in juvenile specialization.

Quite often the supervisor will recognize that one or a few men are very capable, while the majority of the remainder are hard pressed to perform adequately. The solution should involve intensive training or replacement of the poor performer, but most often is manifested in the better personnel being given unequal burdens in the workload. This is reflected not only in the number of assignments, but also in the degree of difficulty involved in each assignment. This is a serious problem for the supervisor, and only the individual with supervisoral excellence will be able to overcome the temptation to resort to unequal work assignment.

This problem can be attacked if the supervisor will make an effort to develop the potential within each member of the unit to perform well in one or several areas of subspecialization. This will not be a panacea, but it will improve the situation. Therefore, the assignment of work is related to the task of identifying and encouraging the development of areas of expertise within the juvenile unit.

Another consideration in work assignment is the need for the supervisor and the personnel under his command to be aware of the fact that a certain expertise will not preclude an assignment in an area other than the subspecialty. A policewoman may be assigned to follow-up on bicycle thefts involving male juveniles, while a male officer may be required to pick up children in a dependency situation.

Case assignments should be made in writing. This is true even in situations where the officers are dispatched via the radio while in the field. Upon their return to the office, the written assignment should be on their desks. Such a system is necessary for the supervisor as a control device, with a copy of the assignment being retained by the commander.

As much as possible, the juvenile operation should be restricted to a preventative patrol or case follow-up. Generally speaking, the initial response should be handled by a patrol unit. The exceptions to this rule are too numerous to be developed, and will be somewhat dependent upon the individual department.

The Supervision of Personnel, Records, and Procedures

The juvenile commander is often faced with a difficult problem in the area of the supervision of the personnel under his command. To begin with, the juvenile operation requires the officers to work both in the field and in the office. The amout of time spent in either will fluctate from officer to officer and day to day. Should the juvenile commander be a field supervisor, or should he concentrate on an office evaluation of the performance of his officers? Obviously there should be a certain amount of time spent in field supervision, but limited. The remainder should be spent in observing the performance of the officers in the office setting and in interviewing personnel in other agencies who are in professional contact with the juvenile personnel on a regular basis. Police reports remain the best single method of supervision evaluation of the performance of the personnel. The juvenile commander should make a conscious effort to evaluate the written reports of his officers as a means of control and on-going supervision.

Police juvenile records should be developed and maintained as a part of the central police records system. Some records may be needed within the juvenile unit, but these should be merely duplicates of what are housed in the central files.

It is suggested that the department adopt a *juvenile contact form* to be utilized to record all of the personnel information that is necessary to aid in the identification of a juvenile. This is very true in jurisdictions that are forbidden to mug or fingerprint juveniles without a court order. Such a form should include information of a personal history nature, parental information, family background, educational information, and data related to previous offenses or probation/parole standing. It should be completed for each juvenile encountered, every time he is officially contacted by the police in a suspected situation, or in a case in which he is to be handled as a dependent child. This form should be filed with the case reporting system employed by the department. A specialized juvenile form can be of invaluable assistance to the juvenile unit and other police personnel, especially follow-up investigators.

Part of the juvenile commander's responsibility in relation to records is to insure that the agency's system is being adhered to, and to utilize the records in a manner that will justify their retention.

The evaluation of existing procedures and the development of new ones exist as a task of the juvenile supervisor. Again, the responsibility may be carried out by utilizing the services of a number of individuals, but the accountability remains with the supervisor. He should also be interested in other procedures that are developed within the total department that may have adverse effects upon the juvenile unit. The same is true in considering the procedures of other agencies within the juvenile justice framework, and those agencies that the police must come into contact with in order to fulfill the police juvenile mission. This is all part of the broad area of coordination of activities that befalls the commander of the juvenile unit.

Liaison

The person who should develop and maintain the fundamental relationships existing between the juvenile unit and other segments of the department and the community is the unit commander. Naturally, other juvenile personnel will be influencing these relationships in their routine contacts, but the task of being officially accoutable for the relationships remains with the supervisor. It is incumbent upon him to develop a program whereby he makes contact on a personal basis with other key figures in the totality of the juvenile system. In this manner, many problems can be worked out prior to affecting the existing relationships, and to establish the relations necessary to afford all parties an opportunity to work in an atmosphere of mutual cooperation. It is quite important for the commander of the juvenile unit to be on a personal basis with the management segment of other agencies and the persons of significant importance in various youth serving institutions.

Program Development

A juvenile enforcement program that has not altered its thrust over the past few years, is one that is static. Juvenile enforcement programs should be viable. The programs should reflect imagination in attempts to meet the needs of the youth and society. The commander of the juvenile unit should strive to keep abreast of new directions and methods. He should incorporate the implementation of new program directions into his planning practices. He should seek methods of encouraging community response to recognized needs, and he should offer a source of leadership within the total police juvenile effort.

These requirements mean that he must have a working knowledge of funding programs, available and untapped resources, and that he should be innovative in his approach to the police juvenile enforcement function. The police have a rightful role in furnishing leadership to the community in all areas of police responsibility. Juvenile operations represent a vital area for this leadership to be displayed.

NOTES AND REFERENCES

1. The Tennessee Association of Chiefs of Police instituted a Police Executive Management Training Program to run in conjunction with Association meetings. The program began in June, 1970 and has been funded via the Tennessee Law Enforcement Planning Agency.
   General police training activities revolve around Basic, Supervision, and Specialized courses of instruction, but fail to reach police managers.
2. *Municipal Police Administration,* 5th ed. Chicago, International City Managers Association, 1961, p. 4.
3. For more on organization, see,
   Raymond E. Clift: *A guide to Modern Police Thinking,* 2nd ed. Cincinnati: The W. H. Anderson Co., 1965, Ch. 3.
   V. A. Leonard: *Police Organization and Management.* Brooklyn, The Foundation Press, 1951.
   John M. Pfiffner and Robert Presthus: *Public Administration,* 5th ed. New York, The Ronald Press Co., 1967, Part III.
   O. W. Wilson: *Police Planning,* 2nd ed. Springfield, Thomas, 1968, Chs. 1-5, and 9.
4. John P. Kenney and Dan G. Pursuit: *Police Work With Juveniles,* 3rd ed. Springfield, Thomas, 1967, p. 70.

5. William B. Melnicoe and Jan Mennig: *Elements of Police Supervision.* Beverly Hills, Glencoe Press, 1969, Ch. 2.
6. A number of specialized training programs are open to police personnel. The opportunities increase each year. The following are merely samples:

(a) Delinquency Control Institute, University of California at Los Angeles.

(b) Delinquency Control Institute, University of Wisconsin.

(c) Police Crime Prevention Institute, University of Louisville.

(d) Youth Officers Course, University of Illinois.

(e) Police and Youth, Mt. St. Mary and Orange County (California) Community College.

(f) Advanced Institute on Police Work with Children and Youth, Pennsylvania State University.

(g) Neighborhood Leadership Training Workshop. Drake University.

(h) Juvenile Delinquency Prevention, Case Western Reserve University.

(i) Social Issues As Youth People See Them, University of California at Los Angeles.

(j) Confrontations Between Youth and Authorities, Syracuse University.

(k) The Battered Child Syndrome, Fresno State College, California.

Chapter Nine

THE POLICE JUVENILE OFFICER

N O discussion of police specialization in the juvenile field would be complete without some thoughts about the personnel who will be so assigned. If juvenile specialization is important to the police mission, then the officers who are to perform the specialized task are equally important. This concept cannot be overstressed. It is imperative that police administrators recognize the importance of the personnel resource who serve as the imput and structure upon which the juvenile effort will be dependent.

CRITERIA FOR SPECIALIZED JUVENILE PERSONNEL

Any attempt to delineate the criteria necessary for the position of the police juvenile officer requires that the tasks involved in the position be analyzed. Already these tasks have presented a glimpse of the magnitude of information, understanding, and skills that relate to the juvenile enforcement endeavor. The tasks required of police personnel to perform in the juvenile officer role are multiple. Juvenile work is exhausting. It is complex. Alone, these two characteristics would create unique criteria for the personnel who are to become involved in the effort. In order to facilitate the presentation of the criteria, items will be considered under three separate headings: (a) Personal Attributes, (b) Educational Background, and (c) Professional Background.

Personal Attributes

The juvenile officer must work with both youth and parents. These two groups comprise his basic clientele. Due to the existence of a significant age differential between the two groups of clients, age becomes a factor in the qualifications of a juvenile

187

officer. The potential juvenile officer should be of a mature age, but within a moderately lower age group. The agrument purported by some indicating that the younger officers should be assigned to juvenile work, as they are closer in age to the youth, holds no validity. Certainly, there will be individual exceptions, but these are situations wherein other qualifications lessen the importance of the age criterion and do not reflect a departure from the premise that maturity and moderate age are needed. Most juveniles, when in difficulty, need a mature, adult confident. They do not need another peer image. In the final analysis, much of their troubles are the outgrowth of peer influence.

On the other hand, a grandfatherly type is generally too old to be effective. The youth who comes to the attention of the police will often be turned off when they encounter the older police officer representing himself as the juvenile specialist.

Age, then, should reflect the middle road. A maturing officer in his late twenties will have between ten and fifteen years of juvenile specialization ahead of him. The fact that he has already attained a sense of maturity will compliment an age differential that will be acceptable from the standpoints of both the youth and the parents.

Since the officer will be required to make contact with the totality of the community, his personal appearance is important. The range of individuals with whom the juvenile officer must come into contact with routinely is so great as to exclude persons from this service who are unacceptable in their personal habits, grooming, and demeanor. The public speaking requirements of the position are enough to support the demand for excellence in personal appearance. Discriminatory as the statement may appear, there is no place in juvenile police work for the sloppy officer, or for a person with offensive habits.

The temperament of the juvenile officer is a crucial area of concern. No police personnel can hope to be effective with youth if they allow the statements or actions of juveniles to cause them to react negatively. One cannot become upset because of the follies of youth. Juveniles will purposely bait officers, and at times in such a manner that only the strongest willed person would be capable of retaining composure. To over react is fatal error and will negate the officer's effectiveness, and on some occasions will place him in a nonfunctioning position.

No officer should be assigned to juvenile work who has either stated or demonstrated no interest toward that area of specialization. While interest itself is not a convincing reason for placement, it is a consideration when combined with other attributes and backgrounds. The author knows of several instances where personnel were assigned to juvenile units after stating their total opposition toward such service. The outcomes in each case resulted in a loss of effectiveness within the unit. Chance probably kept a scandel situation from becoming a reality. This type of arbitrary police management not only disregards the demands of police service, but it also places the resisting officer and others in weakened positions.

The desire to work with youth in a most frustrating and demanding situation should be evident within the interest concept. It is not enough to want to *help kids*. While there is much self-satisfaction in police juvenile work, the nature of the task precludes the assignment of the starry-eyed or the displaced recreational worker.

It would be hoped that the intelligence of the juvenile officer would be a recognized criterion. This qualification is directly related to the nature of the position, and the demand for an assimilation of a large amount of knowledge in an on-the-job encounter. This position requires an insight into human behavior and calls for the use of very broad judicial as well as ministerial powers. The lasting effects upon the juvenile, and consequently the community, are potentials that support this criterion.

The constellation of attributes that has been outlined are not hard and fast rules, but each should be given consideration in respect to its effect upon the total outcome of the program and the ramifications relating to personal strengths and limitations affecting the individual officer.

Educational Background

Certainly the day of the officer without an adequate formal education is in the process of being supplanted by an era in which more and more individuals will be found to enter the service with high school and some college preparation. Many police agencies are recruiting college trained personnel, and some departments have made a certain amount of college work or a degree required prerequisities for appointment to the service.

The demands of the juvenile enforcment enterprise are so extensive as to subject this area of specialization to an educational requirement. While the minimum may remain high school graduation, the optimum is most certainly a baccalaureate degree. Thus, the officer who has attained the four-year-degree in the behavioral sciences or a related field should be given preference for the juvenile assignment.[1] This criterion should be sought at all times, even if it is not always attained.

In lieu of the four-year-degree, educational beckgrounds of either the continuation of formal educational attainment or the holding of a two-year associate degree should take precedence. It is important to stress the effort and individual initative that is displayed by persons who are continuing their formal education in conjunction with their regular work experience. These individuals should not be overlooked.

The subject matter pursued within any college program is a vital consideration for juvenile specialization. Particular areas of educational emphasis offer better backgrounds for the type of work to be performed than do others. The department should make a full examination of the relationship between subject emphasis and the juvenile role prior to making a decision based upon the educational background of the individual. As an example, some police science courses are so traditionally police-oriented that such preparation would place a minor emphasis upon juvenile enforcement related courses. Many of these programs have curriculums that deal only with the procedural aspects of juvenile work, and provide little or no education in the area of behavioral sciences.

The desire upon the part of the individual to pursue both formal and informal avenues of preparation after receiving a juvenile assignment is a part of the considerations necessary in the assessment of the educational background. The static or self-satisfied individual is not desirable.

Professional Background

The thrust of this writing categorically demands that the police juvenile officer be a policeman first. This contention presupposes active and successful police experience *prior* to entry into the juvenile enforcement enterprise.

To begin with, police juvenile work requires excellence in the techniques of investigation. These techniques are best acquired through the patrol function, if the opportunity for full-time investigative assignment has not occurred. The patrol service is the training ground for police officers. This is where police officers learn the subtleties of their trade. Truly professional police personnel have experienced the lessons of the street in the classroom of the patrol car.

It is true that an individual could be brought into police service with the intention of later assigning that person to juvenile work, and first placing him in a patrol situation. However, that patrol situation should amount to more than a few weeks or several months. The patrol apprenticeship for police juvenile officers is so important that to circumvent it is a disservice to the juvenile program and the officer.

A police juvenile enterprise that can be carried on by hiring directly from nonenforcement sources is only partially meeting the overall objectives of police juvenile work. Such persons are often hired on the basis of a degree or some other requirement that the police manager feels cannot be met within the existing ranks of the agency. At one time there may have been some validity to this observation, but with the present numbers of qualified personnel in or entering police service, the original need has been replaced. Therefore, it is strongly recommended that juvenile officers be assigned that duty after first gaining necessary general police experience.

The utilization of individuals with general police experience does place a burden upon the overall selection process. In order to have competent juvenile officers, the level of competency at the entrance stage of general service must be sound. The recruitment and selection of general personnel is a vital area of police management. The better these personnel practices are performed, the better the total police function. Quality police personnel will greatly reduce the difficulties encountered in the selection of juvenile officers.

Other considerations in the area of professional background includes additional police assignments that will tend to transfer skills and knowledge into the juvenile enterprise. As examples, an officer with narcotics experience, in addition to other qualifications, would greatly enhance the juvenile operation during this period of excessive drug contact by youth. An officer, who in addition to his other merits has served in an identification bureau or who is familiar with some of the technical aspects of investigation, would be an asset. The ability to utilize the agency's camera equipment would be helpful.

Previous nonpolice experience that might be found to be beneficial would include tenure in a casework position, or as a correctional staff member. Persons with previous experience working with youth at the recreational level may bring to the juvenile assignment proper attitudes and the desired temperments. Former teaching experience may be an important factor to consider as additional professional experience. Any previous experience working directly with youth should be weighed in its relationship to the juvenile enforcement task, along with actual police work. But, successful and varied police experience remains the most significant professional background for the juvenile officer.[2]

THE SELECTION OF THE JUVENILE OFFICER

Juvenile work is one area of police operation in which no formal or informal political influences should be allowed to affect personnel selection. It is a sad commentary that many police agencies are still suffering the difficulties attendant to political interference. Hopefully, time will be on the side of the police service, and the abuses of political power influence will diminish.

Not only should the police resist external political pressure relating to the selection of juvenile officers, but the normal internal politics emanating as a result of the informal structure and relationships of the organization should not be allowed to play a part in juvenile personnel selection.

Some police agencies may test for specialized positions, but this practice is normally restricted to larger departments. Testing as a part of a selection process is a difficult procedure at best. Most police testing leaves much to be desired, and the knowledge in the field of police testing is far from complete. In order to effectively examine individuals, a measuring device that will test for the desired qualifications must be available. For the most part, the standardized tests that are available through various public and private outlets are not easily adaptable to local laws, procedures, problems, and conditions. For purposes of juvenile officer testing, the use of a subjective essay examination is recommended. The recommendation for essay testing is based upon the need to adapt the device to local conditions, the requirement of testing understanding and application as well as knowledge, and the report writing requirements of the juvenile operation. The essay examination may be locally designed and administered by the police or the local personnel department. It has one drawback, and that is in reference to the difficulty of scoring the examination.[3]

As a part of the selection process, an oral examination should be held. The oral board should be no less than three, nor more than five. It should include a police executive from another department, a juvenile commander not a member of the testing agency, and if at all possible, the juvenile court judge of the local jurisdiction.

The oral board concept should be employed, whether or not a written examination is given.

Prior to any testing program, all nonsupervisory sworn personnel should be granted the opportunity to make a formal application for consideration for a juvenile assignment. Any criteria the departments may select would reduce the number of officers eligible to make application. The application should be accompanied by a written statement in which the officer sets forth the reasons that he feels are important for his consideration.

After the applications have been collected, the chief administrative officer of the department, or the personnel officer if the agency has one, should review the material. The applications should become a part of the officer's personnel file. Each application should be given weight in the final consideration for the assignment.

After the testing program, a list of eligible officers should be submitted to the police manager in the rank order of the outcomes as recorded by the examination process. It should be noted that such an order will occur on the basis of the oral evaluation, even if a written examination is not used.

The selection should be from the top three candidates, at the discretion of the department head.

Departments that are still adhering to mere assignment to juvenile specialization should discontinue that practice and move toward the use of a neutral oral evaluation team as the minimum means of effective selection.

Police agencies should strive to stay abreast of new selection methods, as such procedures or devices are within the field of personnel management.

Rank

It is the practice of many police agencies to assign ranks, normally associated with supervision, to specialized personnel. This is a practice that should be discontinued. There is no reason for a juvenile officer to be given a line rank, *unless his duties also include the supervision of personnel.* The commander of a juvenile unit rightfully should be ranked. In large units where there must be a chain of command and the administrative problems falling under the concept of span of control require it, subordinate first-line supervisory ranks may also be needed. Generally, the commander of the juvenile unit will be the only person involved in direct supervision of personnel and is the only line rank necessary.

Some of the reasons for line rank assignment to specialized personnel that have been stated in the past revolve around the assumption that when two or more specialists are working together, one must supervise; or, that when a specialist enters the picture with regular line personnel who have called for his assistance, the rank concept attached to the specialist will eliminate control problems in the field. These and other arguments in support of line ranking of specialized officers are really rationalizations for higher pay.

There is nothing keeping a police agency from assigning premium pay to specialized classifications. Problems do occur, however, when specialized officers are given ranks, such as sergeant, in order to obtain more pay for the position. Some of the problems are as follows:

1. *Line rank assignments to specialized personnel attacks rank integrity.* When a nonsupervising position is assigned a line rank designation, the integrity of the supervising ranks has been attacked, and the worth of the rank has been lessened.

2. *Line rank assignment for specialization delimits reassignment.* The specialist may not work out well, or may grow stale over an extended period within the special area. Reassignment becomes a problem, and often such persons are reassigned to line positions that are not supervisory in nature. Thus, a sergeant is no more than a working patrolman. Some specialized personnel would make poor supervisors, and their reassignment would hinder the line operation. The problem may be alleviated by providing for premium pay for juvenile officers on the basis of the type of work they perform. Reassignment to a line unit may occur any time, and the premium pay remains with the position of juvenile officer. This way there is no juggling of personnel in an attempt to fit a former specialist with line rank into a line operation.

In answer to the need for rank in order to supervise within the juvenile operation when two officers are working together, this function is a team approach and will result in an informal self-supervising method being an outgrowth of the association. When a specialist is called to assist a line unit, supervision problems can be handled as a matter of departmental policy.

THE FUNCTION OF THE JUVENILE OFFICER

The juvenile officer functions as an auxiliary to the line. He furnishes line units specialized assistance. Juvenile officers are not a part of the line function.

The general responsibility of the juvenile officer involves the investigation of all matters in which a juvenile is either a *suspect* or a *victim*, with the exception of the crime of murder or actual kidnap (the latter to be distinguished from child stealing, normally a family affair; the victim is not the child, but the parent or guardian who has legal custody. There is no intent to harm the child, and seldom does any harm come to the child).

The juvenile operation should be viewed as basically a follow-up function, with the juvenile officer assuming an investigation at some stage beyond the preliminary police effort. In medium and small departments, this cannot always be a hard and fast rule, but as much as possible, a preliminary determination by a line unit should precede referral to the juvenile program.

The concept of preventative patrol should no longer be more than a cursory function of the juvenile unit. Juvenile officers, when they have the time, may engage in such activity, but more often than not their efforts will be required on a follow-up basis. Time limitations and juvenile manpower resources reduce the opportunity for active patrolling as a regular function. Preventative patrols should be carried on by special enforcement units or the regular patrol division. Juvenile officers should assist the line by providing juvenile training and requesting the line to perform patrol functions in areas of recognized need.

The juvenile officer will be required to represent the department in situations involving custody matters. In these situations, which are civil matters, the police should move carefully and only in response to court sanctions.

Liaison between the police and the juvenile court process should be maintained by the juvenile personnel. Thus, general police officers should refrain from contacts with that group, other than the requirements of booking offenders and appearing in court as witnesses.

One of the major responsibilities of the juvenile officer is the determination of what action to take on the many minor offenses that are committed by youth. This implies that a referral system will be utilized between the line units and the juvenile operation. It serves to screen cases for juvenile court actions. It provides a means for police referral to other community agencies. It functions as the basis for follow-up on minor cases. It insures that juveniles with extensive records will come to the attention of the juvenile unit, and that they will not be passed up or overlooked by the line. The referral system provides the juvenile unit with a broad exposure to the actions of youth, while retaining a realistic workload.

As a part of the referral system, the juvenile officer will encounter many situations in which he will be required to offer some direction and counseling to either or both the youth and the parents. These are matters in which the juvenile officer sees no need for further action, and in which he releases the child back to the parents. Such a release cannot take place without some words of advice.

Juvenile operations require a variety of investigative experiences and actions. Offenses range from crime of a serious nature being committed by youth to the protection of the underprotected child. Investigations for juvenile purposes may be more complex than normal adult investigations, but the skills required are the same, with an emphasis upon interrogation.

Things that are not a part of the juvenile officer's role relate to direct involvement in recreational programs, or quasi-probationary activities.

HOW CASES COME TO THE ATTENTION OF THE JUVENILE OFFICER

Most cases coming to the attention of the juvenile officer should result from referrals by line units. There are exceptions to this rule, and one of the most important are cases arising from the school situation. Since the schools operate during the same hours as the juvenile unit, and since the relationship between the schools and the juvenile officer are usually on a personal basis, many cases will be directed to the juvenile unit from the school authorities.

Because juvenile officers normally work in plain clothes and unmarked vehicles, they are in the position to answer calls from the schools without creating problems that will upset the school routine. Therefore, the juvenile personnel should respond to these calls.

Juvenile personnel will encounter "walk-in" cases, where the parent or the youth makes direct contact with the juvenile unit. The contact has been made in order to obtain the special police assistance, and to forestall uniformed police from entering the picture. These obvious wishes should be honored, and the juvenile officer should respond.

There will be occasions when the juvenile officer discovers an offense on the basis of his own action. The fact that he is a police officer demands that he take the appropriate action to deal with the situation. Juvenile specialization does not reduce general police obligations.

When line units are discovered to be referring matters to the juvenile officer, or calling for his assistance in situations that the line is obviously capable of handling to completion, a sign post has appeared indicating that the line is relying too heavily upon the specialist. This is an administrative situation. The juvenile officer should report the matter to his superior and the commander of the juvenile unit should take steps to remedy the situation.

THE ROLE OF THE POLICEWOMAN

The use of women as juvenile officers is an established practice. Juvenile work provides one of the main sources for female involvement in police work. There are, however, some discouraging developments relating to the policewoman in juvenile work. These include the restriction of training, limitations relating to case assignments, and the failure to require the female officer to be properly equipped for duty.

Some concessions must be made to the female in police work. One of the major problems faced by these women is the loss of their feminine identity among their fellow officers. The policewoman must remain a feminine entity to be effective.

A woman assigned as a sworn officer to the juvenile unit should be selected on the basis of an exhaustive selection process, exceeding that of the male officer if she is to be hired directly into police service as a juvenile officer. If there are policewomen within the department, they should be considerd for any juvenile assignment on the basis of their police experience.

The policewoman should be provided the same training opportunities as the male officer. They should be required to attain scores in training that are the same requirements for the male personnel. No woman should be excused from firearms or defensive tactics training. If she is not capable of undergoing the training, she should be dismissed or reassigned.

Cases involving females as suspects, dependent child cases, and misdemeanor offenses perpetrated by young males up to age fifteen, should all be subject to assignment to the policewoman.

A policewoman must be capable of driving the official vehicle. She should know her geographical area as well as the male officers. She should be able to make arrests and transport prisoners. Her knowledge of the law should be on a par with her male counterparts.

When on duty, and off duty if policy so requires, the female officer should be equipped with a police sidearm and handcuffs. If MACE is used, the policewoman should also have that equipment available.

No differential in pay should exist. Line supervisory ranks should only be assigned, if the woman is to perform supervisory functions.

The policewoman must be capable of working alone, as manpower needs and caseloads will preclude her having a male companion every time she goes into the field.

The policewoman can be an asset to juvenile work, but a female officer is *not a necessity*. Male officers can adequately handle female juveniles, if the department policy is adhered to on a strict basis.

The female in juvenile work tends to maintain a long period of tenure. Because she is one of a few, there is a tendency to allow her privileges that are not afforded male officers. This action will lead to morale problems within the juvenile unit. It is imperative that the female function as a police officer. Unless she does, her position cannot be justified.

NOTES AND REFERENCES

1. The newly created Youth Services Division of the Metropolitan Police Department, Nashville, Tennessee established a minimum of a four year degree for incoming officers.
2. John P. Kenney and Don G. Pursuit: *Police Work With Juveniles*, 3rd ed. Springfield, Thomas, 1967, p. 94.
3. In 1969, the Fresno (California) Police Department administered an essay examination for the position of Deputy Chief of Police. This method was considered highly successful.

Chapter Ten

CONTROVERSY AND CONCERN

AREAS OF CONTROVERSY

THERE is no doubt that much controversy permeates the field of the juvenile law enforcement endeavor. Part of this confusion arises from the failure to define the term delinquency with an acceptable and precise meaning. The variety of legislation aids in widening the diversity of opinion. The influence and control emanating from other disciplines establishes philosophies and provides direction affecting the law enforcement role, but without law enforcement's participation in the determination of objectives. Police failure to grasp the desires of societal intervention in the lives of youth, and the effects of police traditionalism are factors in perpetuating controversies.

Within the more controversial areas of police juvenile enforcement, the police should begin to develop guidelines of their own that suit the enforcement goals involved. These guidelines should be acceptable to both the police and the public, and whatever results occur should be subject to evaluation and change.

Several major controversial areas will be presented. There is no presumption that a finality of answers will accompany the presentation, but it is hoped that certain basic principles will evolve that will lend themselves to future police application. The intent of the author is to decrease the diversity of police opinion on these matters, with an eventual unification of philosophy as an ultimate outcome.

Should a Juvenile Be Fingerprinted?

Many individuals violently oppose the fingerprinting of juvenile offenders. Various states have enacted legislation prohibiting the fingerprinting of a juvenile, unless by juvenile court order.

200

The fingerprinting of juveniles is a question that usually provokes heated debate. In those jurisdictions without state laws prohibiting the fingerprinting process, police policy is usually the guide. Some agencies have policies that permits the fingerprinting of all children taken into custody, while other departments restrict the use with specific types of crimes having the control.[1]

Opponents of fingerprinting juveniles tend to be from outside the police field.[2] Arguments against the procedure revolve around the stigma that is attached to fingerprinting by the public, inferring that there is a strong recognition of the criminal element of the procedure. An extension of this argument is that the fingerprints may be a factor in the juvenile's future attempts to obtain employment or receive security clearances.[3]

Several authorities point out the use of the act of being fingerprinted as a status symbol of offending youth.[4]

The majority of opposition, however, tends to agree with the concept of strict control over juvenile fingerprinting with the Juvenile Court having the discretionary power to allow or forbid its occurrence. This concept is well reflected in some state laws.

Although opposed to indiscriminate fingerprinting of juveniles, the views expressed at the federal level take a more middle ground approach. In one of the more widely read publications, the concept of limited police utilization of fingerprints without severe external controls has been advanced.[6]

It is interesting that the same objections relating to stigma were first utilized in opposition to the fingerprinting of adults earlier in the century. The alleged traumatic experience supposedly undergone by a juvenile offender due to fingerprinting has never been empirically studied. It would seem that the fingerprinting trauma potential would not approach the trauma potential involved in the police action, juvenile court appearance, or incarceration. Furthermore, the attempts to delimit the fingerprinting of juveniles seems to have been directed toward the police. Certainly, institutions under the control of state correctional agencies utilize fingerprinting on a wholesale basis. The institutional procedure has never been attacked on a serious level.

This seems to indicate another area of the lack of confidence of other disciplines in the police. This failure to extend the same confidence to police personnel as has been extended to correctional agents may have some merit; however, the track record at juvenile correctional institutions is generally less outstanding than the police record of public service.

Those who would assign the authority to allow fingerprinting of juveniles to the juvenile court usually desire this authority to be used on an individual case basis. It seems this type of procedure is too constricting, and it is one that places an extra burden upon both the police and the juvenile court.

An acceptable approach must be developed that will satisfy the needs of the police and which will also protect the juvenile from indiscriminate practices. Recognition of the importance of fingerprints as a means of identifying the individual should be held at the forefront of any attempts to establish legitimate application of the procedure. Included in the concept of identification are several important considerations.

1. *Fingerprints are important evidence in certain types of crimes.* Fingerprints are not usually utilized as an important investigative factor in many offenses. This eliminates the need to utilize wholesale fingerprinting of juveniles. Fingerprinting should be based upon the type of offense and the effectiveness of fingerprints as an investigative tool in the event the particular youth recommits that type of crime. Fingerprints should not be used in cases of incorrigibility or other delinquent acts that would not constitute a crime if committed by an adult.

2. *Fingerprints can protect the innocent.* Especially in crimes of secret, such as burglaries, the fingerprints of the juvenile may be compared to those found at the scene and result in an immediate elimination of the youth as a suspect. This would also eliminate the need for a police contact with that youth relating to that particular incident. One other thing the existence of fingerprints can do is to serve as a means of identifying a deceased person. With the increased numbers of juveniles who are leaving home and "dropping out," the likelihood of the need for post mortum identification is greater.

3. *All juveniles do one thing that an adult can no longer do— iuveniles become adults.* There is no doubt that a large amount

of crime is perpetrated by youth. By the time a juvenile has reached the upper limits of the statutory designation separating him from adult criminal action, the juvenile may already have confirmed his further lawlessness. Most juvenile offenders tend to remain in their own locality for an indefinite period after leaving the juvenile stage. The lack of fingerprint records in those instances where the youth has established a history of criminal acts in which fingerprints are important investigative tools denudes the police of a very important device.

4. *The increasing demand to lower the age of majority requires new perspectives toward personal responsibility.* Not only is the new concept of the voting rights of the 18-year-old becoming a reality, but the desire to extend to the youthful population full rights of majority is gaining fast acceptance. It is apparent that the total area of youthful offenders needs reexamination. The drive to emancipate the upper youthful age limit should be included in the development of fingerprint practices.

The author would recommend the discretionary use of fingerprints by the police in situations involving crimes where the fingerprint is of investigative or evidential importance, dependent upon the evaluation of the *modus operandi*. This police discretion would apply to all youth who had attained the fourteenth birthday. The fingerprints should be restricted to permanent retention by the local police, with no copies being forwarded to either state or federal central files. In those situations where the age of the youngster was below fourteen, it is recommended that the discretionary power be placed with the juvenile court.

The reason for the permanency of the police fingerprint file for juvenile offenders is the need to protect the integrity of the police records system. The records system is already suffering from numerous attempts at expungement. If this trend continues, police records will become extremely vulnerable.

Should the Police Be Involved in Counselling?

The police and other disciplines that are involved with juvenile problems seem to be at odds concerning the police counselling role.[2] Police juvenile officials are in general agreement that the police should not become involved in long term remedial counselling efforts. There is some misunderstanding on the part of police administrators and the members of other disciplines as to what constitutes counselling. Some police administrators have interpreted the act of a juvenile officer providing the youth and the parent with information of an advisory nature as synonymous with treatment.

It is true that in some instances where the delinquent tendencies are not formidable such advice by a police officer may be all that is required to make a change to a desirable behavioral outcome. This by no means indicates treatment in the sense that the term is professionally applied.

The concept of counselling, as utilized by police juvenile officers, is in the term's broadest semantic application. It is not the narrowly perceived meaning that is understood by the behavioral scientists. The police are not attempting to step out of their role and into the function of another area for which they have no training.

Some people forget that the police do act as a *court of first instance* in many of their functions.[7] This task is personified in the police juvenile officer role, for it is that officer's obligation to not only investigate the offense, but to also seek to make a judicial determination for the purposes of the disposition. In performing this function, the juvenile officer must often decide a course of action other than a referral to the juvenile court.

The majority of police-juvenile contacts are disposed of without further action. This system requires the juvenile officer to explain the meaning of the law, its application in the particular incident, and to provide the youth with some measure of insight into his own actions. One authority has indicated that one successful means of therapy for juveniles has never been so labeled.[8] The act of making a juvenile come to grips with the reality of his own behavior and its effect upon others is a part of the juvenile officer's function. The juvenile must be made to see that the law has been impartially applied, and that *his* actions have brought him into conflict with the legal sanctions of society. He must recognize that he is a part of that society, and that he has the same obligation for self-policing his behavior as do others. These are some of the concepts that should be imparted by the juvenile officer. Whether or not this is counselling per se is not the issue. The issue is the impact that this knowledge may have upon a juvenile's future behavior, and the experience image of the youth-officer contact.

Should Physical Force Be Utilized in a Police Juvenile Contact?

Many police officers are in fear of using force in a juvenile situation. Caution and logical discretion should be used by any police officer in a situation where he believes he is dealing with a juvenile, but this requirement does not preclude the use of necessary or reasonable force.

Certain factors should be taken into consideration. The age, size, and sex of the juvenile have a direct bearing upon the validity of a decision to use force. Whether the juvenile is armed, and with what object he is armed, are important factors. Does the youth represent an immediate threat to the life of the officer or others or is the juvenile apparently capable of inflicting immediate great bodily injury? The seriousness of the offense would relate to whether the juvenile should be subjected to force to affect an arrest.

Officers should be aware that a youth of the middle teen years, who has attained a mature physical size, cannot be granted immunity from physical force on the basis of his age alone. This statement is not intended to evoke excessive force, but it does indicate that if a youth becomes involved in an escalating situation in which reasonable force is necessary, the juvenile status is no longer the criterion governing the police decision to use the force.

Should the Juvenile Offender Be Handcuffed?

It would seem that the same factors of consideration relating to the use of reasonable force would affect any decision to handcuff a juvenile. To pursue this question, one must first determine the reason for the use of handcuffs. Handcuffs are intended for one purpose and that is *temporary restraint.*

If restraint is the purpose of handcuffs, then it would appear that handcuffs should only be used in situations where such restraint is necessary. This is obviously an oversimplified generalization; but no more so than the converse contention that all individuals arrested should be handcuffed.

Limiting the presentation to the juvenile offender, it would be recommended that a youth should be handcuffed anytime it appears that temporary restraint is in order. Police policy should neither demand that all juveniles taken into custody be handcuffed, nor that no juveniles should be so restrained. Individual officer judgment must make the determination on the basis of the circumstances.

Handcuffing a female juvenile might be just as legitimate a police procedure as any other handcuffing incident, depending upon the situation. Some juveniles may require handcuffing before leaving a school situation. Others may have to be restrained at a public place or in their own home in order to insure the safety of the youth, the officer, or others.

Handcuffing may be the key to reducing the number of subjects who are able to escape from custody before incarceration. Officers should recognize the seriousness of the outgrowth of events subsequent to a youth getting away. Most often, the juvenile will increase the difficulties he is already facing as a result of fleeing from custody. The very act of getting away may precipitate a youthful action that will lead to the death of the juvenile or another person.

Wholesale handcuffing is not necessary, but good officer discretion is needed to make the decision of when to handcuff. As in the case of the use of physical force, the determining factor for handcuffing should not be the age of the individual, but rather, the circumstances.

Should the Polygraph Be Utilized as an Investigative Tool in Juvenile Cases?

The polygraph, or lie detector as it is more commonly termed, can be an effective investigative device. There is some question of its value in juvenile cases, and some persons within the field of juvenile enforcement disagree with its use entirely. The question is academic for the majority of smaller agencies, as many of them have no resource in this area. It is true that many state agencies, such as the California Bureau of Criminial Identification and Investigation and the Illinois Bureau of Investigation, offer polygraph services to local police. It is also true that these services are spread desperately thin and very often require advanced appointments that are unrealistic. As a generality, the polygraph is not a tool that is often used in juvenile cases. This is more from the lack of available examiners than from the existence of policy.

There are some instances in which the polygraph has a definite investigative value in juvenile work. Many of these relate to situations in which the juvenile is making a false report of an offense in order to cover other actions (usually of a noncriminal nature) in which he has participated, and which have been forbidden by his parents or other personal authority figures.

The problem in these types of occurrences lies in the fact that the parents of the *victim* usually have been convinced by their child that the offense alleged to have been perpetrated against the youth has actually happened. The youth, in his effort to distract the parents, has concocted a story that removes him from the role of offender and has placed him in the position of being viewed a victim. The parental suspicion index has been effectively neutralized, due to their concern for the welfare of their child and the safety of others. They may be outraged that such an incident could happen.

Seldom does the child intend for the matter to be reported to the police. It is merely a convenient technique *to get the heat off* at home. When it is reported, the so-called victim will normally attempt to establish the veracity of the story to the officers.

An observant police officer may readily see through the fabrication, but the parental concern will not be alleviated until the child makes the admission. Sometimes this is very difficult for the youth to perform. In a similar situation, one would not be surprised to find an adult who would have the same admission problems.

The polygraph has validity in other forms of juvenile investigations, but it is within the scope of the fabricated story as told by an alleged victim that the author has been highly successful in utilizing the machine.

The polygraph results should be a guide to the investigating officer, even though the information is not admissible in court. A good operator will be able to detect signs of deception under normal circumstances. With juveniles these circumstances are subject to many variables. The most obvious variable is the age of the subject. As a general rule, fourteen years is near the minimum age of effectiveness; however, the author's experience includes the use of the polygraph effectively with a twelve-year-old. It should be added that the situation was of a unique nature or the twelve-year-old would not have been submitted to the procedure.

Attitudes sets are another variable. The youth may have a strongly developed morality toward sex. The very word utilized in a polygraph question may indicate a response that could be misinterpreted as being a deception. This variable can only be countered by an experienced operator.

In no instance should the polygraph become a means of short-cutting an investigation, nor should it become an investigative crutch. It can be relied upon in cases where it is an effective tool. In order to be effective, the investigation must have produced sufficient information for the officers to insure that the operator is provided with enough knowledge to perform a valid test.

In working out the arrangement for the polygraph in a juvenile case, the officer should observe all of the individual's rights. Included within the procedure should be the act of consulting with the parents prior to the test being administered. In the event the parents will not give consent, no test should occur unless ordered by a court of competent jurisdiction. This should be a policy rule, regardless of the willingness of the youth to submit.

AREAS OF CONCERN

It is difficult to attempt to evaluate the areas of concern in the juvenile enforcement program, for it could easily be postulated that the totality of the problem is a concern. There do seem to be some current issues that have caught the imagination of both the public and the police. In addition, there seem to exist other concerns that have not received the same widespread attention. This section will address several topics that will fall within each stage of societal interest.

The Television Media

Attempts have been made to establish the effects of television viewing upon the youthful population. The results are inconclusive at this time, and the opinions tend to be polarized. It is not the intention of this writing to editorialize upon the effects of violence and sex as viewed through the medium of television, upon the youthful population. Rather, this section shall address the subtleties of the media's influence.

There must be an axiom within the television industry that demands social saturation. The evidence of this is inflicted upon the viewing audience daily. Social issues are integrated cleverly into a story. During the presentation of the unraveling of the plot, the abortion issue, the homosexual issue, the drug issue, the live together-not marry concept, and a host of other social questions are individually presented on a show by show basis. On one network the kindly doctor is grappling with the antimarriage youth cult, and before the week is over the same theme is utilized by the police shows, the lawyer shows, and possibly a few more physician shows. Each network and each channel has its opportunity to act as a vehicle for social change.

Some difficulties exist within the television enterprise in its attempt to effect social change. To begin with, the figures who are cast in the television program as physicians, lawyers, or police do not portray the reality of the roles as such roles exist in real life. The public is presented with a distorted view of the social problem. They are shown that a controversy exists, but the main character of the series carries the positive image and usually is a person who exhibits tremendous insight into human needs. The actor playing the role that supports the status quo is either cast as an unreasonable person, or otherwise demonstrates his personal inability to be an effective spokesman for the old line.

That the presentations of such issues within series plays tend to run in cycles is as apparent as the television screen itself. That the issues are presented out of context and from a short-sighted perspective may be attributable to time elements and dramatic license. The media obviously desires to overcome this last criticism by utilizing saturation to demonstrate to the viewing audience a concept of universality that may not exist.

To the adolescent mind, already in a state of extreme confusion in the life task of developing a self-identity, television is a one way communication system that requires no audience interplay. The social controversy presentation is intended to capitalize upon the passive receptive mood of youth, while they are captivated by the media in a state of nonparticipation. While the viewer's passive state exists among adults, the social consciousness of the issue is being aimed directly at the youth. Seldom are parents wise enough to discuss the false reality of the program portrayal, for the television set has become an electronic babysitter within our society. Because of this usage, a critique of the program and the issues probably does not occur within the family. As a famous authority stated in reference to the youthful sympathetic acceptance of the story "Romeo and Juliet," youth had failed to grasp the reality of the situation. That reality was Romeo's impatience and impetuousness.[9] The complaint is not with the presentation of social issues, but rather with the manner in which they are transmitted.

One has but to watch the television commercials to note the subtle manner by which the media exposes the audience to altering child rearing practices. The now famous "don't cause a good boy to go wrong" advertisement attempted to reduce the incidence of car theft, but did so by intimating that the so-called good boy would be *caused* to steal a vehicle if the owner left the keys in the ignition. Now, leaving keys in the ignition is certainly an invitation to theft, but no car theft victim should be made to *walk* the streets with a sense of guilt because someone else's child stole the victim's automobile.

Another example may be discovered in the group of commercials that have carried the message of futility or resignation within the parental role. These are the "what can a father or mother do" commercials. The child leaves the house without brushing his teeth, and the mother exclaims to 100 million television viewers, "what can a mother do!" These approaches to child rearing reinforce both youthful and parental conceptions of the inability to take constructive action.

There are those persons who contend that the present youthful generation is better informed than past generations, and they point to the television media as an example of the broadest informative device within our society. In response to the contention of an informed youth because of television, the question must be asked, what adverse effects does television have upon the same youth, relative to violence, sex, drug abuse and other current problems? If it is purported to have no adverse effects, then why would the same media be so effective at informing with understanding? In other words, if children can view violence on television without having their attitudes and behavior affected, what would cause the same system of conveyance to be such an effective method of transmitting positive principles that the positive ones would be the only facts assimilated and affecting youthful behavior? Could it be that the television media transmits both positive and negative motivaters effectively? Or, could it be that because of the passive receptor role of the viewer, little or no motivation of behavior occurs? Logic would seem to dictate that it cannot be a positive transmitter only, in the present state of the media.

Drug Abuse

A most complex question affecting the very soul of the society is involved in the problem of drug abuse. Not many years ago, illicit narcotics and serious drug abuse were of small concern to the juvenile officer. Few youth beyond certain areas of major population centers were involved directly with the illicit drug traffic. Major problems in those days were restricted to glue inhalation and the consumption of alcoholic beverages.

Drug abuse by juveniles and older youth has increased dramatically during the past several years. In California during the period from 1960 through 1968, there was an astronomical increase of 1922.1 percent in juvenile drug violations. The 1969 figures were an increase of 121.9 percent over the figures for 1968.[10] These figures indicate the effects during the early blooming period of drug abuse. Since that time it has been estimated that in the neighborhood of 50 percent of the high school and college youth have experimented with some form of illicit drug.[11]

Available information dealing with the various types of narcotics and dangerous drugs is voluminous. Public educational programs are extensive. Research is being performed and results are being published. The drug issue is one of the most important law enforcement topics of national concern. The controversies surrounding the use of marijuana have reached both the federal and state legislative branches of government. The lessening of penalties for the possession or use of marijuana have been reduced at the federal level, and numerous states are following that procedure.[12]

Many programs are being attempted. Some rise and quickly fade from sight, while others are found to be centered in controversy over the program's very existence. Still, the drug abuse problem continues and the statistics swell.

The problem may have reached a critical stage in the recognition of the drug and heroin abuse existing within the military in Vietnam. More than 3600 service men sought help in the first quarter of 1971, while in Vietnam, for their dependency upon heroin.[13] This is heroin addiction: the ultimate in the loss of humanity to the pleasures of drugs.

What has still not been faced by this society is the challenge the youth have been yelling back at the opponents of drug usage. *What's the difference between our drug abuse and yours?* The answer can only be found in the term *legality*. This is a drug-oriented society. This fact must be faced and dealt with *before* there can be an effective solution to the drug problems of youth.

A noted authority on drug abuse was an early voice crying in the wilderness.[14] His message was simple, but also profound. It called for a realistic examination of the drug problem as it truly exists within our society. In order to do this, however, the established adult society must face facts that will not be easily admitted by its members. These facts relate to the purposeful self-poisoning of large segments of the population in acceptable fashion.

It is entirely possible that little effective progress can be made in trying to cope with the illicit drug problem while the legal intoxication of the public is sanctioned. Any society can be judged by its artifacts. At one time, jeweled snuff boxes were in vogue. Such items are now meaningful only to collectors. The gift counters of numerous stores are found laden with ornate pill boxes. Originally appearing as a feminine fashion, this hardware is now available in manly design.

The use of the most popular and acceptable pain killer has led medical authorities to warn against excessive bleeding as a side effect. [15] The numbers of individuals one encounters daily who are using either tranquilizers or stimulants may only be assumed; but usually these individuals are not prone to hide the facts of the usage. The reverse is true, and many tend to advertise the use of a prescribed drug.

Not only do the news media provide stories of death from the illicit drug activity, but incidents of the fatal effects of mixing perscription drugs with alcohol have become common place. The use of the word alcohol opens a Pandora's box. Certainly, most police officers are aware of the costs in human life and tragedy affected by the misuse of alcohol. Jails and penal institutions are filled with persons whose actions were percipitated by the use of alcohol. It is estimated that at least 50 percent of the annual traffic fatilities are directly attributable to intoxication. These annual figures reach proportions of about 50,000 lives. Such figures exceed the total losses in Vietnam. Yet, the national concern is limited when it is required to face these facts, as evidenced in the failure of many legislative attempts to use harsher means in dealing with drunk drivers.

The driving records of some individuals who are still officially sanctioned to be behind the wheel would cause one to blush if compared with a youthful experimental act of trying one marijuana cigarette.

The author does not condone illicit drug use. There is no attempt herein to lay the foundation for a plea to legalize the use of marijuana. Rather, the intent is to point out a social hypocrisy that is being thrown into the face of the adult world by the youth reared by the members of that world. The parent who is trying to lecture his child on the ills of drug abuse had better hide his cocktail glass until after the words have been spoken. The mother, using her "uppers" in the morning and her "downers" at night, should think twice before becoming involved in a discussion of drug abuse with her children.

Police officers should not allow themselves to over react to the drug problem. While it is a major concern, it should not be cause for reducing police effectiveness. Police personnel should be educated and provided with current knowledge regarding the effects of the various drugs and narcotics. When in contact with youth and other members of the society on the drug issue, factual information should be provided by the police. In the absence of facts, the police should remain mute. Fear tactics will not work. The approach should be as truthful as present knowledge can provide, and it should be low-keyed.

Actions the police should take include increased efforts toward the eradication of suppliers. This places a burden upon law enforcement, as it is much easier to arrest and convict a pusher for possession than it is for the sale. This distinction is not common knowledge outside of police circles, but in the face of legislative actions reducing penalties for the mere possession, the police now have an obligation to educate the public in the difficulties and various ramifications of narcotics investigation.

The police should show some leadership in legislative efforts. Rather than objecting to the lessening of penalties for first offender marijuana violators, police efforts should be directed toward the support of well-formulated legislation at the state and national levels. There is nothing inconsistent with present marijuana knowledge that would preclude lessening possession penalties for first offenders. However, police officials should be quite cautious of supporting such legislation when it also contains segments that would remove the record of the arrest. The police should strive to protect the integrity of the records system, and the expungement of the record of the first offender raises the question of how the police are to know whether an individual is or is not a first offender.[16]

In conjunction with first offender legislation for possession, the police should spearhead the development of such attempts along lines that would provide for a specific maximum amount to be possessed. If the amount in possession exceeds the maximum, the presumption should be that the intent of the possession is for sale or other distribution.

Law enforcement should support and encourage state and federal attempts to destroy or otherwise control the raw narcotics at their source. The drug corporations should be brought under stricter control, and law enforcement should not permit a state of immunity to exist in relation to druggists and physicians who are flagrantly violating drug control legislation.

The juvenile officer must be knowledgeable on the subject, not only pertaining to self-poisoning by means of illicit drugs, but also in relation to the total drug and alcohol orientation of the society. The old wives' tales about drug abuse cannot be effectual arguments with youth. The well-informed juvenile officer can be of real service in dispelling myths and bringing enlightenment to the community.

Juveniles and Sex

Within Maslov's hierarchy of human needs, sex looms as one of the drives requiring fulfillment at the primary level. Youth encounters sex in varying ways. Some of these encounters are quite normal and are sanctioned by the society, while others go beyond the limits of social toleration. In addressing the problems of youth and sex, the concept of promiscuity is but a small segment of a large picture.

Many juveniles are victims of sexual activity. A considerable amount of the victimizing occurs within their own homes and involves parents, stepparents, relatives, friends, or other siblings. Incestuous acts are not uncommon, nor are deviant sexual activities.

Sex play among young children may occur within a family unit or within a neighborhood and exist undetected for long periods. Adult sexuality is often directed toward both young boys and girls. The breadth of sexual offenses committed upon children can best be illustrated through the use of case histories. These are all situations encountered by the author while a working police officer. They all occurred within one jurisdiction. They are representative of similar offenses occurring regularly throughout the country.

While some come to the attention of the police, many go unreported for varying reasons. The true incidence of such offenses is not known.

The youngest child the author ever encountered who was a

victim of a sexual offense was a six-week-old male subject. The offense occurred while the child was in a crib awaiting admission to a public hospital, and it consisted of an act of oral copulation of the penis of the baby perpetrated by an adult male orderly who was a homosexual.

A number of incidents involving kindly old gentlemen in the victims' neighborhood have convinced the author of the regularity of such offenses. The victims may be male or female, depending upon the sexual orientation of the subject. Usually the children range in age from five or six years to puberty. There seems to be an attraction to the young based upon several assumptions on the part of the suspect. First is the ease of contact. Second appears to be the suspect's notion that the victims will not be acceptable witnesses. The third factor is psychological and does not fit all cases. There seems to be some cause for belief that the innocence of the child of tender years is an attraction.

Although unusual, the youngest child in the author's experience, who was acceptable to the court for purposes of testimony, was five years old.

One particularly sordid case was that of a young father, who was the son of a former deputy police chief, who had been committing incest with his daughter for several years until the incident came to the attention of the authorities when the child was eleven. The acts had occurred in the presence of the mother, who allegedly allowed the situation to persist out of fear of the father. This is not an uncommon situation. The so-called fear of the mothers in covering for the actions of an adult male spouse counterpart was never quite convincing, but to take action on a criminal basis would be extremely difficult.

The father of a girl who reported that he was committing incest upon her person while she was in her early teens was convicted, not of the incest, but for having an act of sexual intercourse with a cow. During the course of the investigation, his clothing with the results of the act of bestiality were discovered. He denied any implication with his daughter, but admitted the act with the animal.

There was a father who because of his acts became very friendly with the author. This man had over a dozen children, with the majority being girls. The girls were from two marriages, but some had been born to the first wife, after the man had married the second wife. The two wives were related, and by mutual agreement between the three adults, the first wife had continued to live in the home. The parental records given by the children in the school situation tended to result in much reporting to the authorities. Over a period of years, as the various daughters would reach the age when they would start dating, the stories would be told to the boyfriends or husbands. It developed that the father was continually being reported for having incestuous relations with his daughters. On one occasion, a daughter who had been married about one year admitted that the acts had occurred. It was the strongest case that was ever developed in the particular situation, but the statutes of limitations had expired and no action could be taken. In this instance, the father admitted the acts to the author. Further reports involving other daughters came to light in subsequent years. The father was arrested on so many occasions that at the time of the last arrest by the author, nothing would do but the author view the suspect's pet civet cat before transporting the man to jail. He never admitted the acts, and his denials were corroborated by the two women and other children still in the home. The situation probably still exists.

A whole neighborhood appeared to have been one big orgy in an investigation that began when the attentions of an adult male neighbor toward two twelve-year-old male twins were reported. It transpired that the twins were engaging in passive homosexual activity with the adult neighbor. These acts were in response to money and goods that the twins were receiving from the suspect. In the meantime, the twin's father was carrying on an affair with the homosexual's wife, and this was known both to the twins and the homosexual suspect. Other youth in the neighborhood were brought into the sexuality by the twins. Before the investigation was over, the twins and several other young males had admitted acts of sexual intercourse with chickens, dogs, a goat, and an attempt with a horse.

In light of these few examples, the focus upon normal sexual outlets being a part of youthful experimentation during the later teens does not appear as flagrant a series of violations. Boy-girl sexual relations during the later adolescent period are serious and the society suffers from the results of these relationships. The incidence of venereal disease among youth has reached epidemic proportions; and the problems attributable to the increase in unwed mother cases have potential long-term societal effects that cannot be measured at this time.

Some conclusions may be drawn about the totality of the juvenile sex problem. First, the types of activity involved range the whole of human sexuality. Second, the juvenile is victimized as often as being a suspect. Third, the long-term effects of juvenile sexuality have never been adequately measured, nor can prediction be made as to the effect upon the society of the future. Fourth, the unwed mother and illegitimacy is but a partial segment of a large problem, and both services and solutions are few.

For purposes of the police investigation, several facts are pertinent. The interviewing of the child-victim is a crucial point in the investigation. It must be done with care and tact, but the officer must go into detail to the extent that he will be satisfied that the event must have occurred in order for a victim of tender years to be able to describe the detail. The officer should be certain of the victim's ability to qualify as a court witness, for the majority of the cases involving young children as victims will require the testimony of the child at some stage of the proceedings. Most adult suspects will base their confidence upon the fact that the child will not testify against them when the "chips are down." It is this myth that will force the child's courtroom appearance. For this reason, no officer should tell parents of a sex victim that their child will not have to appear in court. The opposite is more often true.

Most children over six years of age will be able to handle the testimony well, and will qualify as witnesses.

In cases where the victim is involved in a statutory rape situation, the victim should also be handled as a suspect and considered for referral to the juvenile court.[17] The same rule should be applied to the juvenile passive partners in homosexual matters, after the so-called victim has passed puberty. The reason for the latter referral is to determine if the juvenile has or is developing homosexual tendencies, and to provide remedial treatment if such tendencies are detected.

In situations where the sexuality is occurring in the home situation, the victim should be immediately removed from the home and referred to the juvenile court under the conditions of a dependent ward.

Juvenile officers must be capable of handling the variety of sexuality represented and encountered in the course of the juvenile police enterprise. This demands that they be skilled interviewers and interrogators, and that they have a well-developed insight into the mechanisms of human behavior.

Abuse and Neglect

The subject of children and the suffering inflicted upon them, often by the very caretakers who are present to provide them with care and supervision, is a whole facet of the juvenile problem. It is a subject area so intense and sophisticated that the attempt to include it within police juvenile writings has not adequately covered the problem. The coverage of the topic as now presented will be little more than a superficial introduction. Police personnel who are encountering the problems of neglect and abuse are referred to several books that deal more explicitly with the total ramifications of the phenomenon.[18]

There are many children within our society who live in squalor or filth, and who are physically neglected to the extent of permanent emotional damage to their personalities. These children represent the broad spectrum of neglected children, and they are in dire need of the efforts of society to offer them protection. A high proportion of the delinquency encountered in later years may be attributable to the home conditions and the neglect experienced by the juvenile during the formative years.

Abuse of children involves an intentionally inflicted physical trauma by a human vehicle. Usually a family oriented situation, the *battered child syndrome* is a more limited, but also more severe area of child protection need.

Even in light of recent legislation in many states placing the responsibility for the investigation of matters of neglect and abuse in the hands of welfare agencies, the police still are involved. The main reason for this continued involvement is the around-the-clock availability of the police.

The need for police involvement has been strengthened by the U. S. Supreme Court decision causing the amount of proof in juvenile court to be equal to criminal cases.[19] This requires a knowledge of the rules of evidence and of criminal investigative techniques to be employed in relation to a juvenile court hearing. These are skills that the caseworker does not possess.

Not attacking the dimensions of the casework approach in child protection, most authorities in the area of child abuse are in agreement that many cases *require immediate intervention* in the parent-child relationship. This usually does not occur in casework situations.

The difficulty involved in the delegation of the responsibility for the protection of abused children to casework agencies from the outset of the report is the result that is being observed in police agencies across the country. That result is the further withdrawal of the police from this area of child protection, and the failure of law enforcement to include this problem as a priority area of juvenile enforcement. This action increases the police orientation toward the prosecution of the adult offender, rather than developing a police priority of protection of the child.

This is unfortunate, for the efforts to reduce the incidence of child neglect and abuse have not resulted in a significant lessening of the number of occurrences. The attention given this social phenomenon during the sixties seemingly has waned. This lack of publicity has possibly lulled many into a state of complacency. But, the facts are that the incidents continue to occur.

For the police juvenile officer, an awareness of the target of child abuse is important. While older children are subjected to physical abuse, the serious area exists within the child age group below three years. This is the area of the problem where the child is being attacked within his own environment, during a period when the child cannot physically escape nor verbally communicate the nature of the offense.

Since there is an effort on the part of other disciplines and professions to exclude the police from the information of such an occurrence, the police juvenile officer should be more alert than ever to the existence of such an incident.

Other than the parents or guardians, the only source of ultimate protection within the society is the juvenile court. If the cases are not coming to the attention of the court during the early abuse discovery period, the child is being left in a perilous situation. This failure to bring the situation of obvious abuse to the attention of the juvenile court is the result of the casework approach, and the desire to retain the family unit intact. While this latter end is good, it should not be maintained at the obvious risk of the victim.

The police have a definite role in the protection of children. It is best articulated through the efforts of enlightened juvenile police personnel.

The Neurologically Handicapped Child and Delinquency

Until very recently, the problems of the neurologically handicapped or brain damaged child were recognized by only a handful of experts. Even at this writing, the general public has little grasp of the existence of such persons, and the research and development in the professionl attempts to aid these individuals is somewhat scarce.

Basically and oversimplified, the brain damaged child suffers from the effects of an injury sustained after conception, and often after birth. In the more severe cases, the effects are quite noticable. In the majority of instances; however, the child develops along somewhat normal patterns, and is affected in subtle ways that may indicate that he is slow learner, but not mentally retarded.

The damage is neurological, which is to say that it is usually evidenced by an inability on the part of the child to properly transmit, interpolate, and act upon normal sensory messages. Early evidence of the handicap may first appear in the child's inability to perform simple motor control tasks, such as opening a door or tying shoes. As the child's age progresses upward, the parental tolerance of the inability to perform will diminish. This will create tense situations between the child and the parent.

These situations will be increased when the child enters school.

Unless the child is fortunate to have a very observant and well-prepared teacher, early grade problems may not be recognized as signs of the handicap. School manifestations of the handicap usually involve reading and writing skills, as well as mathematics. The child may read or spell words backwards. He may even make certain letters backwards. Thus, *was* is either read or written as *saw*, while dog may be interpreted as *bog*.

These mistakes are quite simple, but for the neurologically handicapped child, to overcome the errors may be close to an impossibility. To ever do so, the child must have the time necessary to develop new circuits by which to transmit messages and receive response signals. This cannot be taught, but must be the result of an unconscious compensation.

The simple mistakes, both at home and at school, usually persist for a number of years. The child's total life experience is one of error or failure to perform to the acceptable standards of parents, teachers, and classmates. The child may not mature as rapidly as others, but surprisingly enough, most of the neurologically handicapped children are quite enthusiastic about school and other tasks required of them during their early and middle childhood years. In fact, this enthusiasim is also another source of irritation between the child and the adult world. Many times, when asked to do something the willing child will rush off to perform, only to discover that he has not obtained all of the message or complete directions. After awhile, he may stand in the middle of a room, rather than return and ask what he was sent to get.

It is no wonder that an authority discovered a high incidence of later years delinquency among this group, a finding later tested by others.[20] As the child grows older, he has the same trouble in the perception process as earlier encountered in the reading situation. The child does not perceive information on input with the same degree of accuracy as normal children. This decreases the youth's ability to make effective judgments and decisions. Coupled with academic and other life style failures, the end result is a frustrated individual with a poor self-image, who is easily led, and may have developed other personality abnormalities. The opportunity for delinquency is immense.

One authority has placed the brain damaged school population at about 20 percent.[21] Assuming this were true, and that the total number of juveniles arrested in California were 277,649 in 1965, another writer has indicated that as high as 55,530 of those delinquents were within the brain damaged population upper limits.[22]

The mere possibility of such staggering numbers demands that the police juvenile officer expose himself to that information that will best develop the background by which the police juvenile enterprise will be able to assist in the treatment of these offenders within the juvenile justice system.

NOTES AND REFERENCES

1. Sophia M. Robinson: *Juvenile Delinquency.* New York, Holt, Rinehart, and Winston, 1960, pp. 216, 217.

2. *Municipal Police Administration,* 5th ed. Chicago, International City Managers Association, 1961, pp. 207-208, 229.

3. H. A. Block and F. T. Flynn: *The Juvenile Officer in America Today.* New York, Random House, 1956, p. 263.

4. John P. Kennedy and Dan G. Pursuit: *Police Work With Juveniles,* 3rd ed. Springfield, Thomas, 1967, p. 140.

5. Sheldon Glueck: *The Problem of Delinquency.* Boston, Houghton Mifflin Co., 1959, p. 540.

6. Richard A. Myren and Lynn D. Swanson: *Police Work With Children.* Washington, D. C., U. S. Department of Health, Education, and Welfare, 1966, p. 87.

7. John R. Ellington: *Protecting Our Children From Criminal Careers.* New York, Prentice-Hall, 1948, pp. 226-228.

8. Lee R. Steiner: *Understanding Juvenile Delinquency.* Philadephia, Chilton Press, 1960, p. 181.

9. Karl Menninger, M. D., in the Keynote Address to the 40th Annual Governor's Conference on Youth, University of Illinois, June 10, 1971.

10. *Drug Arrests and Dispositions in California 1968.* State of California, Department of Justice, Bureau of Criminal Statistics, Sacramento, p. 22.

11. Director John E. Ingersoll, Federal Bureau of Narcotics and Dangerous Drugs, as quoted in the *Southern Standard,* McMinnville, Tenn., November 5, 1970.

12. Arkansas, Colorado, Florida, Idaho, Indiana, Minnesota, Nebraska, Utah, Washington, and West Virginia reduced marijuana penalties during the first six months of 1971.

13. This figure was released by Roger T. Kelley, Assistant Secretary of Defense, U. S. Defense Department and quoted in the *St. Louis Post Dispatch*, June 10, 1971.

14. Duke Fisher, M. D., in an address to the 1968 Annual Training Conference of the California State Juvenile Officers Association.

15. Aspirin has come to the attention of medical authorities as a major cause for bleeding, when used in excess.

16. C. J. Flammang: On the proposed marijuana legislation. *Tennessee Law Enforcement Journal, 15* (2): 6-7, 23, 1971.

17. When a juvenile girl, below the age of legal consent, willingly submits to an act of intercourse, the offense is statutory rape.

18. For extensive treatment of this subject, see,

   C. J. Flammang: *The Police and the Underprotected Child.* Springfield, Thomas, 1970.

   Vincent J. Fontana, M. D.: *The Maltreated Child,* 2nd ed. Springfield, Thomas, 1971.

   Ray E. Helfer, M. D. and C. Henry Kempe, M. D.: *The Battered Child Syndrome.* Chicago, University of Chicago Press, 1968.

19. *Winship v. New York,* decided by the U. S. Supreme Court on March 31, 1970 set the degree of profit in Juvenile Court to be *beyond a reasonable doubt.*

20. Sara Geiger, M. D.: Early recognizable personality deviations. *Federal Probation,* XXV: December, 1961.

   Mary Dutcher: Neurological aspects-symptoms and detection. *Papers in the Behavioral Sciences for Teachers in Correctional Work.* Boulder, University of Colorado Press, 1963.

   Donald Kenefick and Maniel Glaser: *The Violent Offender.* New York, National Council on Crime and Delinquency, 1965.

21. Joan Beck: *Minimal Brain Disfunction.* Los Angeles, California Association for Neurologically Handicapped Children, 1967.

22. Robert E. Kelgord: Brain damage and delinquency. *Journal of California Law Enforcement, 4*(2): 53,58, 1969.

Chapter Eleven

NEW DIMENSIONS

T HE exploration of the many factors influencing behavior, the presentation of the normalcy of growth and development, and the variables within the family, the culture, and the society have served to dramatize the ecology in which modern youth must develop their adulthood. In rounding out the constellation of multiple factors related to youthful problems, the complexities of the general system of criminal justice as applied to youth present other factors that have both direct and indirect effects upon the life task of the young, which is the evolution of an individual self-image.

In review of the information presented, the enormity of the problems faced by the youth and the society provide an insight into the inadequacies of the present approach to the control and prevention of delinquency. Stereotyped methodology and time worn cliches are no longer capable of holding the promises that were once envisioned. The society has incorporated into its midst technological advances that have given rise to an increase in the cultural lag that is normally encountered in an industrial structure. The very prosperity so highly countenanced has introduced new and complex factors influencing behavior. That youth behavior is the most vulnerable within the society is not surprising, for the youth are the most unstable group in terms of personality development.

The ever increasing crime statistics, no matter how poorly that system has evolved, provides a stark picture of the reality of youthful involvement in antisocial behavior. This nation can no longer afford the luxury of traditional approaches in an attempt to barely hold the line. The time has come for new dimensions

225

to be added to a system that has really lost when it loses one individual to pro-criminal orientations.

There has finally been a recognition that cultural differences do exist within modern America, and that these differences are in stark contrast to other cultures to be found within the same neighborhood, the same community, and the same sphere of influence. The nation's youth are no longer willing to be passive observers, ingesting the hypocrisy of the adult society while attempting to reconcile adult behavior to the distortions of the dual standards that are directed at the youthful population.

This nation is now reaping the harvest of permissiveness, affluence, and the results of misguided progressives. That harvest is confusion—a confusion that permeates the very being of the society, forming a mire from which the system is having difficulty extricating itself.

From the attempt to integrate the society has flourished hate and increased bigotry evident among the racial groups. The nation is fast being polarized into two camps, with self-arming practices being employed at both extremes. Militants emerge, attack the system, and fade off into oblivion as a result of power struggles within their own systems. Effective leadership does not prevail, even in the highest seats of government. Domestic strife is overshadowed by international events that reflect a vacillating national interest.

The now famous *generation gap* has reached out to throttle the last vintage of family unity. A term coined to express an inability to communicate with or understand the motivation of large segments of the youthful population, it more nearly represents an *experience gap*. The major difference between the generations is the lack of inhibitions so readily demonstrated by the younger population. It is this difference that provides the hope for the future of this society, for as the necessary experience is gained, effective and innovative leadership will emerge from the present youth group.

In the meantime, society must provide the resources and services that will overcome the effects of the dilemma facing the incoming generation. The numbers of children who are being raised in a poverty existence, denied not only the benefits of material realities, but also being denied the true opportunities for attaining their potential. A welfare system that degrades dignity and serves to develop its future clientele under the guise of assistance. A selective service system that is inherently not favorably improved over the methods employed during the Civil War, with many persons being granted deferments, while others serve inflicting hardships upon themselves and members of their families. A system of civil and criminal justice that is archaic and incapable of providing the mechanics necessary to insure equal protection and justice. An economy that has become so troubled that the youthful generation entering it cannot possibly compete without parental or other private aid. These are but a few of the legacies that the wisdom of recent leadership have presented to the youth; and, the new generation is expected to view these complexities, accept their realities, and react in a positive manner. To do otherwise would be to jeopardize the equilibrium of the mythical middle class value system; a value system that even the members of that class do not pass on to their own offspring.

To develop new methods of coping with youthful problems requires the evaluation of the totality of the social system. It demands innovation. It will require courage.

The police have a role in the future thrust that will direct the society toward more effective intervention in the lives of youth who are demonstrating an inability to establish patterns of beneficial behavior. This role will only successfully be portrayed through new insights, innovative techniques, and courageous leadership. Anything short of that effort will do no more than perpetuate the intolerable. The traditional police attitudes and approaches toward youth and their problems will no longer provide the solutions that are so desperately necessary.

THE YOUTH SERVICES CONCEPT

A number of years before the President's Crime Commission, the author was requested to develop a proposal to provide innovative police services for a community. The results were a preliminary design that set forth some concepts relating to the police capability to become involved in a program that would attempt to develop an anticrime atmosphere within the community. The proposal, while not fully developed, represents new dimensions in police service. It is thought to be worthwhile to include the text of the proposal within this writing, not as a representation of a model, but rather to try to demonstrate the conceptualization of the police as an agency capable of offering leadership in community service.

Proposed Establishment of a Sheriff's Crime and Delinquency Prevention Unit

The following proposal is designed to produce a new effort and approach to the prevention and detection of antisocial behavior based on the concept of the total individual and his relationship to his environment.

This program will also set forth a new role to be demonstrated by the officers comprising the Unit. An outline of some of the envisioned duties and responsibilities of the Unit will be discussed.

PROBLEM: The rising crime rate, increase in acts of violence, and the continuing acceleration of youthful participation in serious offenses are well-documented on the national, state, and local levels. The effect upon our community and its individual members is a physical, emotional, and monetary burden which is proportionate to the lawless discord.

No community will continue to be capable of withstanding the increased costs, both from crime losses and from the enforcement perspective.

The present waste in human productivity is one of the nation's most pressing problems. The conservation of human resources must become a national priority.

NEED: A major need is the constructive awareness of the problem on the part of the community, and the community's active participation in the preservation of order and the assumption of its role in the prevention of crime and delinquency.

PROPOSAL: The establishment under the administration of the Sheriff, of a Unit of Enforcement charged with the responsibility to provide the following:

1. Investigation and other specialized police services as may be required for the control of criminal acts.

2. Research and development of concepts which will aid in the prevention of crime and delinquency.
3. The professional force necessary to initiate, motivate, guide, and provide direction to the efforts of the community toward the objectives of the program.
4. Organization and coordination of the existing community resources into effective prevention activities.
5. The establishment of a County Crime Prevention Commission, with authority provided by the Board of Supervisors. The Unit's personnel would develop an advisory committee to provide professionalized law enforcement services to the Commission.

OBJECTIVES: To reduce the immediate incidence of criminal and delinquent acts within the community. CONTROL

To provide for the development of good police practices, standards, and training; to insure the organization of the community resources into effectual prevention activity; and to establish a permanent awareness of individual responsibilities for crime prevention among the citizenry. PREVENTION

To develop an anticrime atmosphere within the community. PREVENTION

In describing the personnel to be attached to the Unit, the proposal stated:

Due to the Unit's role as a flexible specialized task force, coupled with the mission to attain its intended objective, the qualifications for personnel assigned to this Unit would necessarily be high. Individuals should have obtained the basic college degree, and their backgrounds should include varied and successful police experience. Each officer should have a record demonstrating a high degree of adaptability.

Each member of the Unit would be required to demonstrate leadership and initiative. The tasks involved would demand that foresight and depth of understanding be utilized in the promulgation of prevention programs. The ability to grasp and accept concepts foreign to their experience must be evident. The nature of the work would call for a continuous approach to duty, and the principles involved in meeting the objectives of the Unit.

The proposal developed the need for incorporating methods of evaluating the success of the program. It called for research efforts to determine needs and courses of action. Upon the identification of a need, the Unit would be responsible for involving those groups or agencies within the community which would most readily affect an adequate solution of the problem. This would require the Unit members to provide technical assistance and advice.

The proposal recognized the existence of numerous public and private groups that tended to work independently, often duplicating services. The Unit would serve as the organizational and coordinating arm of the Prevention Commission, drawing upon the existing services in a manner that would produce a more effective anticrime force.

The proposal developed other activities and provided additional direction. It ended with the following statement:

> Within the scope of these broad and revolutionary proposals lies the opportunity for law enforcement to enter into a total involvement toward the assumption of its rightful role as the community leader in the prevention and control of crime and delinquency. The necessity to abandon the traditional perspective of enforcement and to enter into an area of the full acceptance of the responsibilities of leadership requires the recognition of the urgency of participation and of the efforts of other levels of government to upgrade the society in which we live.

This concept was prepared in 1964. That it did not become a reality is another perspective upon the state of the art during that period. However, the concept of unifying the efforts of the community through law enforcement leadership, in an attempt to induce the prevention of crime and delinquency at all age levels, has been espoused by the President's Crime Commission. Thus, several years after the presentation of this proposal, the national task force drew similar conclusions that resulted in the recommendations for the development of a Youth Services police approach.

The Youth Services concept recognizes that crime is a youthful occupation. It also presents an awareness of the futility of attempting to gear one program for the juvenile and another for the young adult. Therefore, the concept of providing police services to all youth, rather than continuing the juvenile specialization and approaching the young adult and older youth in the same manner as much older adults, is a challenging enterprise.

Youth tend to idolize youth. They tend to group together and view the adult society as perpetually hostile. What occurs among the college population is soon discovered among the high school students, and in time filters downward to reach the younger population groups. This includes fads of dress, music, entertainment, speech, and actions. It is just not practical to try to handle this large and somewhat differing, but paradoxically interrelated group of youth, as two separate entities.

Naturally, the juvenile court system will continue to exist in some manner, but still much of the police contact with youth does not end up in court situations. The police must open their services to the young adult. The police should attempt to develop programs that will serve to alter attitudes. Law enforcement must become involved on college campuses, not as the occasional lecturer, but as an integral part of the academic life.

The same is true at the high school and junior high school levels. It is true at the dropout's headquarters. It is true in the ghetto and the suburb. The police must begin to relate to *people*, not to offenders. Since the majority of the police contacts result in youthful encounters, then the police must begin to relate to the youth.

This is not an easy task. It will have to begin with the institution of Youth Service Units within police agencies. Programs will have to evolve slowly. The police effort must extend beyond the mere apprehension and prosecution of offenders.

One of the more successful programs the Youth Services Unit could institute would be a meaningful method for youthful grievances against the police to be heard and acted upon. At the present time, most youth have no means of approaching the police with a complaint. They are shut off from any meaningful grievance vehicle. The Youth Services Unit could provide such a vehicle.

Such an effort would have to be an honest attempt to allow the youthful voice to be heard within the inner-police community. It would have to be built with a means for acting upon the complaints that were legitimate. If it is developed in such a manner as to merely patronize youth, it will only add to the present hostility between the youth and the police.

The Youth Services Unit could spearhead the involvement of youth in police-related tasks on a volunteer basis. Many police officials are prone to question youthful background records of violations and arrests, culling the more delinquent backgrounds from any participation in such programs. One questions the validity of denying delinquent youth the opportunity to learn why the police exist and how the police relate to the community in which the particular youth is a member. It can truly be postulated that some working police officers are engaged in more flagrant violations of the law than many of the youthful offenders could conceive. If law violations are the criteria for allowing persons to participate in police activities, then the police had better begin looking inwardly in many sections of this nation.

Law enforcement recognition of the interrelationship and interdependency that tends to exist informally between the juvenile population and the young adult population would go a long way in providing impetus to the implementation of Police Youth Services. The concept of service is foreign to many police officers, but it is an integral part of the police effort and is extremely important in innovative approaches to the youthful problem.

Services should include the recognition of youth needs within the community, and the police effort toward stirring the community conscience to meet those needs. Services for unwed mothers, services for young people who are transient and in need of assistance, resources for providing youth with the needs for continuing their educations or for seeking employment are all examples of services that the police could strive to develop within the community structure.

Working with the schools to encourage meaningful programs of a vocational and educational nature to be instituted provide youth with a variety of training or educational opportunities. As examples, the automobile is a large part of the youthful culture and also poses some police problems. A cooperative auto shop where youths would be trained to work as mechanics, while also discovering the skills of management and financial responsibility, would serve training and educational purposes while relieving the high costs of auto repair. The same concept could be incorporated into dry cleaning cooperatives, and a number of other enterprises. The establishment of a youth-operated credit union would build financial responsibility on the part of the operators and the clientele.

The Youth Services Unit should strive to develop methods of credit practices of merchants in the community, in relation to the youthful population. Businesses who are using methods that rely upon youthful financial inexperience should be brought to the attention of the youth of the community.

The police certainly would not be expected to design and provide all of the services, but they should be instrumental in determining needs and initiating action by other groups.

The Youth Services Unit should strive to develop methods of utilizing untapped volunteer assistance within the community. Older people can be used in emergency foster care situations. They can also be organized into home care assistants, shoring up disorganized family structures while official agencies are processing cases. Young adults can serve as *police workers,* riding with the Youth Service officers and acting as a paraprofessional aide. Upper classmen and graduate students in colleges welcome the opportunity to perform in an observer's role or the role of an intern. It is not necessary that a college be located within the community. The Youth Services Unit could easily contact many schools and make the arrangements for college credit to be granted for in-service experience on a volunteer basis.

The police are continually agonizing over manpower shortages, while there exists an untapped wealth of manpower in every community. The trick is to organize methods of effective utilization. This will never occur as long as the police believe that only a person wearing a badge can perform any part of the police function.

The concept of a Youth Services Unit reaching out to embrace the needs of the youthful population is innovative. There is a wide variety of forms that such a program could take. There exist pitfalls and some would be encountered, but no effort is without risk if it is also worthwhile.

Police legislative advice should reflect the knowledge and expertise gained through the Youth Services concept. The police should be able to identify necessary legislation, and recognize legislation that is detrimental or of no value to the youth or the enforcement enterprise.

It is hoped that the future of police work will include an understanding of the youthful population and of the relationship the police have with that group.

A YOUTH COURT

Just as the police should see the relationship between the juvenile community and the older youth group, so should the judicial system. Consideration should be given to the development of *a youth court system* that would encompass both the juvenile system and the young adult system of justice. In all probability, the upper age limit should be 21 years, but that is truly an arbitrary figure. The facts are that little separates the thinking and actions of the juvenile in the adolescent period and the young adult, other than the magic birthdate where the juvenile exceeds the upper limits of the first group. All of a sudden the former juvenile is placed in the position of being handled as an adult for all intents and purposes. Society has not prepared the youth to face the change. The system of justice has done nothing to allow the change to be a gradual transition.

The criminal justice system is overburdened with cases. Court dockets are filled to overflowing. Even in the most minor incidents, the courts are becoming arenas for contests. Everyone desires his day in court.

That many of the youthful situations are minor, as in the case of juveniles, cannot be denied. The incorporation of the two systems into a youth court could provide a needed answer to many of the problems confronting the criminal justice system at this time.

Minor incidents could be heard by nonjudicial hearing officers, similar to the present Juvenile Court Referee in the California Juvenile Court. Minor traffic cases could be heard by Traffic

Hearing Officers. This method of disposing of minor cases would eliminate tying up the time of the jurists who are necessary for the more complicated matters. It would allow for a reduction in the number of juries that would be necessary within any jurisdiction. It would retain jurisdiction over the youth during the period when they are better situated for learning their responsibilities under the law. This would reduce the negative effect in the transition from this system to the adult procedure.

Police and court records could be maintained under a Youth File, reducing the stigma that the young adult receives by an appearance within the adult judicial setting. Probation services could be intensified to work with the youth at the local level. Appearance in youth court would not receive the notoriety that an adult court action is given, and the effects of the court action would not be as debilitating to future rehabilitative attempts.

Coupled with other services of a social and correctional nature, the youth court concept extends the period in which a youth is to be given an opportunity. This extension is not inconsistent with the extended period of vocational or educational preparation necessary to enter the productive economic society. If it takes a person up to or past 21 years of age to prepare himself to make a living, why not grant that same adjustment period for violators?

Naturally, safeguards similar to those presently found within the juvenile court system should be incorporated. The young person who is an extreme case or adamant to change could be declared unfit for the youth court and remanded to the adult process. The youth court would be granted broad discretionary powers, and could order the youth to follow certain prescribed programs necessary to forestall further criminal or antisocial activity.

It is admitted that the youth court concept is possibly advanced, but it is based upon a growing need to alter the present system of dealing with youthful offenders. It represents no greater an opportunity for failure than the present system has already established.

BIBLIOGRAPHY

Abrahamsen, David: *Psychology of Crime*. New York, John Wiley and Sons, 1964.

Amos, William E.; Raymond Manella; and Marilyn A. Southwell: *Action Programs for Delinquency Prevention*. Springfield, Thomas, 1965.

Amos, William E. and Charles F. Wellford: *Delinquency Prevention*. Englewood, Cliffs, N. J., Prentice-Hall, 1967.

Barnes, Harry E. and Negley K. Teeters: *New Horizons in Criminology*, 3rd. ed. Englewood Cliffs, N. J., Prentice-Hall, 1959.

Bloch, Herbert A. and Gilbert Geis: *Man, Crime and Society*. New York, Random House, 1962.

Bloch, Herbert A. and Arthur Neiderhoffer: *The Gang*. New York, Philosophical Library, 1958.

Bowman, Leroy: *Youth and Delinquency in an Inadequate Society*. New York, League for Industrial Democracy, 1960.

Burchinal, L. G.: *Rural Youth in Crisis*. Washington, D.C., Childrens Bureau, Department of Health, Education and Welfare, 1965.

Cary, Lee J. and Robert H. Hardt: *The Central Registry*. Syracuse, Syracuse University Youth Development Center, 1961.

Cary, Lee J.: *Work Camps for Young Offenders*. Syracuse, Syracuse University Youth Development Center, 1960.

Cavan, Ruth S.: *Criminology*, 3rd ed. New York, Thomas Y. Crowell, 1962.

Cavan, Ruth S.: *Juvenile Delinquency*. Philadelphia, J. B. Lippincott, 1962.

Cavan, Ruth S.: *Readings in Juvenile Delinquency*. Philadelphia, J. B. Lippincott, 1964.

Chapman, A. H.: *Management of Emotional Problems of Children and Youth*. Philadelphia, J. B. Lippincott, 1965.

Clinard, Marshall B.: *The Sociology of Deviant Behavior*. New York, Holt, Rhinehart and Winston, 1963.

Clinard, Marshall B. and Richard Quinney: *Criminal Behavior Systems*. New York, Holt, Rinehart and Winston, 1967.

Cloward, Richard A. and Lloyd E. Ohlin: *Delinquency and Opportunity*. New York, Free Press of Glencoe, 1960.

Cohen, Albert K.: *Delinquent Boys*. New York, Free Press of Glencoe, 1955.

Conant, James B.: *Slums and Suburbs*. New York, McGraw-Hill, 1961.

Curry, J. E. and G. King: *Race Tensions and the Police*. Springfield, Thomas, 1962.

Dudycha, G. J.: *Psychology for Law Enforcement Officers*. Springfield, Thomas, 1960.

Eldefonso, Edward: *Law Enforcement and the Youthful Offender.* New York, John Wiley and Sons, 1967.

Flammang, C. J.: *The Police and the Underprotected Child.* Springfield, Thomas, 1970.

Gibbons, Don C.: *Changing the Lawbreaker.* Englewood Cliffs, N.J., Prentice-Hall, 1968.

Gibbons, Don C.: *Delinquent Behavior.* Englewood Cliffs, N.J., Prentice-Hall, 1970.

Gibbons, Don C.: *Society, Crime and Criminal Careers.* Englewood Cliffs, N.J., Prentice-Hall, 1968.

Glueck, Sheldon and Eleanor: *Unraveling Juvenile Delinquency.* New York. Commonwealth Fund, 1940.

Glueck, Sheldon and Eleanor: *One Thousand Juvenile Delinquents.* Cambridge, Harvard University Press, 1934.

Glueck, Sheldon and Eleanor: *Predicting Delinquency and Crime.* Cambridge, Harvard University Press, 1959.

Glueck, Sheldon (Ed.): *The Problem of Delinquency.* Boston, Houghton Mifflin, 1959.

Glueck, Sheldon and Eleanor: *Unraveling Juvenile Delinquency.* Cambridge, Harvard University Press, 1950.

Healy, William: *The Individual Delinquent.* Boston, Little, Brown and Company, 1915.

Higgins, Lois L.: *Policewoman's Manual.* Springfield, Thomas, 1961.

Holman, Mary: *The Police Officer and the Child.* Springfield, Thomas, 1962.

Hsu, Francis L. R.: *Psychological Anthropology.* Homewood, Ill, The Dorsey Press, 1961.

Kempe, C. Henry and Ray Helfer: *The Battered Child Snydrome.* Chicago, University of Chicago Press, 1968.

Kenny, John P. and Dan G. Pursuit: *Police Work With Juveniles,* 3rd ed. Springfield, Thomas, 1967.

Kvaraceus, William C.: *The Community and the Delinquent.* New York, World Book, 1954.

Kvaraceus, William C. and Walter B. Miller: *Delinquent Behavior.* Washington, D.C., National Educational Association, 1959.

Kvaraceus, William C. and William E. Ulrich: *Delinquent Behavior.* Washington, D.C., National Education Association, 1959.

Lippitt, R.; Gene Watson; and Bruce Westly: *The Dynamics of Planned Change,* New York, Harcourt, Brace and World, 1958.

Lohman, Joseph D.: *Juvenile Delinquency.* Cook County, Ill., Office of the Sheriff, 1957.

Lou, H. H.: *Juvenile Courts in the United States.* Chapel Hill, N.C., University of North Carolina Press, 1927.

Lunden, Walter A.: *Statistics on Delinquents and Delinquency.* Springfield, Thomas, 1964.

238 *Police Juvenile Enforcement*

Mc Carthy, Raymond G.: *Teen-agers and Alcohol.* New Haven, Yale Center of Alcohol Studies, 1956.

Mc Cord, William and Joan: *Origins of Crime.* New York, Columbia University Press, 1959.

Menninger, Karl: *The Vital Balance.* New York, The Viking Press, 1964.

Merrill, Maud: *Problems of Child Delinquency.* Boston, Houghton Mifflin, 1947.

Moles, Oliver M.; R. Lippitt; and S. Withey: *A Selective Review of Research and Theories Concerning the Dynamics of Delinquency.* Ann Arbor, University of Michigan, 1959.

Mulherene, Henry J.: *Handbook for Police Youth Bureaus.* Albany, Division for Youth, State of New York, 1958.

Myren, Richard A.: *Processing and Reporting of Police Referrals to Juvenile Court.* Springfield, Thomas, 1962.

Myren, Richard A. and Lynn D. Swanson: *Police Work With Children.* Washington, D.C., Childrens Bureau, Department of Health, Education and Welfare, 1962.

Nye, F. Ivan: *Family Relationships and Delinquency Behavior.* New York, John Wiley and Sons, 1958.

O'Conner, George and Nelson A. Watson: *Juvenile Delinquency and Youth Crime.* Washington, D.C., International Association of Chiefs of Police, 1964.

Perlman, I. Richard: *Delinquency Prevention.* Washington, D. C., Childrens Bureau, Department of Health, Education and Welfare, 1960.

Pfiffner, John M.: *Delinquency, Urban Pathology and the Administrative Process.* Los Angeles, Youth Studies Center, University of Southern California, 1964.

Pfiffner, John M.: *Some Role Alternatives for the Police Juvenile Activity.* Los Angeles, Youth Studies Center, University of Southern California, 1964.

Pfiffner, John M.: *Parameters of the Role of the Police in Dealing with Juveniles.* Los Angeles, Youth Studies Center, University of Southern California, 1963.

Powers, Edwin and Helen L. Witmer: *An Experiment in the Prevention of Delinquency.* New York, Columbia University Press, 1951.

Quay, Herbert: *Juvenile Delinquency.* Princeton, D. Van Nostrand, 1965.

Redl, Fritz and David Wineman: *Children Who Hate.* Glencoe, Ill., Free Press, 1951.

Robison, Sophia M.: *Juvenile Delinquency.* New York, Holt, Rinehart and Winston, 1960.

Roucek, J. S.: *Juvenile Delinquency.* New York, Philosophical Library, 1958.

Salisbury, H. E.: *The Shook-up Generation.* New York, Harper and Row, 1958.

Savitz, Leonard: *Dilemmas in Criminology.* New York, Mc Graw-Hill, 1967.

Shaw, Clifford, R.: *Delinquency Areas*. Chicago, University of Chicago Press, 1929.

Shaw, Clifford R. and Henry D. Mc Kay: *Juvenile Delinquency in Urban Areas*. Chicago, University of Chicago Press, 1942.

Shaw, Clifford R. and Henry D. Mc Kay: *Social Factors in Juvenile Delinquency*. Washington, D.C., U.S. Government Printing Office, 1931.

Shulman, Harry M.: *Juvenile Delinquency*. New York, Harper and Row, 1961.

Taft, Donald R. and Ralph W. England: *Criminology*. New York, The Mc Millan Company, 1964.

Tappen, Paul W.: *Crime, Justice and Corrections*. New York, Mc Graw-Hill, 1960.

Teeters, Negley K. and John O. Reinemann: *The Challenge of Delinquency*. Englewood Cliffs, N.J., Prentice-Hall, 1950.

Tunley, R.: *Kids, Crime and Cops*. New York, Harper and Row, 1964.

Turner, William W.: *The Police Establishment*. New York, Putnam Sons, 1968.

Vedder, Clyde B.: *Juvenile Offenders*. Springfield, Thomas, 1963.

Vold, G. B.: *Theoretical Criminology*. New York, Oxford University Press, 1958.

Watson, Nelson A. and R. N. Walker: *Training Police for Work With Juveniles*. Washington, D.C., International Association of Chiefs of Police, 1965.

Wattenberg, William E.: *Relationship of School Experiences to Delinquency*. Detroit, Wayne State University Press, 1960.

Wheeler, Stanton: *Controlling Delinquency*. New York, John Wiley and Sons, 1968.

Whyte, William: *Street Corner Society*. Chicago, University of Chicago Press, 1955.

Wilson, O. W.: *Police Administration*. New York, McGraw-Hill, 1963.

Winters, John E.: *Crime and Kids*. Springfield, Thomas, 1959.

Witmer, Helen L.: *Psychiatric Clinics for Children*. New York, The Commonwealth Fund, 1958.

Witmer, Helen L. and Edith Tufts: *The Effectiveness of Delinquency Prevention Programs*. Washington, D.C., Childrens Bureau, Department of Health, Education and Welfare, 1954.

Wolfgang, M. E.; L. Savitz; and N. Johnston: *The Sociology of Crime and Delinquency*. New York, John Wiley and Sons, 1962.

Young, Pauline V.: *Social Treatment in Prevention of Delinquency*. New York, McGraw-Hill, 1952.

Zeisel, Hans: *Delay in the Courts*. Boston, Little, Brown and Company, 1959.

APPENDIX

A POLICE COMMUNITY LEADERSHIP ACTION

A Proposal to Develop Positive and Significantly Better Attitudes Toward the Police at the Junior High School Level

INTRODUCTION

Man is a social animal. If he were not he would perish, as he possesses no instinctive patterns for survival. He must learn such behavior through social interaction. In doing so, he acquires more than the mere ability to survive; he learns how to live within his culture.

The process through which an individual acquires cultural knowledge is socialization. The term is appropriate because it recognizes the primary importance of the social factor in learning cultural behavior.[1]

Children see the role assigned by the culture and reflect attitudes of rejection which often lead to violation of social norms through aggressive behavior.[2]

Because the proper socialization of the young is among society's most important task, society structures that task in a systematic manner. At a cursory glance, it may seem that much of the child's social training is left to random or casual social processes. In reality, his experiences of social interaction are firmly controlled by society. Folkways and mores are instruments of such control, but institutions are the most influential societal agents in this regard.[3]

Much of the socialization process affects the development of attitudes. These attitudes are formed initially through the influence of the primary group: the home and the family.[4]

The decline of the effect of the formative role of the primary group in a complex urban society has brought increased need for the structure of institutions in an orderly arrangement as a concomitant of the function of socialization.

Children learn their attitudes through the socialization process. This learning is conveyed through inadvertent example as well as through deliberate teaching.[5]

Prepared by the Municipal Technical Advisory Service, the University of Tennessee. C. J. Flammang, Police Consultant.

Attitudes are learned reactions and so they may be weakened or strengthened, or even unlearned.[6]

Children of the early adolescent period of development are more flexible and open to attitude change.[7]

In contrast to the early adolescent period of personality development, by the middle or late adolescent period personality structures are usually definite and stable enough to predict the individual's social behavior and attitudes in different situations.[8]

One of the principal purposes of any culture is to pass on its way of life to the young. This includes the attitudes and values of the group as well as its artifacts and institutions.[9]

The school is one of the principal socializing agencies of our culture, having a unique opportunity to influence behavior and to mold the character of the youngsters in its charge.[10]

CRIME AND DELINQUENCY

In the opening sentence of the Preface to the *Uniform Crime Reports* (1967), J. Edgar Hoover indicated, "Perhaps never before in our history has there been such widespread concern over crime and the capability of our criminal justice agencies to contend with it." The statistics presented in that document tend to accentuate this concern. This does not mean a concern based on panic, but a rational concern which emphasizes the positive aspects of proper utilization of social institutions for the development of attitudes, as well as programs to assist in the efforts to contain the increase in crime and delinquency.

Significantly, the statistics for the section, "Total Arrests by Age" during 1967, relating to the seven major felonies, indicated that 23.1 per cent of those persons arrested within the categories mentioned were fifteen years of age or under.[11]

More startling was the finding that 49 per cent of all arrests in those categories were persons under eighteen years of age.[12] This means the age group exceeding eighteen years of age accounted for only 51 per cent of all the major arrests in the United States in one year.

In reference to assaults on police officers, the report indicated the following:

> One of the serious problems facing the law enforcement officer today is the growing segment of public disrespect for the police officer and

the failure of the citizens to come to the aid of officers being attacked as they attempt to perform their lawful duties. These attitudes certainly are, in large measure, responsible for the nationwide increase of 11 per cent in the rate of assaults on law enforcement officers last year.[13]

While recidivist rates for all age groups were high, the report indicated that 70 per cent of those persons under eighteen years of age who were released from custody in 1963 had been rearrested at least once by 1967.[14] It has been estimated that the financial figure spent each year on the apprehension, conviction, and control through custodial care and correctional services of delinquents approximates the amount spent on the support of public education nationwide.[15]

THE NATURE OF ATTITUDES

An everyday occurrence is to discover someone's attitude toward a particular person, object, or topic. Some attitudes, such as the attitude one holds regarding himself, may be of importance to that individual, but of little significance to others. Most attitudes, however, are much broader and more important. Pressey and Robinson have stated:

. . . they may be exceedingly broad like attitudes of hostility or friendliness or anxiety or curiosity or conservatism regarding almost anything. As the personality becomes integrated, attitudes tend to become more consistent.[16]

This leads one to a first clue about the nature of attitudes. They are related to the personality. Therefore, attitudes are capable of indicating certain personality characteristics that are intangible. Attitudes reflect values and ideals that are important to the individual. These values, in turn, tend to be the key to attitude expression.

Attitudes may be expressed in any number of ways, but the result will always be either favorable or unfavorable, along a continuum. A neutral attitude is not an expression of an attitude, but rather the lack of such an expression. Attitudes are external manifestations of personality and character dispositions either for or against something which is value-oriented.

Attitudes are more learned and more variable from person to

person, and although they tend to have more of a background of specific experience than emotions, they have less intellectual content than concepts.[17] Both attitudes and moral judgment are based on a system of values; but attitudes differ from moral judgement in that attitudes, once formed, remain intact until altered. Moral judgment, on the other hand, occurs in the context of decisions in which we judge some action.[18]

Attitude Development

Attitudes are learned responses. They may be acquired through careful study, analysis of facts, and thoughtful decisions, but more often involve an emotional response.

Newcomb hypothesized that attitudes and concepts grow together within the individual's development of maturity. Rather than attitudes being determined by available information or vice versa, both are acquired as related aspects of individual adjustment to the community.[19]

A natural first question concerns the point where attitudes begin to develop. It must be recognized that the development of attitudes begins very early. By age eight months, a baby shows consistent preference for particular games or toys. Definite attitudes between sisters are evident by the age of three years.[20] As early as the second year, boys and girls will display a definite preference for toys related to their sex.[21]

The Development of Attitudes Through Early Primary Group Relations

Because of this early stage of attitude development, not only are cultural influences important, but also the effects of subcultures upon the attitudes of the young child are important. The subcultures with their crosscurrents and unstable truces frame the social world within which the child develops. The family makes the earlier and more profound impact. Children learn attitudes primarily from people whom they admire and wish to emulate as models.[22] Evidently younger children most usually admire someone they know personally. But with increasing age the weaknesses of persons thus known come more to be seen, and the historical and public characters have greater influence.[23]

Everything a child experiences has its share in shaping attitudes. Attitudes are influenced by such factors as age; home; written material; media such as radio, T.V. and movies; financial status; unemployment; group opinion; customs; and geographic location.

Attitude Development and the Peer Group

The quality of experience is probably an additional influential factor in attitude development.[24] Thus, the manner or form of the experience or environmental influence can cause the development of an attitude. This may be readily seen in an example of a person who has been the victim of a robbery by a minority group member and who develops an emotional prejudice against that ethnic group.

To gain acceptance by the peer group, the child learns that he must accept the values and interests of the group. Depending upon these group values, attitudes will develop either for or against an object. The peer group requires that a person verbalize his likes or dislikes; and the member cannot afford to be different because this will jeopardize his status in the group.

Attitude Development and Culural Influence

There is a cultural orientation of attitudes. The importance attached to culture in attitude development is most important and most subtle of all determinants of attitude. Attitudes are the result of the total complex of beliefs of a nation, class, or community.[25]

In every culture, children are subjected to pressures to develop a personality pattern that will conform as closely as possible to the standards set by the culture. From these pressures, the child learns to behave in a socially approved way in that culture and to have attitudes that are sex-appropriate.[26]

In general, adolescents tend to follow the pattern of attitudes held by their parents. However, it has been found that in the few cases of divergence from the parents' views, the cause seems to be not so much a difference of opinion, as an expression of rebellion and hostility toward parental authority.[27] Actually, most people short-circuit the process by imitating attitudes that they observe in people whom they admire or love. Adolescents especially imitate the opinions of their age mates. Society thus furnishes the models. Every child's basic nature is overlaid by the culture in which he grows.[28]

The evidence indicates that the development of attitudes is the learned result of the influential interplay of the parents, the family, other persons, and the various groups with whom the individual comes into contact. These factors are coupled with the effects of the generalized cultural pressures that have affected not only the individual, but all of his other influences and attitude determinants; and how these individuals and groups have interpreted and passed on the values of the society.

The Alteration of Attitudes

The child of preadolescent years has been exposed to a narrow range of attitudes. The source of these attitudes has been a group of persons quite close to the child, and his values have seldom been questioned by the child. The moral ideas and attitudes of preadolescents correspond to those of adults. However, preadolescents are still thinking about values in external, nonmotivational terms. They know what adults expect, even if they do not meet these expectations.[29]

Values can be taught by utilization of group processes in laboratory means, provided we understand the viewpoint of the child. It is in this stage of development that the beginnings of the "generation gap" appear. The preadolescent child of the middle of the school years will begin to question many of the standards and rules he previously accepted. This often leads to conflict with the adults in his environment, and from the experience of these conflicts the child gradually forms new attitudes of response. Thus, toward the end of the elementary school period, the serious search for the self-concept begins. As a child approaches puberty, he is already undergoing some changes in attitude. With the onset of the radical changes of puberty, there is a devastating effect on the pattern of social development. Some of the changes in attitude and behavior are so pronounced that the child literally reverts to behavior characteristics of the preschool year; some are more suggestive of the attitudes or actions of the delinquent; some are so new and different as to be a radical experience for the individual.

The pubescent child develops an alteration of attitude that is quite antagonistic toward everyone—parents, siblings, teachers, relatives, society in general, and even peers. The child seems to delight in being uncooperative. Earlier social insight disappears, and often isolation replaces social participation. For the majority of children, out of this chaotic and rapid upheaval will appear new and wholesome attitudes, which by the middle or late adolescent period will be generally set.

The most flexible period of attitude alteration comes during the period of late middle childhood through early adolescence. It is important that this child's efforts to understand be encouraged and guided.[30]

Despite the significant influences of cultural factors on the development of attitudes, despite the deep-rooted functional nature of many attitudes, and despite the inherent tendency of attitudes to preserve themselves, attitudes can be changed.[31]

The success of any effort to alter attitudes will depend upon the theoretical soundness of the measures taken and not the energy expended. The reeducative process has to fulfill a task which is essentially equivalent to a change in culture. Research into attitudes and beliefs shows that young people reflect faithfully the attitudes of their elders, but also that they tend to modify these points of view as they grow older and are influenced by various individuals and agencies outside the home.[32]

On the assumption that the individual's attitude has some meaningful value for him, he will attempt, if possible, to retain it. If the potency of the force leading to the alteration of one of the basic components of the attitude is great or persistent, rejection of that force is impossible. When this is the case, fragmentation may occur; but if the force exerted is sufficient, the resistance will cease and the alteration will take place.

It can then be posited that it is possible to devise a force that may then be applied toward the attitude to such an extent that the attitude must give away. The application of these external factors would so alter the comfort of the person with relation to the attitude held as to cause change. The fact that the early adolescent is already undergoing the discomfort of old attitudes in no way diminishes the priority of that stage of development as being the best period for attitude change. In fact, the early adolescent period is enhanced as a priority period of change, *in that change will occur anyway.*

Attitude Development and the School

Schools can try to understand the emotional dynamics of attitude development and act accordingly. All through the school years, attitudes and ideals are forming and changing as a result of many influences, some of them in the school. The school can be a very constructive instrument, if it has the understanding and will to make the effort; and if it can work cooperatively with the home and the community.

One obvious way for the school to affect attitudes is to put before the students material for that purpose. Research has shown the school can, with an almost frightening ease, influence the attitudes of students.

The teacher's function in shaping attitudes is crucial. While the family establishes basic attitudes, the school plays a large part too—especially in adolescence.[33] One way an adolescent asserts independence is by rejection of the views of the parent. At that point, the youth is in the position to alter his attitudes in favor of others. His attitudes may be strongly influenced by the school, especially on those issues that are not discussed in depth in the home.

Attitudes may be even more drastically altered when the curriculum is planned to that end. In one study a majority of high school students reported a change in attitude after seeing the picture "Gentleman's Agreement.[34]" Field trips have also been shown to be effective.[35] The use of class discussion seems to be effective, as the individual with a poor attitude is subjected to the counter-arguments of his classmates.

Most educational and behavioral authorities place the school high as an institution for affecting attitudinal change. It must be concluded that the school is a potent force in the alteration and change of attitudes.

POLICE COMMUNITY LEADERSHIP

Historically, the police have failed to take the leadership role in the community that they are capable of carrying out. As one reviews the makeup of various committees, commissions, and other groups who formulate policy on the local, state, and national levels in relationship to law enforcement, one continually discovers the lack of meaningful police participation. While this is partially the fault of the community or the government, it is also partially the fault of the police themselves.

Remaining within the isolated shelter of the closed police society, law enforcement has refrained from becoming actively engaged in bringing to the community programs and innovation that would assist the citizens in formulating plans to combat crime and delinquency.

The proposal presently under discussion has two objectives. The first is the long range goal of altering negative attitudes toward the police, thus bringing about a total community change over a period of years. The second is the meaningful involvement of the police in a community leadership role.

Obviously, the second objective will be attained long before any results of the first objective can be measured. For police purposes, the second objective is of immediate importance. It is through this objective that the police can bring community focus upon a positive approach which has been sought by the police to lead the community in the direction of upgrading local efforts to combat crime and delinquency.

This is a unique opportunity for a police organization. To forego involvement in this opportunity would be tragic.

The Police Role in the Program

The police role in the institution of this program revolves around its leadership role in stimulating the institutions surrounding and within the community to participation. In order to do so, it will be necessary for the police department to name a coordinator or liaison officer who will assume the leadership function. This officer should be of command rank, and he must have authority delegated from the office of the Chief in order to be able to proceed in an effectual manner.

The first thing the officer should do would be to obtain a copy of the completed findings of the original Office of Law Enforcement Assistance Grant, No. 52, emanating from the Justice Department, Washington, in 1965. Within this report will be found the full results and effectiveness of the research and development of this program.

The second function of the coordinator should be to contact the representatives of the local school district and present them with a critique of the planned program. By this means, the police should be capable of instilling enthusiasm and cooperation within the school officials which will lead to the necessary studies to determine the overall need for the curriculum which has been developed.

The third function of the coordinator should be the recruitment of college or university graduate students, in either the Department of Education or Psychology, to form a nucleus of available talent to perform the necessary fundamental attitude survey. The importance of this step cannot be overstressed, as the adoption of the curriculum at a later date will be highly dependent upon the outcome of the research of the attitude survey. Such a survey cannot be performed by persons who are not knowledgeable in the area of academic research.

It would seem advisable for the police coordinator to contact Dr. Robert Portune, Chairman, Department of Secondary Education, University of Cincinnati, and determine his willingness to serve as a consultant throughout the life of the program.

In developing this proposal, the cost of student assistance from the local colleges or university, as well as the expenses of the computer and Dr. Portune's consultation, should all become a part of the grant proposal. In addition, in-kind matching of city funds on the cost of the coordinator's salary, the educational institution's salaries, various supplies, equipment, facilities and transportation should also be computed.

During the initial stages of the attitude survey, the police coordinator should function as a central focal point to which all information could be channeled, and from which would emanate effective coordination and leadership. After the results of the attitude survey, it would be important for the police coordinator to continue the leadership role in trying to get the schools to institute a pilot program utilizing the basic curriculum.

THE PROPOSAL

The Portune ATP-Scale

The instrument to be utilized to measure the attitude of the students involved in this proposal will be the *Portune Attitude Toward the Police Scale*. This device was developed by Dr. Robert Portune, University of Cincinnati, and it has been used in numerous studies of this type throughout the United States.

The device was the result of the Thurstone-Chave method of attitude scaling, with adaption of the Likert method. It was developed after identifying a junior high school population in Cincinnati, Ohio that most closely approximated the socioeconomic structure of the community. From this school, 250 statements regarding the police were obtained from a random sample of the students. These statements were analyzed and any statements that were factual were discarded. The only ones retained were definite statements of opinion. The results left 105 simple statements of student opinion toward the police. The statements were then printed on IBM cards for the purpose of data processing.

From the same school, a second random sampling of 100 students was obtained. These students became the group judges necessary to the Thurstone-Chave method of developing attitude scales.

Each of the students selected was given the cards with the simple statements. Their task was to formulate an opinion range scale on a nine point basis from favorable to unfavorable. The students distributed the cards over the nine point scale, thus equaling 10,000 individual judgments. The cards were distributed in nine separate packages. These packages were individually programed to discover statements that were most nearly in agreement under each category. By this means, key statements were identified.

By switching to the Likert method of scale development, the intensity of feeling was included. This was accomplished by using a five point choice range as follows: Strongly agree; Agree; Uncertain; Disagree; and Strongly disagree.

The final selection resulted in ten favorable and ten unfavorable statements regarding the police. The five point choice range applied to each statement. This became the *Portune ATP-Scale*.

The scale has the following scoring system: for the favorable statements, Strongly agree = 4 points; Agree = 3 points; Uncertain = 2 points; Disagree = 1 point; and Strongly disagree = 0 points. For unfavorable statements, the order is reversed with Strongly agree being assigned 0 points and Strongly disagree being assigned 4 points. The score range is from 0 to 80 on a continuum, with 80 points being extremely favorable attitude toward the police.

The reliability factor of the Portune ATP-Scale is .90 based on 3,000 cases.

The Portune ATP-Scale

1. Police keep the city good. SA A U D SD
2. Police accuse you of things you didn't do. SA A U D SD
3. The police are stupid. SA A U D SD
4. Police protect us from harm. SA A U D SD
5. The police really try to help you when you're in trouble. SA A U D SD
6. The police are mean. SA A U D SD
7. The police offer you money to tell on other kids. SA A U D SD
8. Police use clubs on people for no reason at all. SA A U D SD
9. The police keep peace and order. SA A U D SD
10. Without policemen there would be crime everywhere. SA A U D SD
11. You can rely on the police in times of distress. SA A U D SD
12. Policemen are dedicated men. SA A U D SD
13. Police try to act big shot. SA A U D SD
14. The police are always mad at kids. SA A U D SD
15. Police help me to help myself. SA A U D SD
16. Police represent trouble instead of help. SA A U D SD
17. Police are brave men. SA A U D SD
18. The police are protective of our country. SA A U D SD
19. Police don't give you a chance to explain. SA A U D SD
20. Police try to get smart with you when you ask a question. SA A U D SD

The Application of the Portune ATP-Scale

The application of the ATP-Scale is an attempt to measure the attitudes of children in the late middle childhood period, and of youth in the early adolescent stage toward the police. Assuming that three grade levels occur within the junior high school (seventh, eighth, and ninth), it would be advantageous to administer the attitude measurement to seventh graders during the first month of their junior high school experience and to ninth graders during the same period. In the event that the scale would be utilized during a later period of the school year, it would be important to consider the effect of six to eight months of the junior high school experience upon the seventh grader. This effect may alter the reliability of a proper attitude measurement as the child would be already exposed to some of the negative attitudes within the junior high school situation.

To overcome that situation, it should be considered a reasonable system to administer the scale to sixth grade students during the spring term or semester. By this means, the students in the sixth grade would be caught at a time prior to exposure to the junior high school situation. At the same time, by measuring the ninth grade students during the spring term or semester, they would be recorded prior to their exposure to any high school situation.

It is important to choose a random sample of the population to be measured. One way to ensure the random sampling is by selecting classes which cover subject matter that is required for all students. Thus, it would be conceivable that the seventh and ninth grade social science classes could be administered the scale with retention of the random sampling requirement. A population measurement approximating 100 in each grade level would be deemed sufficient.

In either the sixth or seventh grades, students would be of the age group approaching or already within the stage of puberty or early adolescence. The age levels would range from ten to fourteen years.

Ninth grade students would be expected to be ending puberty and already in the early adolescent period of development. The age level should range from a low of around fourteen years to a high of around seventeen years.

The schools in which the attitude survey is to be made should be chosen on the basis of their representation of the comprehensive student population of the school district. In the event that elementary schools' sixth grade classes are utilized, those schools that serve as feeder schools to the junior high school should be chosen.

The classroom survey should be conducted by school personnel, preferably the classroom teacher. The actual estimated time to survey a class of 40 students would fall into a period of about fifteen minutes.

In addition to the favorable and unfavorable statements contained within the Portune ATP-Scale, certain other areas of information may be questioned as a part of the device. These areas would be intended to provide information beyond the scope of the attitudes that could be applied to the total investigation project. The additional information might relate to some personal and environmental factors. Some of this additional information might be the school name; age and sex; race or descent; whether a family owns a home or not; favorite subject; regular church attendance; and/or occupation of parent or guardian.

The use of this information would be to determine if there was a difference between the attitude of the boy or girl toward the police in either grade. Race or descent would seek to determine whether any significant difference existed between the attitudes of students toward the police depending upon ethnic background. Home ownership information would be sought in an attempt to include the social status attributed to home ownership or the process of purchasing a home, as opposed to renting, in the comparison of attitudes toward the police. The favorite subject might give information showing the existence of a significant difference in attitude toward the police depending upon whether a student listed an academic or a nonacademic subject as a favorite. It might also be found to be significant toward the attitude, depending upon which academic subject were listed. Church attendance would be included to determine whether such attendance appeared to significantly better the attitude of youth toward the police. The use of the information relating to the occupation of the parent would be to assist in determining a significant difference in the attitude of a student, depending upon the economic and educational background of the parents and the exposure of the student to what is presumed to be an adequate and culturally acceptable economic environment.

Certainly other factual information might be determined, but the suggestions listed above would be of importance to any attitude survey.

It is conceivable that a coded cover sheet could be utilized in obtaining personal information in-depth on each student surveyed. This information could be filed with the Police Department or the Juvenile Court for a long range follow-up study to determine how many students surveyed, who showed good attitudes, encountered trouble with the law within the next five years. These are part of the variations that can be employed in a program of this type.

After the physical distribution and survey, the graduate students in question would be utilized to tally the information and prepare it for statistical review.

Statistical Computation

The *null hypothesis* should be utilized to determine the significance of the differences between the means of groups of the population sampling. The null hypothesis simply asserts that the mean of the sampling distribution of differences between sample means is zero. The test of this hypothesis consists in deciding whether or not the difference between the two sample means could, because of sampling error, reasonably be expected to occur in a sampling distribution of differences in which the mean is zero. However, something more precise than an inspectional check obtained from the drawing of a distribution is needed; and that is a precise statement of probability. To obtain this, the z-score technique, permitting the use of the normal curve, is utilized. This technique, when applied to test the differences between means, is called the t-ratio.

The results of the t-ratio are then applied to the Fisher and Yates statistical table at a particular level of significance. From this table, it is possible to conclude whether or not the sample means differed significantly.

In the event the difference was significant, it may be presumed that the significance involved was not the result of sampling error. This would indicate that the difference between the two means would occur at levels of significance of 1 percent or 5 percent, either 99 or 95 times out of 100 attempts at sampling populations, depending upon which level of significance was chosen.

Another system that would answer some of the questions desired is one of the most widely used method of statistical analysis of findings from experiments in which conditions are varied in three or more ways. This is by *analysis of the variance*. The basic fact which underlies the technique is that the total variability of a set of scores from several groups may be divided into two or more categories. In the type of experimental design that should be utilized in the study, there would be two categories of variability: the variability of subjects within each group, and the variability between different groups.

As the cornerstone in the analysis of variance, the sum of squares is utilized. The sum of squares, represented by SS, is simply the sum of the difference between each score and the mean squared, or the sum of the square deviations from the mean. Since the total variability in an experiment may be divided into two parts, the variability of the subjects within the groups, and the variability between different groups, both of these will produce sums of squares. In addition, the total variability also produces a sum of squares.

The technique has one disadvantage. The size of the sum of squares depends upon the number of measurements upon which it is based. It is necessary to use a further statistic that is not so greatly dependent upon the number of cases. This quantity is the mean squared, represented by MS. By finding one mean square value to represent variability within groups, the size of their ratio may be used as the basis for determination of significance of the data.

It is then necessary to compute the F-ratio, which is a numerical expression of the relative size of the means squared between groups and the means squared within groups. After calculating the F-ratio, the null hypothesis is retained or rejected by reference to the Merrington and Thompson table of percentage points of the inverted beta distribution.

Procedure After the Results of the Survey

Obviously, if the results of the survey indicate that there is no significant difference between the attitudes of ninth grade and seventh grade junior high school students toward the police, there would be no reason to continue onward with this proposal. It is probable that something does occur within the life of the early adolescent individual, external to the school situation, which adversely affects his attitude toward authority figures in general and the police specifically.

If the results of the survey of the attitudes indicates a significant negative difference within the ninth grade junior high school population as opposed to the seventh grade junior high school population, it is then apparent that the youth are being sent into the high school situation during which time their attitudes will become set with significantly negative attitudes toward the police. These negative attitudes will probably then continue the rest of the individual's life.

In order to alter these attitudes and devise a system whereby attitudes during the junior high school years will not drop off toward the negative, the institution of a specially designed curriculum into the junior high school should then be considered.

THE CURRICULUM

At the conclusion of the original Cincinnati research, and funded under the OLEA Grant, one outstanding police juvenile officer and one outstanding junior high school social science instructor from each of fifteen regions throughout the United States were brought to Cincinnati, Ohio. These persons spent a total of 23 weeks preparing and designing a self-discovery curriculum block to be placed within the junior high school social science core curriculum. The total curriculum amounts to 3 six-week sessions. One session each appears within the social science course at each of the three grade levels of the junior high school, seventh, eighth, and ninth.

The first curriculum or block of instruction that appears in the seventh grade is entitled "The World of Rules." This is followed by "The World of Games," and culminates with "The World of Laws" in the ninth grade. It is within the ninth grade section that the local police, for the first time, appear in the classroom.

A pilot program instituting the curriculum should be initiated.

As a part of this program, the Portune ATP-Scale should be administered to all students participating, before and after exposure to the curriculum designed. By this means, any significant changes in the attitudes of the students toward the police could be recorded.

It is hoped that this recommendation will receive serious consideration, not only for the immediate results to be attained by a better youthful understanding of the role of the police, but also for the long range benefits leading to better adult citizenship.

NOTES AND REFERENCES

1. John M. Wilson: Socialization and juvenile delinquency. *Delinquency Prevention.* Englewood Cliffs, New Jersey, Prentice-Hall, 1967, pp. 37-50.
2. Louis Kaplan: *Foundations of Human Behavior.* New York, Harper & Row, 1965, p. 138.
3. Wilson, *op. cit.* p. 39.
4. Charles H. Cooley: *Human Nature and the Social Order.* New York, Charles Scribner's Sons, 1902, p. 152.
5. Kaplan, *op cit.*, p. 156.
6. David H. Russell: *Children's Thinking.* New York, Ginn & Co., 1956, p. 171.
7. Robert Portune, University of Cincinnati, in a presentation before the Delinquency Control Institute, Indiana University of Pennsylvania, June 18, 1968.
8. Russell, *op. cit.*, p. 174.
9. William E. Amos: Prevention through the school. *Delinquency Prevention.* Englewood Cliffs, New Jersey, Prentice-Hall, 1967, pp. 128-149.
10. *Ibid.*, p. 129.
11. Federal Bureau of Investigation, *Uniform Crime Reports* (1967) U. S. Department of Justice, Washington, D. C., p. 121.
12. *Ibid.*
13. *Ibid.*, p. 50.
14. *Ibid.*, p. 38.
15. R. L. Rowland and I. R. Perlman: Statistics on public institutions for delinquent children, 1958, U. S. Children's Bureau, *Statistical Series No. 59,* 1960.
16. Sidney L. Pressey and Francis P. Robinson: *Psychology and the New Education.* New York, Harper & Bros., 1944, p. 162.
17. Russell, *op cit.*, p. 173.

18. Herbert Fegil: Aims of education for our age of science; reflections of a logical empiricist. *Modern Philosophies in Education.* Chicago, The National Society for the Study of Education, 1955, p. 324.

19. T. M. Newcomb: The influence of attitude climate upon some determinants of inforlation. *Journal of Abnormal Social Psychology, 41:* 291, 1946.

20. M. B. McFarland: Relations between young sisters as revealed in their overt responses. *Journal of Experimental Education,* (6) pp. 173-179, 1937.

21. G. Murphy; L. B. Murphy; and T. M. Newcomb: *Experimental Social Psychology: An Interpretation of Research upon the Socialization of the Individual.* New York, Harper, 1937, pp. 239-243.

22. Ruth Cavan: *Juvenile Delinquency.* New York, J. B. Lippincott Co., 1962, p. 41.

23. Pressey and Robinson, *op cit.,* p. 40.

24. Dorothy Rogers: *The Psychology of Adolescence.* New York, Appleton-Century-Cross, 1962, p. 200.

25. Pressey and Robinson, *op. cit.,* p. 277.

26. Elizabeth Hurlock: *Child Development.* New York, McGraw-Hill, 1956, pp. 70-72.

27. Lewella Cole and Irma Nelson Hall: *Psychology of Adolescence.* New York, Holt, Rhinehart & Winston, Inc., 1964, pp. 453-454.

28. Rogers, *op. cit.,* p. 437.

29. Ira J. Gordan: *Human Development from Birth Through Adolescence.* New York: Harper & Row, 1962, p. 239.

30. *Ibid.,* p. 320.

31. David Krech and Richard S. Crutchfield: *Theory & Problems of Social Psychology.* New York, McGraw-Hill, 1948, pp. 175-181.

32. Cole and Hall, *op. cit.,* p. 472.

33. Rogers, *op. cit.,* p. 200.

34. I. C. Rosen: Effect of the motion picture 'Gentleman's Agreement' on attitude toward jews. *Journal of Psychology, 26:* 525-536, 1948.

35. L. J. Epstein: Attitude changes attendant upon variation in experience. *Journal of Education Research, 34:* 453-457, 1941.

INDEX

child's right to privacy, 114
disintegration of familial controls, 79
economic status, 42
father role, 47-50
financial dependency, 87
identifying with others, 40
mobility, 76
mother role, 44-47
nuclear family, 76
ordinal position within, 56-63
permissiveness, 112-116
primary function of, 42
psychological factors, 40, 41
size factors, 42
sociological factors, 41-44
socialization process, 78
sphere of influence, 71, 72
subsidized marriage, 84
working mother, 91
First offender, 110

G

Gault, 130
Generation gap, 84, 226
Geographic association, 71
Ghetto, 74
Goals of youth, 31, 116

H

Heterosexual social development, 33-36
father role, 47-49
Homosexual social development, 35-37
father role, 47-49
legal sanction, 111

I

Illinois Bureau of Investigation, 207
Incorrigibility, 125
Individual differences, 22, 26, 27
Infant mortality, 94
Institutions
as sources of information, 148-150
of socialization, 73
Interrogation, 152
Investigation of delinquency, 151-154

J

Joy riding, 116

Jurisdiction of Juvenile Court, 125, 126, 168
Juvenile Contact Form, 183
Juvenile court
age limits, 125, 168
appearance rates, 10
concurrent jurisdiction, 126
Court of Chancery, 123
detention hearing, 131
findings of, 130
finding of unfitness, 126
first court, 124
history of, 123-125
juvenile court hearing, 127-130
original jurisdiction, 125
parens patraie, 124
petition, 124, 127
philosophy of, 125
system, 123
variety of law, 123
wardship, 130
Juvenile court Judge, 137
Juvenile court referee, 234
Juvenile court years, 9, 10, 125, 168
Juvenile delinquency *see* Delinquency
adolescent delinquency, 28-30
arrests for, 10-12
broken homes and, 91
cultural effects and, 74
definition of, 8
development, 16, 17
early manifestations of, 24
extent of, 9-12
family determinents, 42-50
juvenile court years, 9, 10, 168
juvenile criminality, 8, 9
perception of system, 136-138
planned delinquency, 28
pleasure index, 29
recreational delinquency, 21
school delinquency, 25
threat symbols and, 101
Juvenile hangout, 147
Juvenile officer
advisory role, 204
and fingerprinting juveniles, 200-203
and handcuffing juveniles, 205, 206
and juvenile modus operandi, 151
and the polygraph, 206-208